# UNDERWORLD

# Underworld:

*Death and burial in Cloghermore Cave, Co. Kerry*

MICHAEL CONNOLLY and FRANK COYNE

*With* LINDA G. LYNCH

First published in 2005
Wordwell Ltd
PO Box 69, Bray, Co. Wicklow
Copyright © Wordwell

ISBN 1 86985787 9

British Library Cataloguing-in-Publication Data.

A catalogue record for this book is available from the British Library.

Typeset in Ireland by Susan Waine

Cover design: Rachel Dunne

Copy-editor: Aisling Flood

Printed by ebrook, Dublin

IN MEMORIAM

Marie T. Connolly
Niall Connolly
William Groves

# CONTENTS

# ACKNOWLEDGEMENTS

The authors thank the following: the Groves family, Cloghermore, for allowing us to excavate on their lands and for their interest and support throughout the excavation; Mr John Sheehan, Department of Archaeology, University College Cork, for his extensive library on all things Scandinavian and his report on the silver hoard; Ms Margaret McCarthy, Archaeological Services Unit, University College Cork, for her report on the animal bone from the site; Ms Linda Lynch, Aegis Archaeology Ltd, for her report on the human remains; Dr Andrew Chamberlain, University of Sheffield, for his work on the human remains and on the site in 1999; Dr Arthur MacGregor for his comments on a number of the artefacts from the cave; Dr Patrick Wyse-Jackson, Geology Department, Trinity College Dublin, for his comments on and identification of stone types from the site; Mr Adrian Kennedy for his work on conserving many of the artefacts from the cave; Dr Patrick Wallace and Mr Eamon Kelly, National Museum of Ireland, and Mr Steffan Stumann Hansen for their comments on the artefacts from the site; Ms Marion Dowd and Ms Maeve Sikora for allowing the use of information from their MA theses. The authors would also like to acknowledge the excavation team and the funding provided by Aegis Archaeology Ltd toward the radiocarbon dates from the second season of excavation.

Finally, we would like to thank the National Monuments Service, Department of the Environment, Heritage and Local Government, for funding the two seasons of excavation at Cloghermore and the publication of this important site. In particular, we thank Mr Victor Buckley, Dr Anne Lynch and Mr Conleth Manning; without their interest in the site and efforts to secure funding, this excavation and publication would not have been possible.

*Illustration credits*
All figure illustrations: Frank Coyne
Plates 1–33: Michael Connolly
Plates 34–9: Frank Coyne
Plate 40: Thomas Tyner, AV unit, UCC
Plate 41: John Sheehan, Department of Archaeology, UCC
Appendix 2, Plates 1, 3–6: Linda G. Lynch
Appendix 2, Plate 2: Andrew Chamberlain

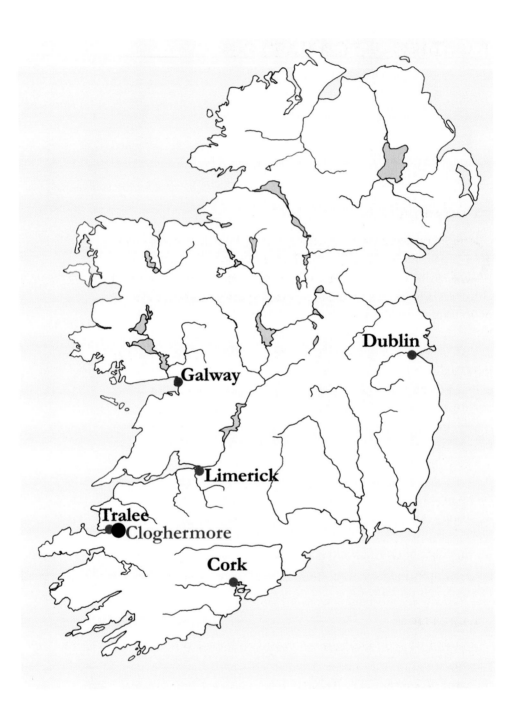

FIG. I
Location map of
Ireland showing major
population centres
with site marked

# I    THE EXCAVATION

## I.I INTRODUCTION

Cloghermore Cave has been visited by local people and caving enthusiasts for at least the last 70 years and probably longer. However, the presence of skeletal material in the two end chambers of the system was not reported to any archaeological body or institution until 1998, when a number of human bones and a broken iron axehead were brought to Kerry County Museum in Tralee by two local caving enthusiasts. After this, the cave was inspected and was found to contain a large quantity of human and animal skeletal material. At this time the cave was sealed to prevent any further public access and became the subject of a preservation order issued by Dúchas, The Heritage Service (Connolly 2000). Given the disturbance of the site and the shattered and fragmentary nature of much of the visible skeletal material, Dúchas decided to undertake a limited excavation of the site. The excavation took place in August 1999 under licence number 99E0431 with a view to recovering the visible skeletal material and investigating the date of the site. Further funding was made available in 2000, and effectively the two end chambers of the system were completely excavated between April and June 2000 (Connolly and Coyne 2000, 16–19).

## I.2 LOCATION

The site is in the townland of Cloghermore, in the parish of Ballymacelligott and barony of Trughanacmy, 6km east-south-east of the town of Tralee in County Kerry (Ordnance Survey 6-inch sheet 30, coordinates 799mm east, 101mm north; National Grid reference Q906128). The cave system is under a large limestone reef measuring 308m east–west by 128m north–south. The main entrance to this system was one-third of the way along the length of the limestone reef, which is at 51m OD at its highest point and affords expansive views in all directions (Fig. 1).

The reef is 2.2km east of the archaeological complex on a similar reef at Ballycarty, where a passage tomb was excavated in 1996 and which also includes at least two other similar sites—a henge and a 1.9ha multivallate enclosure (Connolly 1996; 1999). No archaeological sites are recorded on the reef in the Record of Monuments and Places for County Kerry; however, during the Dúchas-sponsored survey of the Lee Valley a number of meandering banks, two enclosures and at least two cairns were noted on the reef (Connolly and Coyne 1996; Pl. 1). Indeed, one of the major results of this survey was the identification of a large number of previously unrecorded sites, which were discovered on and around limestone reefs similar to those at Ballycarty and Cloghermore. The presence of caves and 'holes' that periodically filled with water was noted close to a number of the main archaeological complexes (Connolly 1997; 1998).

PL. I
*Aerial view of the Waulsortian mudmound/reef at Cloghermore from the west. The D-shaped enclosure is situated in the field in the centre, on top of the reef.*

## 1.3 GEOLOGICAL SETTING

The area between Tralee and Castleisland, to the east (the Vale of Tralee), and the Magherees and Camp on the Dingle Peninsula, to the west, is underlain by a succession of limestones and shales that were deposited during the Lower Carboniferous.

This narrow strip of low-lying terrain is sandwiched between areas of considerable topographical relief to the north-east and the south. Older sediments, including the Old Red Sandstone of Devonian age, which forms the bulk of the Slieve Mish Mountains, are exposed to the south, while to the north-east younger black shales that were deposited during the Upper Carboniferous form the Stacks Mountains.

Cloghermore is underlain by Waulsortian limestone of Early Carboniferous age, which in the Tralee area reaches 600m in thickness (Thornton 1966). Within this unit occurs limestone of two differing styles. At the base of the unit are well-bedded limestones (the Castleisland Limestones of Hudson *et al.* 1966) that are pale grey, partially dolomitised and highly fossiliferous, with corals, goniatites, nautiloids and brachiopods. These bedded limestones grade or interdigitate with developments of unbedded, massive, pale grey limestones that formed discrete banks of aggregated lime mud known as Waulsortian mudmounds.

Waulsortian mudmounds are found in western Europe, North America and Asia (Lees and Miller 1995) and were most extensively developed in Ireland (Sevastopulo 1982). They grew from the seabed through the accumulation of limy mud and developed relief of up to 200m. Waulsortian mudmounds occurred individually, where they reached a thickness of several tens of metres and an area of several hundreds of metres, or as large banks, where several mounds coalesced, with thicknesses of 1km and areal extent of 30,000km² (Pl. 2).

Waulsortian limestone contains abundant and diverse fossil assemblages, the distribution of which is often determined by depth: bryozoans and crinoids are most common in the basal portions, and foraminifera and algae are found in the upper portions. Bryozoans, brachiopods, cephalopods and gastropods are common, and corals are rare (Wyse-Jackson 1999).

## 1.4 DESCRIPTION

### The cave system

The cave system was surveyed by the Mid-West Caving Club, Limerick, in 1983 and described as consisting of 375m of fossil

**PL. 2**
*Aerial view of the reef at Cloghermore from the north-east. The entrance to the cave system used by caving enthusiasts and locals is situated one-third of the way along the cliff-like northern side of the reef.*

passages that run in a north-west/south-east direction for around half of its length before turning to run north–south for the remainder (Condell 1985).

Entrance to the system was through a narrow cleft on the northern side of the reef. Bones are visible throughout much of the system, but these are mainly animal bone and may have been dragged in by animals or washed into the system from above. However, the two small chambers at the southern end of the system, the 'Two-Star Temple' and the 'Graveyard' (*ibid.*), contained large quantities of bone (Fig. 2). The route through the system from the existing entrance to the two bone-bearing chambers at the southern end was difficult, and it was clear that this was unlikely to be the route along which the bones placed in these chambers had been carried. Therefore, it was decided to seek an alternative entrance at the southern end of the system with the help of a radio location device. Interestingly, this showed that the system terminated inside a D-shaped enclosure, which had previously been identified in a sloping field on the south side of the reef.

## The enclosure
The enclosure is clearly visible on the south-facing side of the reef and is composed of a broad, D-shaped bank the straight side of

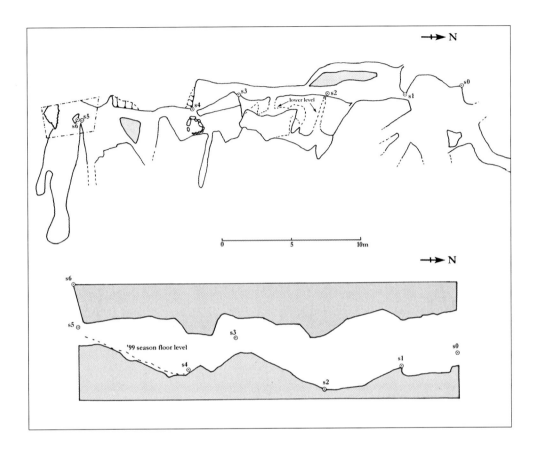

FIG. 2

*Plan and section of Cloghermore Cave.*

which is crowned by a modern drystone field wall (Fig. 3). It offers a spectacular view of The Paps to the south-south-east and of Knockawaddra and the eastern end of the Slieve Mish Mountains to the south-south-west; the view to the south is obscured by a second limestone reef (Pl. 3). The enclosure appears to have been scarped out of the side of the reef, and there is a sharp slope from the top of the bank on the north side of the site into the interior. Indeed, there is a 3.4m drop in height from just outside the bank on the north side to the level area in the southernmost part of the interior. There is a very faint depression outside the bank to the north-north-east, which may be evidence of a ditch; this feature is visible for a length of 18.6m and is 1.6m wide and 0.32m deep. There are no visible internal features. Internally the enclosure measures 16.8m north–south and 28m east–west. The bank is best preserved to the north-north-east, where it is 1.5m high internally, 0.55m high externally and 12.20m wide. The total dimensions of the enclosure are 34.8m north–south and 44.80m east–west.

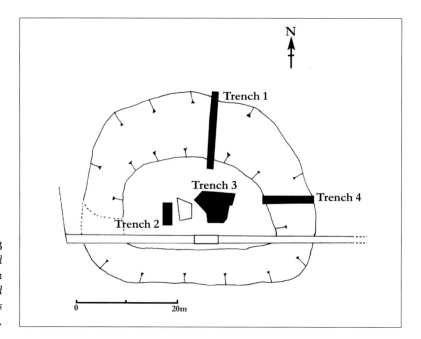

FIG. 3
*The D-shaped
enclosure, with
entrance shaft and
trench locations
shown.*

## 1.5 THE EXCAVATION

### Cave entrance shaft

Use of a radio location device showed that the end of the cave system
was situated centrally within the D-shaped enclosure, so a trench
measuring 2m by 3m was opened at this point. After the topsoil was
removed, a layer of smallish angular stones was uncovered. This was
a deliberately constructed feature, almost like cobbling. This layer of
stones was 0.11m deep and came down onto a dark brown, silty loam,
0.20m deep, which clearly had been deliberately deposited. This
deposit contained some bone fragments, stones and charcoal and
produced three artefacts: two perforated bone needles and a struck-
flint pebble. The deposit in turn covered a redeposited boulder clay,
0.20m deep, which also contained bone fragments, stone and
charcoal and produced a small fragment of copper alloy. This deposit
sealed a spread of large limestones, up to 0.30m deep, that had the
appearance of having collapsed from a structure; again, bone
fragments were found among the stones (Pl. 4). Under this deposit
were three large slabs of limestone: two lying flat, and the third, at
the western side of the trench, was at an angle as if it had been
disturbed. Voids around the two recumbent slabs clearly showed that
they sealed an entrance of some sort (Fig. 4).

The larger of the recumbent slabs was the more western and
measured 0.90m by 0.50m by 0.23m; the smaller slab measured 0.80m

PL. 3
Aerial view of the surface of the reef. The D-shaped enclosure is situated in the field in the centre right of the photograph.

by 0.70m by 0.13m. The slab that was to one side of the other two measured 0.50m by 0.47m by 0.28m. Removal of these slabs revealed an almost completely infilled shaft. The shaft was almost D-shaped, with the northern side, which was composed of bedrock and some pieces of drystone walling, forming the straight side. The remaining arc of the shaft was composed almost exclusively of drystone

PL. 4
The capstones covering the artificial entrance shaft to the cave system, inside the enclosure.

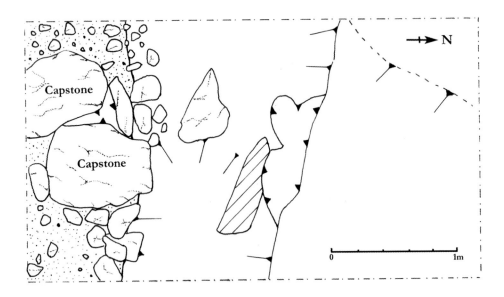

FIG. 4
*Plan of the entrance shaft sealing layer showing* in situ *capstones.*

walling. It was clear that the walling on the northern side was necessary only to facilitate the placing of the capstones and that the western side had almost completely collapsed into the shaft; however, the walling on the eastern side was intact.

A narrow opening to the cave system below could be seen, but using it would first involve the removal of the collapse and infill from the shaft. The upper layer of soil in the shaft was a moist clay up to 1.2m deep; it had the appearance of being a deliberate fill and sealed a dark brown soil that contained charcoal. This in turn covered a shallow (0.10m) deposit of orange, scorched silt, which produced a burnt, water-rolled quartz pebble and contained significant quantities of bone and charcoal. This deposit overlay the natural boulder clay, which in turn covered the limestone bedrock. After the removal of this material from the shaft, it could be seen that the extant entrance to it measured 1.17m north–south and 1.60m east–west at the top, narrowing to 0.59m north–south and 0.84m east–west at the base. The depth from the ground surface was 2.57m, and the depth from the *in situ* capstones was 1.77m.

The extant drystone walling was composed of irregular blocks of limestone in roughly ten rudimentary courses (Fig. 5). It measured 1.77m in maximum height and narrowed from 1.30m at the top to a very narrow 0.60m at the base. The extant walling also displayed clear evidence that corbelling was used to facilitate the closing of the shaft by the capstones (Pl. 5). It was also clear that, inverse to the

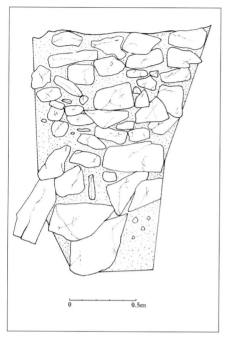

usual arrangement in a corbelled structure, the base of the shaft was much narrower than the top, because the walling was supported by the earth and bedrock sides of the original cut while the bottom half of the shaft was quarried out of the bedrock. Once the shaft had been cleared of soil and stone, it could be clearly seen that it allowed entry to the cave system through a narrow opening on its north-north-eastern side. This narrow opening led into a long gallery, the floor of which sloped steeply downward and was composed of a brown soil, some of which had probably fallen inward, and loose stones of a similar size to those used in the drystone walling of the entrance shaft. Indeed, there was a substantial depth of soil and sediment, which sloped sharply all the way down along this gallery and into the chamber known as the Graveyard. The slope was also littered with bone, which was planned and collected. This collapsed material was removed to facilitate access along the gallery, and a number of finds were recovered, including whetstones, one half of a quernstone, a fragment of post-medieval pottery, some iron fragments and an antler pin-beater.

**The cave system**
As well as the removal of collapse from inside the cave entrance, three separate test-pits were dug within the cave system during the

FIG. 5
*Elevation of drystone walling of the entrance shaft.*

PL. 5
*The entrance shaft showing drystone-walled and natural rock sides.*

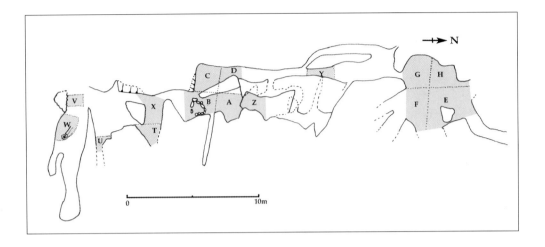

FIG. 6
*Plan of the cave showing excavated areas.*

1999 season: two in a recess to the east of the entrance, and one in the chamber known as the Graveyard (Fig. 6). An attempt was made to excavate a pit in the chamber known as the Two-Star Temple; however, there was no soil cover over most of this area, and where it existed it was found to be only 30–40mm deep and rested on a very solid stalagmite floor. The soil from an area measuring 1m by 1m was removed from the Two-Star Temple and sieved. It produced a stone spindle-whorl, an iron arrowhead and some other small iron fragments, as well as small fragments of crushed bone (a result of people walking on the unburnt remains).

## Area S

The two pits in the recess to the east of the entrance were excavated because of the existence of a thin covering of stalagmite over what appeared to be a substantial area of collapse. It was hoped that this indicated the antiquity of the collapse and that undisturbed archaeological strata would be preserved underneath. Both pits measured 1m by 1m, and the stratigraphy in both was the same: a 1.65m depth of inwashed sandy soil and roof-collapsed stones overlying a shallow layer of yellow/light brown clay, which rested on the cave floor. A few pieces of bone were recovered from the inwashed/collapsed layer in the more western of the two pits.

## The Graveyard

The most productive area of excavation was the Graveyard, where a pit measuring 1.15m north–south and 1.40m east–west was excavated in the floor of the chamber, immediately at the base of the sloping deposit of collapse and infall, which ran downward, to the north, from the entrance (Area X). This chamber had initially appeared to be the most trampled and disturbed. The western half consisted of a raised shelf composed of huge rocks, which had obviously fallen from the roof of the cavern. This stone platform area sloped upward from south to north, toward the passage, which exited from the chamber and led on to the Two-Star Temple (Fig. 7).

The floor of the eastern half of the chamber was on average 0.90m lower than the collapse forming the western side. The floor was composed of very trampled mud and stones, some of which had fallen from the roof. Most of the soil/mud on the floor, as well as some of the stones, may have rolled down from the entrance.

It was obvious that some of the larger stones on the floor had been lifted and moved around the chamber, and the extent of the trampling clearly indicated relatively recent disturbance. Indeed, on one night during the 2000 excavations three large holes were dug in the area of excavation by unidentified individuals (Pl. 6).

During the removal of the surface bone, the chamber had been divided into four quadrants: A (north-east), B (south-east), C (south-west) and D (north-west). Initially, a pit measuring 1m by 1m was opened in the floor of Quadrant B, but this was extended to enable the removal of large stones, the final pit measuring 1.15m north–south and 1.40m east–west.

FIG. 7
*Plan of the Graveyard.*

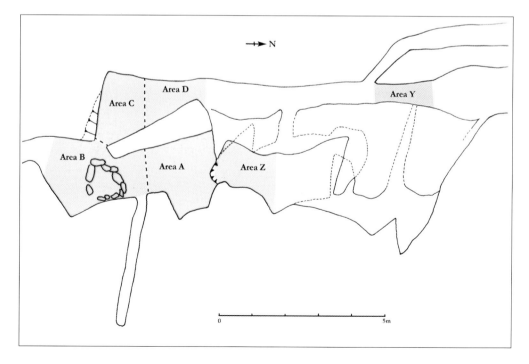

PL. 6
*The Graveyard before*
*excavation.*
*Quadrants A and B*
*are on the right-hand*
*side of the central*
*area of roof collapse;*
*Quadrants C and D*
*are on the left.*

QUADRANT B

The muddy, dark brown clay was 0.11–19m deep and contained large quantities of unburnt human and animal bone. It came down onto a light grey, ashy layer, which contained cremated and unburnt fragments of bone. This layer overlay five large stone slabs, which rested on a horseshoe-shaped setting of stone, forming a capping. The slabs measured between 0.76m by 0.62m by 0.21m and 0.47m by 0.35m by 0.15m; they rested on a semicircular setting of twelve stones, which, when taken with the eastern side wall of the cavern (the two ends of the semicircular setting rested against the cavern wall), gave a roughly D-shaped feature measuring 1.16m by 0.66m.

This setting contained a deposit rich in charcoal and cremated bone, which was 0.14–19m deep. This deposit was generally black in the eastern side of the setting, which it filled and indeed overflowed. Sieving of the deposit here resulted in the recovery of large quantities of cremated bone fragments and wood charcoal (Pl. 7). In the western half of the pit the grey/ashy layer overlying the slabs capping the setting contained a greater density of cremated bone, and sieving resulted in the recovery of three amber beads and three copper-alloy fragments The slabs were also partially covered by a pink ash deposit containing large fragments of cremated bone and huge quantities of charcoal; this deposit, 0.13m in maximum depth, was also found over and around the stone setting.

The main deposit inside the setting was composed of a pink/grey ash and cremated bone, 0.33m deep; 1.4kg of cremated bone was recovered from this deposit (Pl. 8). The cremation deposit

overlay a bright yellow boulder-type clay, 0.14–0.19m deep, which in turn overlay a lens of pure wood charcoal on average only 0.04m deep. This was the basal deposit and rested on a stalagmite floor that had formed over a mass of roof-collapsed stones.

During the second season, Quadrants A, C and D were excavated to the depth of the roof collapse.

## QUADRANT A

Only in Quadrant A was there any depth of soil, and excavation here involved the removal of a similar depth of material to that removed from Quadrant B during the previous season. The area excavated here measured 2.55m north–south and 1.4mm east–west (Pl. 9). The southernmost part of Quadrant A, where it abutted the limit of excavation in Quadrant B, contained the same stratigraphy as Quadrant B, with the trampled mud overlying a black charcoal-rich deposit—the overflow of the cremation deposit from the stone setting—and a layer of wood charcoal. However, over most of Quadrant A there was only a single soil layer, the trampled, brown, muddy soil found throughout the cave from the Graveyard to the entrance shaft. This soil layer was up to 0.80m deep and rested on and between roof-collapsed rocks that had been welded in place by the action of flowstone within the cave.

This layer of soil produced quantities of human and animal bone, as well as amber and bone beads and a silver hoard comprising two ingots and four pieces of hack silver, two of which were linked together. This hoard was recovered from a small cleft between two large boulders on the cave floor, while the amber beads were again associated with the cremated material.

PL. 7
*The stone setting in the Graveyard during excavation.*

PL. 8
*The cremation deposit inside the stone setting during excavation.*

QUADRANTS C AND D

These two quadrants were on the western side of the Graveyard, on a narrow shelf, 0.90m above the original ground level of the eastern half of the chamber, formed by two massive blocks of collapse from the roof and numerous other smaller boulders. The shelf sloped upward from the south toward the narrow passage that led from the Graveyard to the Two-Star Temple; it measured 3.60m north–south and 1.75m east–west. There was very little soil in these two quadrants. What occurred was found mainly between the stones forming the raised shelf; however, by moving those stones not set in place by flowstone, a depth of up to 0.90m was excavated (Pl. 10). The soil was almost entirely composed of the brown earth found as the upper layer over most of the excavated area, although some pockets of more charcoal-rich material occurred in some of the deeper clefts.

These quadrants also produced both human and animal bone but in smaller quantities to the eastern side of the chamber. Finds from this area included a broken decorated bone comb, a decorated and perforated ivory ball, a bone bead and numerous iron fragments.

*Area X*

This area comprised the long, narrow passage that sloped steeply upward from the southern end of the Graveyard to within *c.* 1m of the base of the entrance shaft (Fig. 8). This passage measured 7.0m north–south and on average 1.20m east–west. The upper levels of the slope were composed of the brown soil found in all of the excavated areas, which was 0.50–0.70m deep. This brown soil rested mainly on the cream-coloured, sandy sediment that was the basal soil layer in the cave system. This sediment appeared to form the steep slope from the entrance shaft to the Graveyard and was *c.* 3.5m deep at the entrance. At its southern extent the brown soil rested on pockets of this sediment, which contained charcoal and had obviously been redeposited, in one instance on a small, subcircular area of fire-reddened sediment and ash measuring 0.38m by 0.30m and 0.16m deep. The sediment in this area inside the entrance was very level, and the sharp slope did not occur for a distance of 1.58m from the base of the entrance shaft.

The brown soil produced large quantities of human and animal bone, as well as an amber bead, a stone bead, a bone bead, iron knives and other iron fragments. Although the upper level of the sediment layer produced the odd piece of bone, it was mainly sterile (Pl. 11).

However, it is of note that the underlying sediment appeared to

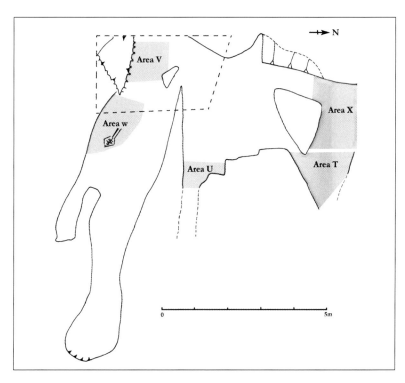

PL. 9
*Quadrants A and B of the Graveyard.*

PL. 10
*Quadrants C and D of the Graveyard.*

FIG. 8
*Plan of the entrance gallery (Areas T, U, V, W and X).*

have a very rudimentary step cut into it at two locations. The first step occurred at the point where the sediment began to slope steeply down to the north, 1.8m from the base of the entrance shaft. The second occurred a further 2.7m farther on, where the passage narrowed to pass the huge boulder on top of which was Area T. The upper steep was 0.33m wide and 0.43m high, and the lower step was 0.27m wide and 0.31m high.

## Area T

On the eastern side of Area X, close to the point where the sloping entrance gallery exited the Graveyard, there was a very large, almost triangular boulder, which reached almost to the roof of the gallery. The area around this boulder was treated as part of Area X; however, in the narrow space above and behind this boulder there was a raised shelflike area, which seemed to be part of a now blocked offshoot passage. This raised area was 1.85m above the floor level of Area X at the boulder and measured 2.4m by 3.1m; it had a triangular shape, narrowing from the boulder back.

Area T produced human and animal bone, including part of the skull of a small horse, as well as two iron rings and some other iron fragments.

PL. II
*Area X, the long, sloping passage/gallery leading from the base of the entrance shaft to the Graveyard.*

PL. 12
*Area U before
excavation. Human
bone can be seen
embedded in the mud
floor.*

## Area U

This area comprised a short offshoot passage on the eastern side of Area X. The passage was 4.9m long (east–west) and 1.4m wide (north–south). It narrowed slightly and decreased in height toward its eastern extent, which was blocked with stones and appeared to form the top of a shaft.

The soil in the passage was composed of the brown clay that occurred over all of the excavated areas. This soil rested directly on the cream-coloured, sandy sediment, which, owing to the slumping forward of sediments from the area at the southern end of the cave, sloped sharply downward to the north (Pl. 12). The brown clay was on average 0.35m deep and produced quantities of animal bone and human bones of adults and children, as well as iron fragments, a decorated bone handle, a stone spindle-whorl, a pendant whetstone, the shaft of a bronze pin, a metal stud with possible textile attached, a blue glass bead with yellow paste decoration and a decorated bone gaming-piece.

## Area V

Area V was immediately inside the entrance to the cave and abutted

Area W to the east. Area V was distinguished from Area W stratigraphically in that the sediment layer underlying the brown soil was rich in charcoal and contained large quantities of bone. This redeposited sediment covered an area measuring 1.3m north–south and 0.95m east–west (the southern extent of this layer was not uncovered because this would have involved the removal of material at the base of the entrance shaft, which would have undermined the drystone walling) (Pl. 13). Close to the western extent of this layer a subcircular area of burning, measuring 0.35m by 0.27m, was uncovered, consisting of fire-reddened sediment framed by narrow bands of white/grey ash and charcoal. This material proved to be on average 0.14m deep and rested directly on the redeposited sediment.

Excavation of this redeposited sediment showed that it filled a subrectangular pit, which had been cut through the surrounding sterile sediment. The pit was deepest toward its southern end (0.75m) and, owing to the fact that it was cut into a bank of sediment, which sloped down toward the Graveyard, became shallower toward its northern extent Excavation of the pit produced large quantities of animal bone, including very young animals, and the bones of at least one child, as well as iron knives, bone combs, a bone point, a bone pin, an antler spindle-whorl and a decorated bone gaming-piece.

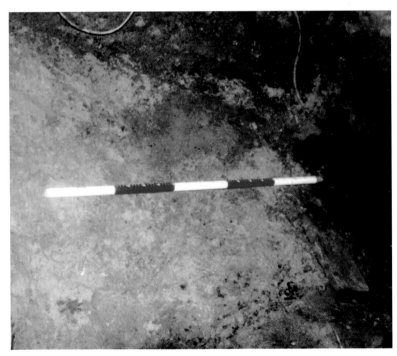

PL. 13
*Burning on the top of Pit V before excavation.*

## Area W

This small area was situated immediately inside and to the east of the cave entrance. It contained the only articulated burial uncovered in the cave system (Fig. 9; Pl. 14). The stratigraphy in Area W was the same as that in Area X, the brown soil resting directly on the cream-coloured, sandy sediment. The skeleton lay on the sloping sediment with the legs to the north-west. The upper half of the body lay in a very shallow, U-sectioned depression, 0.98m long, 0.41m wide and 0.21m in maximum depth. Two stones, bedded in the sediment, lay on the north-eastern side of the torso and either were part of a setting or were used to prevent the body from rolling downslope. The stones measured 0.25m by 0.24m by 0.16m and 0.33m by 0.25m by 0.21m. Finds from the area included a copper-alloy ringed pin, a boat-shaped whetstone, a small iron knife and a small copper-alloy button, all directly associated with the articulated burial.

## Area Y

As already noted, there was very little soil within the Two-Star Temple, and this was also the case over much of the narrow passage (Area Y) that separated this chamber from the Graveyard. Over most of its length the passage floor was composed of roof-collapsed rubble

FIG. 9
*Plan of the articulated burial in Area W.*

PL. 14
*Area W before excavation. Scattered human and animal bone can be seen resting on the sediment floor.*

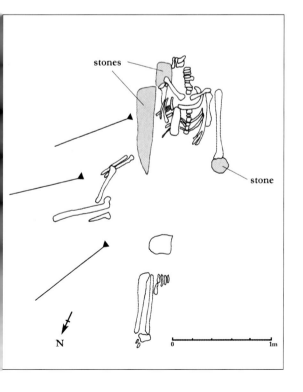

stones

stone

N

0     1m

covered to varying degrees by flowstone. The passage dropped sharply from the Two-Star Temple to a point roughly midway along its length, where it began to rise steeply toward the Graveyard. The area at the base of these opposing rubble slopes contained pockets of the brown soil found elsewhere in the southern end of the cave system. This soil was removed and was found to be 0.19–0.28m deep, covering an area measuring 1.3m north–south and 0.7m east–west. The soil contained a small number of bone fragments and produced iron fragments, bone comb fragments and a perforated triangular bone plaque, probably a strap-end.

### Area Z

At the northern end of Quadrant A there was a large boulder (1.64m by 1.2m by 0.75m) that partially blocked the entrance to a small, low offshoot passage, which terminated in a dead end after a length of 3.8m. This short passage was at a lower level (0.38m) than the original floor level of the Graveyard. There was a small quantity of the brown clay in the front of this passage, covering an area measuring 2.60m north–south by 1.25m east–west (Pl. 15). This brown soil lay directly on a cream-coloured, sandy sediment, which was the basal soil layer over much of the cave system and, in Area Z, varied in depth between 0.30m and 0.47m. The soil in this area produced quantities of human and animal bone, as well as beads, iron fragments and a well-preserved copper-alloy loop-headed ringed pin.

## The enclosure excavation

During the 1999 season, only one trench was excavated across the enclosing bank. This was placed at the north-north-east, where the slight depression indicated a possible ditch for a length of 14m.

### Trench 1

The excavation revealed that the feature consisted of two banks with a rock-cut ditch in between and that the depression outside the bank was in fact a very shallow drain-like feature, which can only have been used to divert away from the enclosure rainwater flowing down the slope (Pl. 16). Indeed, the southern side of the enclosure currently floods up to a depth of 0.4m during the winter, but this depth of flooding is undoubtedly facilitated by the presence of the modern wall on top of the straight-sided bank to the south. There was a berm between this drain and the outer bank, and three very shallow post-holes/pits were uncovered in this area. These post-holes

appeared to have been truncated, and the charcoal flecking and mottling of the sandy silt that overlay them may be remains of the post-hole fills.

Both banks were composed of stone and soil, the larger, inner bank being constructed on top of a natural crest of bedrock. The stone for both banks was, in part at least, provided by material quarried from the ditch and also from material quarried from the interior of the enclosure. The drain-like feature that formed the outer element was 1.00m wide (north–south) and was exposed across the trench for a length of 1.5m. It was filled with a brown sandy silt that contained some unburnt animal bone. The feature was 0.25m in maximum depth; the side nearest to the enclosure sloped gently down to the base, while the outer face was almost vertical. The berm was 1.7m wide, and the three shallow post-holes measured (from north to south) 200mm by 180mm by 60mm deep, 175mm by 150mm by 60mm deep, and 90mm by 100mm by 70mm deep. The middle post-hole produced fragments of cremated animal bone and a worked flake of rock crystal; and all three produced small fragments of charcoal.

PL. 15
*Area Z, a very narrow offshoot passage at the rear of the Graveyard.*

PL. 16
*Trench 1, across the northern side of the D-shaped enclosure. The earth-and-stone banks and intervening rock-cut ditch can be seen in the centre of the photograph.*

The face of the outer bank, visible in the ditch, was formed of three rudimentary courses of drystone walling resting on the underlying bedrock. The limestone slabs measured on average 0.35m by 0.20m by 0.15m. The extant height of the walling was 0.40m. The outer bank was on average 0.40m high externally, 0.80m high internally and 1.57m wide. The ditch was filled with two distinct soil layers. The upper, a grey/brown sandy silt, was 0.40m deep; the lower, a light brown silt, was 0.25m deep and contained flecks of burnt/cremated bone. The rock-cut ditch was 1.3m wide and 0.85m in maximum depth. The inner bank was composed of a mixture of soil and limestones (average dimensions 0.18m by 0.15m by 0.12m), to form a much larger bank, 7.40m wide. The bank was on average 0.85m high externally (in the ditch), and the fall from the crest of the bank to the interior of the enclosure was over 3m.

During the 2000 season a further three trenches were opened in the area of the enclosure: two, Trenches 2 and 3, inside the enclosure, and one, Trench 4, across the enclosing element.

*Trench 2*

This trench measured 4.00m north–south and 1.80m east–west and was opened inside the enclosure on the western side of the entrance shaft to the cave. Over most of the trench the topsoil rested on a layer of angular limestone cobbles (average dimensions 0.25m by 0.10m). This layer of stones was on average 0.20m deep and was more concentrated in the southern half of the trench. It was also identical to the layer of stones uncovered above the capstones of the entrance shaft to the cave. At the eastern extent of the trench the stone layer rested on a loose layer of light, black soil, which ran the length of the trench from north to south (4.00m) and extended 0.85m from the eastern edge of the trench. The soil overlay redeposited boulder clay at the south and the fill of the cave entrance shaft at the north (Pl. 17).

Excavation revealed that a semicircular cut had been excavated through the boulder clay to facilitate access to the cave and the subsequent construction of the drystone walling of the entrance shaft. Within Trench 2 this cut measured 1.60m north–south and 0.85m east–west and contained one soil layer, a black soil with stones and occasional charcoal. This layer was excavated to a depth of 0.50m, at which point it was decided that to continue might cause the collapse of the drystone walling immediately to the east. The stratigraphy of this cut was the same as that encountered immediately above and around the entrance shaft during the 1999 season of excavation and indicates that a large, circular depression had been excavated around the entrance to the cave system.

### Trench 3

This trench was opened on the eastern and south-eastern sides of the entrance shaft and was the largest trench opened on the surface: the final dimensions were 4.50m north–south and 7.50m east–west. Similar to Trench 2, the topsoil layer rested on a layer of limestone cobbling that overlay the light, black soil layer. This was the stratigraphical sequence over all of the trench except the south-east corner, where there was a ditch-like feature that ran north-east/south-west for a length of 3.50m and was filled with a topsoil-like material to a depth of 0.71m (Pl. 18).

Where the trench abutted the eastern side of the entrance shaft to the cave, the cut that was noted in Trench 2 was again uncovered and similarly contained a black soil. The feature measured 1.60m north–south and 0.65m east–west and clearly confirmed that a circular depression had been excavated around the cave entrance to facilitate access and the construction of the drystone walling of the shaft. Two large stones situated within the cut in Trench 3 may well

PL. 17
*Trench 2, opened on the western side of the entrance shaft. The line of the backfilled pit that had been excavated around the entrance shaft is clearly visible as a dark, charcoal-rich layer.*

PL. 18
*Trench 3, on the southern side of the entrance shaft. The sealing layer of stones, charcoal, animal bone fragments and earth is clearly visible.*

have formed the portals of a formal entrance feature while the cave was in use, before its final sealing.

Centrally placed within the trench were the remains of a fire/ pyre. The feature was situated in a subcircular depression, measuring 1.60m north–south and 1.90m east–west, cut into the redeposited boulder clay. A flue extended eastward from the depression for a distance of 0.80m. It was 0.20m wide where it exited the depression, and it splayed outward to a maximum width of 0.80m at its eastern extent. The depression contained a black/brown sandy silt with patches of burnt soil, ash and charcoal. Fragments of cremated bone, burnt iron fragments and part of a burnt bone spindle-whorl were recovered from the pyre remains.

Elsewhere in the trench, 22 stake-holes and post-holes and two slot-trenches were excavated, which were found mainly to be cut into a redeposited boulder clay. The holes varied in diameter from 0.06m to 0.80m, and a number of the post-holes contained stones, which were probably used as packing for wooden posts. Most of the post-holes had flared tops, suggesting that the posts had been deliberately removed at some point (Pl. 19). The shorter of the slot-trenches was 0.90m long, 0.25m wide and 0.15m deep. It contained two post-holes, one at either end. It was situated immediately south-east of the cremation pyre and ran east–west. The side-plates of a decorated

PL. 19
*Trench 3, which extended around the eastern side of the entrance shaft. In the centre of the photograph the two short slot-trenches and post-holes are visible. The pyre pit and flue are also visible in the centre of the photograph. Again, the backfill of the pit excavated around the entrance shaft is visible as a charcoal-rich layer. The two large holes nearest the shaft represent a large post-hole and probable standing stone socket.*

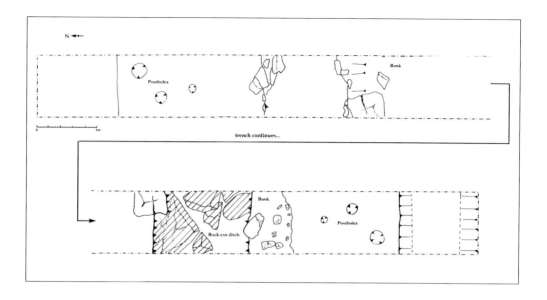

FIG. 10
*Plan of Trench 4.*

bone comb were recovered from this slot-trench. The longer slot-trench ran north-west/south-east and was truncated by the later flue of the cremation pyre. The trench was 3.40m long, 0.30m wide and 0.15m deep and contained three post-holes.

## Trench 4

This trench was opened across the D-shaped bank of the enclosure, on its eastern side, and was 10m long and 1.5m wide (Fig. 10; Pl. 20). The morphology of the bank in this trench was very different from that encountered in Trench 1, where the various features were very clearly defined and remained substantially intact. The trench showed the bank here to be much more flattened and disturbed but also less substantial than that encountered in Trench 1.

There was no evidence of the external gully and berm noted in Trench 1, and the outer bank was very flattened, 2.15m wide and only 0.25m in maximum height. The stones of the bank were set in a reddish-brown, sandy silt matrix.

Immediately inside this bank, to the west, was the ditch, which in this case was dug through the underlying boulder clay but not cut through the bedrock. The ditch was 1.05m in maximum width and 0.50m deep and was filled with a brown/red sandy silt with charcoal flecking.

The inner bank was much less substantial than that encountered in Trench 1, but the construction was the same: stone and earth piled

PL. 20
*Trench 4, opened
across the eastern side
of the D-shaped
enclosure.*

onto the underlying bedrock. The bank was 2.25m wide and had a maximum height of 0.45m. Again, the bank was very flattened and did not attain the height of the bank in Trench 1, which is partially explained by the fact that, unlike the bank in Trench 1, it was not built into the natural slope of the land.

# 2   INTERPRETATION

## 2.1 THE ENCLOSURE

The D-shaped enclosure that surrounded the entrance shaft to the cave was excavated at two points: one at the north (Trench 1), where the bank was best preserved, and the other at the east (Trench 4). As already described, Trench 1 gave a clear picture of the morphology of the enclosing element: two banks of earth and stone divided by a rock-cut ditch. Outside the banks there was a gully or drain-like feature with a level area between it and the outer bank. Three truncated post-holes were uncovered in this area, which provided burnt material that gave a radiocarbon date of 1130±60 BP (Beta-137054) (Pl. 21). In Trench 4 the bank was more flattened and disturbed. The outer gully/drain was not uncovered, but the double bank with intervening ditch was again noted, although the ditch here was dug into the underlying boulder clay.

The enclosing elements clearly were not substantial enough to have been defensive in nature, and the enclosed area (28m by 16.8m) was too small to have contained much but the cave entrance and the structures uncovered in Trench 3. Therefore, the enclosing element may have been purely ritual in nature, delimiting the ritual area of the cave. Alternatively, it may have functioned purely as a method of preventing run-off water from further up the slope of the outcrop from flowing down into the cave entrance shaft and the area of ritual immediately around the cave. However, given the annual flooding of the cave and water entering from elsewhere, this may have been a thankless task. The former suggestion seems more reasonable, given the labour involved and the complexity of the enclosing element: a single bank rather than two banks separated by a ditch would have been sufficient to keep the area free of water (Pl. 22).

The radiocarbon date from the post-holes does not necessarily date the construction of the enclosing element. A clearer indicator of the date of the banks and ditch is probably provided by the fragments

of cremated animal bone in the fills of the post-holes and the ditch between the two enclosing banks. The recovery of a whetstone of a similarly fine-grained micaceous siltstone to examples from the cave, in the make-up of the inner bank in Trench 1, coupled with the central location of the entrance shaft to the cave, suggests that the enclosure is coeval with the tenth-century use of the cave.

## 2.2 THE CAVE ENTRANCE

Excavation within the D-shaped enclosure demonstrated that the entrance to the cave at this point was primarily an artificial feature. There may originally have been a small break in the rock in this area, but it was expanded and widened at some point in the history of the use of the cave.

The evidence from Trenches 2 and 3 showed that a circular area around the opening to the cave had been excavated, possibly to provide easier access to the site but more likely to facilitate the construction of the drystone walling of the entrance shaft. This depression had subsequently been backfilled. The backfill material was identical to that which immediately overlay the capstones of the entrance shaft, which suggests that the depression was excavated to allow the construction of the drystone-walled shaft, which was roofed with three large slabs. The depression was then filled, and the slabs were sealed with black soil containing charcoal, cremated animal bone and some artefacts. This black soil was clearly the result of burning in the immediate area and probably originated from the pyre uncovered in Trench 3, where the animal bone uncovered inside the stone setting in the Graveyard had been cremated. The roofing of the shaft with three slabs seems to suggest that it was intended that the cave should be accessible at a future time. However, the fact that the sealing layer above the slabs seemed to be intact indicated that the cave had not been entered by this route after its initial sealing— but, given the fact that one of the closing slabs was in an upright position, this is far from certain.

It appears that all of the burials placed within the cave by this route were *in situ* before the cremation of the animal bone in the pyre uncovered in Trench 3 and the construction and sealing of the drystone-walled entrance shaft. Therefore, the latest burials in the cave, the cremation of the animal bone, the construction of the drystone walling and the closure of the entrance shaft are all broadly contemporaneous. The latest radiocarbon dates from the burials within the cave are, interestingly, all from areas immediately inside the entrance, the latest being from Area T (1020±40 BP; Beta-150539).

## 2.3 ACTIVITY WITHIN THE ENCLOSURE

There can be little doubt that the activity within the D-shaped enclosure and some of the burials within the cave are coeval. The excavation in Trench 3 clearly showed that the pyre site uncovered here was the site of the cremation of the animal bones subsequently deposited within the stone setting in the Graveyard. Indeed, cremated animal bone and a fragment of a cremated bone spindle-whorl (175) were recovered from the remains of the pyre (Fig. 11; Pl. 23). As discussed above, it seems likely that soil from the site of the pyre was used in the backfill of the depression excavated around the cave entrance and the sealing layer over the capstones of the entrance shaft. The excavation in Trench 3 also indicated that a wooden post and walled structures were erected immediately to the east of the cave entrance shaft, within the enclosure, before the construction of the pyre (Pl. 24).

The stratigraphy in this area is quite clear, given that the long,

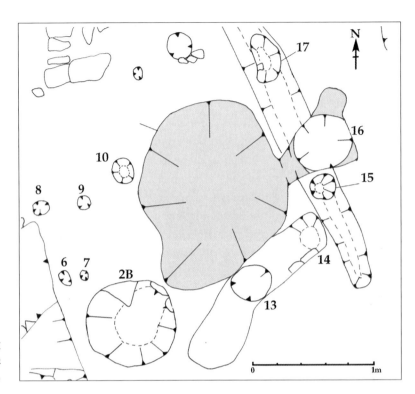

FIG. 11
*Plan of the cremation
pyre site.*

PL. 23
*The cremation pyre
site during
excavation.*

PL. 24
*Stone socket and large
post-hole in Trench 3,
close to the entrance
shaft.*

north-east/south-west-running slot-trench was cut by the flue of the cremation pyre. Subsequently, the largest and deepest post-hole on the site (16) was excavated through the flue of the pyre and part of the underlying slot-trench. Clearly, the slot-trench represents the earliest activity in this area, with the large post-hole probably representing the latest activity. However, the time gap between events in this area may well have been extremely short, as the activity here is clearly associated with the second phase of burial. As already stated, material from the pyre, as well as being deposited within the stone setting in the Graveyard, was scattered within the fill of the circular depression excavated around the cave entrance. Charcoal and fragments of cremated bone were also recovered from a number of the sockets and post-holes, particularly the large post-hole through the flue and long slot-trench (16) and the large stone socket (2B).

Therefore, the earliest structure on the site appears to be associated with the long slot-trench, which contained two post-holes (15 and 17). This structure probably consisted of a plank wall, with the planks either set vertically in the trench or nailed horizontally to the two posts in the trench. Alternatively, the two posts may represent a gap through this wall. The exact purpose of such a structure is unclear, but, together with the post-holes to the north-east (18, 19, 21, 22 and 23), it may have formed part of a lean-to or flat-roofed structure on the site before the final funeral rituals. Alternatively, it could have served to divide the ritual area into two distinct parts: one for use before the burial, and the other for use in the burial rituals. In this way the wall would also have helped to screen the cave entrance from view, while the five post-holes may independently have supported a temporary roofed structure or bier-like platform.

The smaller slot-trench did not intersect the larger one but abutted it to the south-west at a point 0.40m from the south-eastern extent of the larger trench. The shorter trench was also slightly curved rather than straight. This seems to suggest that it is not a walling trench or an integrated part of the wall set in the longer trench. However, it is clear that the pyre cut flattened to observe the line of this trench, indicating that the trench and its two posts (13 and 14) were in use when the pyre was constructed. Therefore, there is a possibility that this trench and its posts, together with the two post-holes and stake-hole on the opposite side of the pyre cut (10, 11 and 12), held a platform over the fire or formed the corners of a wooden pyre structure. In the south-western half of the trench the underlying limestone bedrock was close to the surface, and the basal boulder clay dipped down to the south-west into the depression excavated around the original cave entrance. In this area a soil fill containing charcoal, flecks of cremated bone and stones occurred, similar to that noted in Trench 2 and immediately above the capstones of the entrance shaft.

The post-holes and stake-holes in this area of the site were generally small and in most cases relatively shallow, although three post-holes (1, 2 and 8) are reasonably substantial. Again, it is difficult to suggest a definite structure in this area, although these features may have served as the main structural elements of a passage to the cave entrance, the passage avoiding the north-eastern side of the trench, where the body may have been placed before burial. Indeed, the presence of the long wall-trench and the ditch feature on the south-eastern side of the trench is suggestive of access to the cave from the north-north-west, and such a route may well have been clearly defined. There were also two large, irregular depressions, which contained packing-stones, and, in the case of 2B, charcoal and flecks of bone. Both were partially rock cut and appeared more likely to be deliberately fashioned stone sockets rather than post-holes.

These sockets may have held small standing stones or pillars, but it is unclear when these were erected. However, the presence of fragments of cremated bone and charcoal in the fill of 2B suggests that it was in use after the use of the pyre and had some ritual significance. Yet the possibility that a number of the features in this area relate to the excavation of the circular depression and subsequent construction of the entrance shaft, or the lowering of bodies, animal remains etc. into the cave, cannot be discounted. The large post-hole (16) through the flue of the pyre site had a similar fill to 2B: cremated bone and charcoal. This post-hole seems to represent the last activity in the area and may have held a memorial post or grave-marker, as indeed may the stone socket 2B.

There is clear evidence that the structures represented by the post-holes and slot-trenches did not rot or burn *in situ*, and the flared tops to many of the post-holes suggest that they were dismantled deliberately before the construction of the pyre. Indeed, the timber from the structure may have provided the fuel for the pyre (Fig. 12). Charcoal from the remains of the pyre provided a date of 1160±60 BP (Beta-150535), very similar to that from Area T and clearly linking the later burials in the cave with the sealing of the entrance and the erection of structures on the surface.

The other interesting feature to emerge from the excavations in Trench 3 was a ditch-like feature filled with topsoil, which was situated in the south-east of the cutting and ran across the excavated area for a length of 3.50m (Pl. 24). This feature occurred immediately inside (north) of the modern stone wall that crowns the broad bank that forms the straight side of the D-shaped enclosure. The presence of the wall and a water cistern at this point ruled out further

FIG. 12

*Plan of Trench 3.*

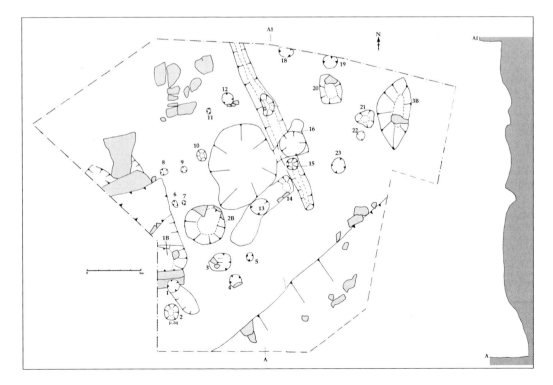

excavation in this area, and only the northern side of the feature was uncovered; however, it suggests that the enclosure was internally ditched, at least on its southern side.

## 2.4 THE CAVE

There was no clear stratigraphy within the cave, and, although this made it easier to excavate the material, it precludes the possibility of suggesting a detailed sequence of deposition within the cave. This was compounded by the fact that there had clearly been much disturbance inside the cave, with collapse moved and evidence of digging in the excavated areas. Indeed, during the 2000 season of excavation the cave, which had been fitted with locked wooden doors, was broken into at night, and two large holes excavated in Area X.

Over all of the excavated areas the upper soil layer was a brown clay that had been trampled and, owing to flooding of the cave, was in effect mud. This soil was only 13mm deep in the small area in the Two-Star Temple in which it occurred, where it rested on a flowstone-covered stone floor, which was visible throughout the rest of the chamber. In the Graveyard, Area X, Area W and Area V this soil was up to 0.80m deep, but only in the Graveyard did it again rest on a stone floor. Elsewhere in the excavated area this brown mud rested on a cream-coloured, sandy sediment that at the southern extent of Area X was up to 3.7m deep. This sediment had probably been washed into the cave over the years and was in most cases sterile, although the upper layers of sediment at the base of the entrance shaft were flecked with charcoal and were clearly redeposited.

In Area S, where two pits were excavated through this sediment to a depth of 1.65m, it was found to rest on a sediment that was light yellow in colour and rested on the cave floor; presumably the stratigraphy was similar underneath the upper sediment throughout the system.

All of the artefacts and most of the skeletal material, both human and animal, were recovered from the upper layer of brown clay; even in areas such as Quadrants C and D in the Graveyard, where there was little or no soil, any material recovered was found in pockets of this soil between the stones. The exception was the Two-Star Temple, where most of the skeletal material was found lying directly on the cave floor (Pl. 25). Indeed, excavation clearly showed that before the deposition of this brown clay the Graveyard chamber would have looked the same as the Two-Star Temple: with little or no soil or

PL. 25
*Bone and charcoal on
the flowstone-covered
floor of the Two-Star
Temple.*

sediment and stone floors visible over most of the chamber.

This brown clay was the same as the general topsoil on the surface of the reef—the soil that the enclosing bank was partly composed of and the soil through which the circular depression that facilitated construction of the entrance shaft was excavated. Therefore, this soil may well have fallen into the cave system at the time when the area on the surface was excavated to enlarge the entrance to the cave and to construct and subsequently seal the drystone-walled entrance shaft. Yet, given that the naturally deposited sediments did not settle in the Graveyard, it is unlikely that infalling soil would have managed to so completely cover the floor of this chamber. It seems more likely that the soil was deliberately brought into the cave at this time, either to cover the burials inserted in this final phase of activity—the earlier burials in the chamber becoming covered by and mixed into the soil during this operation— or to cover the earlier burials and provide a clean surface. The presence of a tenth-century silver hoard in a cleft in the rock floor of the Graveyard, covered by a 0.65m depth of the brown soil and stones, seems to support this argument (Pl. 26).

As the lack of any sizeable deposit of inwashed sediment in the Two-Star Temple and the passage connecting this chamber to the Graveyard shows, only minimal amounts of the soil was carried any farther into the system through the action of water and human activity. It is therefore very probable that this brown clay is associated with the final phase of activity at the cave, the insertion of burials in

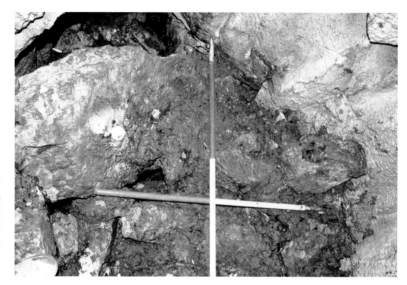

**PL. 26**
*Quadrant B, showing stones and mud piled against the large stone that partially sealed the entrance to Area Z.*

the tenth century. This would imply that there are a mixture of earlier and later burials in the Graveyard, and possibly other areas where the brown clay occurs, but that the burials in the Two-Star Temple are earlier than those inserted in the tenth century.

Indeed the two radiocarbon-dated pieces of bone from the Two-Star Temple are earlier, producing dates of 1260±50 BP (Beta-137049) and 1220±40 BP (Beta-137051). The distribution of artefacts within the cave appears to support this argument in that the only two artefacts from the Two-Star Temple were recovered from the minimal deposit of brown clay near the entrance to the chamber from the passage linking it to the Graveyard. No other excavated area of the cave produced so few finds, which suggests a difference in the burial style between the Two-Star Temple and those areas where the brown clay was deposited. This difference was also visible in the arrangement of the bone within the two chambers. In the Two-Star Temple the disarticulated bone usually occurred in larger groupings and was often placed in clefts and alcoves within the chamber; there was far less bone scattered across the central area of the chamber than was uncovered in the Graveyard. It is probable that this more coherent arrangement of the disarticulated human remains was also the case in the Graveyard before the deposition of the brown clay and the insertion of the later burials.

## 2.5 THE STONE SETTING

The only identified structure within the Graveyard was a subcircular

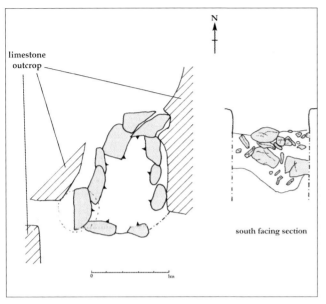

setting of stones, which was covered by a number of larger slabs and contained the main deposit of cremated animal bone, charcoal and ash (Fig. 13; Pl. 27). Human and animal skeletal material was found in the soil above and around this stone setting, although no unburnt bones were recovered from within the setting itself. The amber beads (41, 44, 48, 64 and 69) were all recovered from charcoal- and ash-rich deposits around the setting. As already noted, the cremation deposit produced more than 1.4kg of bone, which analysis has shown to be composed exclusively of cremated animal bone (see Appendix 3). However, there is clear evidence linking the cremated animal bone, and consequently the stone setting, with the activity on the surface— the pyre site etc.—which it has already been suggested is contemporary with the latest phase of burial within the cave (Pl. 28). Indeed, the discovery of amber beads associated with the cremation deposit would, on the basis that all of the finds come from areas associated with the brown clay and the later phase of burial, support a tenth-century date for the setting and cremation deposit.

FIG. 13
*Plan and section of the stone setting in the Graveyard.*

PL. 27
*The stone setting in the Graveyard during excavation.*

## 2.6 AREA X

Both human and animal skeletal remains, as well as artefacts, were

PL. 28
*The cremation deposit inside the stone setting.*

recovered from the brown clay in Area X, and this material clearly relates to the final phase of burial in the cave; however, the question arises of whether there were burials in this area before the insertion of burials in the tenth century.

Area X has to be viewed as the access way to the chambers of the Graveyard and the Two-Star Temple, and therefore burials could not be placed in this area until access to the cave via this route was no longer required. The fact that two crude steps were cut into the sediment underlying the brown clay in Area X demonstrates its use as an access way. However, the steepness of the slope, which necessitated the steps, would have made it very difficult to rest any burials in Area X unless they were buried in the sediment or later brown clay. It is also worthy of note that the sediment at the base of and immediately inside the entrance shaft had the appearance of having been levelled; indeed, much of the sediment in this area was charcoal flecked and probably redeposited.

Therefore, the evidence suggests that the basal sediment slope of Area X had been remodelled to allow easier access. Indeed, the levelling of the area at the base of the shaft and inside it would, more importantly, have allowed the drystone walling of the shaft to rest on a level foundation (Pl. 29). This indicates that the work on the sediment slope, particularly the levelling of the upper area near the

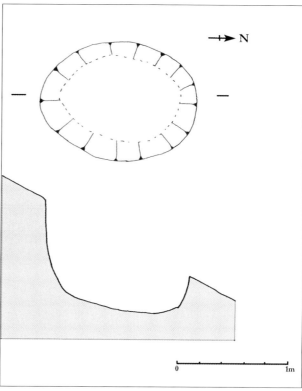

entrance, is contemporary with the construction of the drystone-walled shaft and the later phase of burial.

## 2.7 AREAS T, U, V, W AND Z

These areas were all given separate identifications to the main gallery of the cave (Area X) and the two chambers named by the Mid-West Caving Club because they were clearly discrete areas with defined boundaries within the overall layout of burial in the cave. In the case of Areas T, U and Z these boundaries were natural in that they were a result of the structure of the cave: dead-end passages or alcoves in Areas U and Z, and the raised shelflike area in Area T. In the case of Areas V and W the boundaries were artificial: the pit dug through the sediment in the case of Area V (Fig. 14) and the shallow grave-cut in the case of W. Area W has the added difference of being the location of the only articulated skeleton from the site.

## 2.8 THE BURIALS

Human skeletal remains were recovered from all of the excavated

PL. 29
*Area X, the long, sloping entrance gallery, looking down toward the Graveyard.*

FIG. 14
*Plan and section of the pit in Area V.*

areas of the cave except Area Y, the small deposit of brown soil situated midway along the passage connecting the Graveyard and the Two-Star Temple. The skeletal remains were found resting in, on or under this brown soil in all areas except the Two-Star Temple, where the soil occurred only immediately inside the entrance to the chamber from the connecting passage. This suggests that burial within the cave was centred on the two chambers—the Graveyard and the Two-Star Temple—with the connecting passage not being used.

The lack of the brown soil in the Two-Star Temple, as discussed above, also suggests a temporal difference between the burials here and elsewhere in the cave; the small amount of fragmented animal bone recovered from the Two-Star Temple compared to the volumes from elsewhere in the cave supports this interpretation (Appendix 3). Indeed, the small amount of animal bone from the Two-Star Temple could well have been deposited there by the annual flooding of the cave or visitors to the cave and is probably evidence of a difference in burial rite also.

This two-phase use of the cave as a place of burial is substantiated by the radiocarbon determinations from the site, which suggest that the earliest use of the cave may date to the fifth century but is centred on the period AD 635–815, with the later phase of burial centring on the period AD 880–1010. As shown above, the dates from the Two-Star Temple indicate use of the chamber in the eighth century. However, although twenty radiocarbon dates were taken from the cave, only a small proportion of the total volume of skeletal material was dated, and, because of the disarticulated nature of the remains, the dates are not helpful in interpreting phases of burial. Indeed, two or more dates could be from the same individual. Therefore, the short time-span between the two phases of burial may be a reflection of the material that was dated rather than indicating two distinct phases of burial within the cave, and the site may well have been in continuous use.

Interestingly, even though four trenches were excavated on the surface, only four fragments of human bone were recovered, while animal skeletal material was more common, particularly in Trench 3. This clearly shows that, even though there is evidence that rituals relating to burial within the cave took place on the surface—cremation of animals, use of the post-and-wall structure—all burial clearly centred on the cave interior. It is also worth pointing out that the radiocarbon dates taken from the trenches on the surface clearly date the activity within the enclosure to the tenth century.

# 3 SITE DISCUSSION

## 3.1 CAVES

The archaeological study of caves in Ireland is a relatively minor field, and few archaeological finds from such sites are recorded. This, even though caves themselves are common features throughout the countryside, especially in limestone areas where caverns have been created by water action, as is the case in the Cloghermore area.

The cave at Dunmore, Co. Kilkenny, is probably the best known site with Scandinavian associations because of the reference in the Annals of the Four Masters for the year AD 928 (dated in the Annals of Ulster to AD 930): 'Godfrey, grandson of Imhar, with the foreigners of Ath Cliath, demolished and plundered Dearc Fearna, where one thousand persons were killed'. Dunmore Cave has generally been accepted as the Dearc Fearna of the annals and the site of a massacre carried out by the Scandinavians of Dublin in AD 928. There has been a long history of the recovery of human bone from the cave, and a number of excavations have been conducted.

Wynne Foot (1870–1, 78) excavated near the Well in the Rabbit Burrow in 1869. E.T. Hardman (1875, 168–76) excavated in the same area and also that beside the 'Market Cross' stalagmite column. Monks (1946–7, 55–60) excavated in the Rabbit Burrow, the Market Cross chamber and the Crystal Hall; and the Market Cross chamber, the Rabbit Burrow and the Recess, Area A, were excavated in 1973 (Drew and Huddart 1980). All of these excavations, together with chance finds, have produced large quantities of disarticulated human bone, as well as quantities of animal bone, yet none of the excavators notes the occurrence of an *in situ* burial. Indeed, Drew and Huddart (1980, 17) note that the remains consisted of scattered or piled-up areas of human bone, often interspersed with cattle, sheep and pig bone.

A total of 45 individuals were represented in the bone assemblage from the 1973 excavations: over 57 per cent were children, and 63 per cent of the adult bones were identified as those of females. This led the excavators to suggest that the cave had been used as a refuge by women, children and, possibly, old men (*ibid.*). However, an interesting group of bones was recovered in 1996 from a cavity in the chamber known as the Town Hall (Buckley 2000, 5). Analysis showed that the deposit consisted almost entirely of animal bone, with a small amount of human bone. Most of the human bone came from a foetus of about 36 weeks' gestation, but there were also three fragments of adult long bone and a fragment of adult rib. This arrangement of bone deposited in a cavity is very similar to that from the pit in Area V at Cloghermore (Appendix 2), although the Cloghermore deposit also contained a number of finds. Dowd (1997, 184–5) has interpreted the large number of children's bones from certain parts of Dunmore Cave as possible evidence that these areas were used as a *ceallúnach*, or children's burial-ground. However, given the fact that a number of the children in these areas were over 7 years of age (Drew and Huddart 1980), this thesis is questionable.

The recorded finds from the cave include glass beads, a woodman's axehead, a silver hoard comprising coins and one piece of hack silver, ringed pins, an amber ring, a bone bead, two small bobbin-shaped pieces of wood and iron fragments. More recently, in 1999, a hoard of 43 silver and bronze items was discovered in a recess deep in the cave. The hoard was dated to AD 970 on the basis of coins minted in the north of England and included hack silver, ingots and conical buttons made of fine silver wire (Buckley 2000, 5).

The finding of foetal bones in a cavity with a small amount of adult bone and animal remains would argue against the traditional view of the human remains being the result of a massacre. Indeed, the massacre is dated to AD 928 in the annals, but the recently discovered hoard is dated to AD 970, which clearly indicates use of the site only 40 years or so after the recorded massacre. The fact that the cave has been accessible and often visited, coupled with the numerous piecemeal excavations and removal of bone, makes any clear interpretation of the site very difficult. However, the artefacts recovered from the site are comparable with material from the Cloghermore assemblage, and many display Scandinavian influence, while the presence of human and animal remains together is also comparable to Cloghermore. Therefore, the possibility that Dunmore Cave was a place of Irish burial with the subsequent insertion of Scandinavian or Hiberno-Scandinavian burials cannot be ignored.

Another cave site with similarities to Cloghermore was excavated at Carrigmurrish, Whitechurch, Co. Waterford, by Ussher in 1881 (1885–6, 362). The site is described as a 'rath situated on a high limestone knoll'. In the centre of the site there was a depression flanked on one side by a rock, which subsequently proved to be hollow. This led into a system of galleries that Ussher interpreted as the 'kitchen midden' of the rath. When excavated, the cave was found to be full of earth and stones, from which what appeared to be a conical shield boss of Viking type was recovered, along with a variety of other pieces including two jet bracelets, a knife, a spearhead, some iron nails, a ringed pin and a bronze buckle. The finds clearly date this cave deposit to the Viking Age, and the location of the cave inside an enclosure on a limestone outcrop mirrors that at Cloghermore. Shield bosses are most commonly associated with Viking burials, and the other finds from the site would fit into such a context quite comfortably. Indeed, the finding of a single skull at the site may indicate the presence of at least one burial within the cave. The site at Carrigmurrish clearly offers a number of interesting parallels for Cloghermore, most importantly the only clear parallel for the location of the entrance to the cave inside an enclosure.

Other caves explored in the early twentieth century have also produced human remains and artefacts of Scandinavian or Hiberno-Scandinavian character. A number of limestone caves in County Clare were investigated by a committee of the Royal Irish Academy appointed to explore Irish caves (Scharff et al. 1906). In the so-called Alice and Gwendoline Caves the scattered and disarticulated remains of a single individual were recovered, although it is interesting that the skeletal remains consisted mainly of bones from the fingers and feet. The Gwendoline Cave also produced an amber bead and two metal 'bracelets'. One of the bracelets is of gold (ibid., plate V, fig. 16) and is described as a simple slip of flat gold bent around until the squared ends meet. It was found in a recess between two stones and was covered by a slab, which led Westropp to conclude that it was 'manifestly buried for concealment' (Scharff et al. 1906, 67). The other bracelet is of bronze and consists of a thin band, relieved by 'X crosses, lozenges and chevrons'. It was found in material that was interpreted as the debris of a kitchen midden thrown down through a shaft from a settlement on the surface. Sheehan (2000, 34–5) has interpreted both of these 'bracelets' as being of Hiberno-Scandinavian character, the gold one being an arm-ring of broad-band type, and the copper-alloy one a copy of a coiled arm-ring.

Sheehan (*ibid.*) also notes the recorded recovery of part of a brooch of probable Hiberno-Scandinavian origin from 'about 10–12 feet under the surface in a quarry' at Clonloghan, near Newmarket-on-Fergus, Co. Clare (Bøe 1940, 132). Given the above description of the findspot, it is likely that this object also came from a cave.

Human remains were also recovered from Elder Bush Cave, Newhall townland, Co. Clare, where it was again noted that the bones were mainly from the hands, arms and feet. It was also noted that the bones were usually associated with 'the bones of domestic animals and charcoal' (Scharff *et al.* 1906, 16–19). Other artefacts such as knife blades, hones and bone pins were recovered from the Clare caves, and human remains were recovered from many of the areas investigated. However, it is interesting that no formal burial was recorded, and the human remains are described as being 'scattered'. This scattering of the bone may be due to water action, later disturbance or animal activity, as is suggested in the report. However, it is more likely that the burials within these caves were disarticulated at the time of or shortly after burial, as at Cloghermore.

In the cave known as The Catacombs, at Edenvale, the bones of at least three adults and one child were recovered; some of the bones are described as being 'scorched'. Among the artefacts recovered from this cave was a 'bronze strap, a buckle or brooch of bronze, plated in silver and engraved with an interlace pattern'. The object is probably a buckle and dates to the ninth/tenth century. A bronze pin was recovered from the nearby Bats' Cave in Newhall townland (Scharff *et al.* 1906).

One of the earliest scientific excavations of a cave was that undertaken by the Third Harvard Archaeological Expedition to Ireland at Kilgreany, Co. Waterford (Movius 1935). The excavation was prompted by the finding, by the University of Bristol Spaeleological Society in 1928, of human remains that were suggested to be Palaeolithic. The excavations at Kilgreany produced material from the prehistoric and the Early Christian period; however, Movius felt that the main occupation of the cave was during the Early Christian period and that most of the archaeological material was assignable to this period.

A number of the finds from Kilgreany are paralleled at Cloghermore. An object described by Movius as a bone 'button' (272, fig. 6, no. 3) is identical to the bone spacers/beads from Cloghermore, and an object described as a lathe-turned bead (272, fig. 6, no. 2) is very similar to the gaming-pieces recovered from Cloghermore but without the central peg. Part of a decorated bone comb side-plate (272, fig. 6, no. 4), a sandstone spindle-whorl (274, fig. 6, no. 14) and two amber beads (262, fig. 7, nos 19 and 20) are also directly comparable with the material from Cloghermore, and the perforated, baluster-headed pin fragment (277, fig. 7, no. 16) appears to be part of a ringed pin that, if the ring was of the plain type, would be of a similar date to the plain-ringed, loop-headed pin from Cloghermore (Fanning 1994, 15–25). Movius also recovered 'an extraordinary quantity of human material, probably representing disturbed burials', as well as the bones of extinct and domesticated animals (Movius 1935, 281). He considered the presence of extinct fauna with much later material to indicate a very disturbed stratigraphy, caused by the periodic flooding of the cave (ibid.), a situation very similar to that at Cloghermore.

A cave excavated by Coleman (1942) near Midleton, Co. Cork, had what was described as a 'black habitation layer' that contained animal bones and seashells and produced bone pins (fig. 4, nos 6, 7 and 8), a shale spindle-whorl (fig. 4, no. 4), bone comb side-plates (fig. 4, nos 1A and B) and an iron knife (fig. 4, no. 3), similar to those recovered from Cloghermore Cave. It also produced fragments of what the excavator described as a bronze silver gilt brooch (73, no. 14) and a decorated bronze bar (74–5, no. 13), which he interpreted as part of the mounting from a shrine dating to the eighth century. The animal remains in the cave were interpreted as food of the inhabitants, and on the basis of the finds the cave occupation was dated to the eighth or ninth century.

Clearly, the evidence from Kilgreany, and probably from the Clare caves, indicates multi-period use; the picture from Dunmore Cave is unclear, but the artefact record suggests that the use of the cave dates mainly to the ninth–tenth centuries; and the evidence from Midleton suggests use during the eighth–ninth centuries. The caves at Kilgreany and Dunmore and a number of the Clare caves had undoubtedly been used for burial during the ninth–tenth centuries, and it is striking that in all three cases no articulated burial was noted. In all cases, as with all except one burial at Cloghermore, the bones were scattered or heaped and intermixed with the bones of animals. The cave at Midleton, however, seems to have been a habitation rather than a burial site. Nonetheless, all of the caves discussed above have produced some artefacts that either are of Hiberno-Scandinavian character or, as in the case of the possible mounts from a reliquary or shrine from both Kilgreany and Midleton, would be more likely to occur in a Scandinavian or

Hiberno-Scandinavian cultural context. The presence of these finds associated with disarticulated human and animal bone in the case of Kilgreany, Dunmore and a number of the Clare caves is directly comparable with the evidence from Cloghermore. The evidence suggests that, as at Cloghermore, the majority of the burials are of local people, but possibly according to a pagan rite.

O'Brien (2003) has suggested that up until the late seventh–early eighth century there were small numbers of high-ranking, probably Christian, burials being placed in and around prehistoric monuments among their pagan ancestors, as evidenced at Knowth, Co. Meath, and Ballymacaward, Co. Donegal. She also notes that members of the laity in general were still being buried in family cemeteries up until the end of the seventh century, although from the eighth century onward Christians were expected to be buried close to a church. Therefore, on the basis of O'Brien's examples of Christian burial in places of earlier, non-Christian burial, the burials in these caves may be Christian. However, in the case of Cloghermore, the evidence of the defleshing of the bodies—probably by being interred elsewhere—the wholesale disarticulation of the skeletal remains and the placing of them in a cave with no definite evidence of earlier use suggest that these burials, at least, may well be according to a non-Christian rite.

The presence of artefacts that would sit comfortably in a Scandinavian context, such as the hoards at Dunmore and the mount from a shrine or reliquary at Kilgreany, surely raises the question of whether there are burials of Scandinavian character within the caves also. The sites at Kilgreany, Dunmore and Cloghermore may well have been chosen as burial sites by pagan Scandinavian or Hiberno-Scandinavian groups because of the fact that they were already burial sites and thus well-recognised features and sacred places in the landscape. Indeed, the volume of human skeletal remains from Kilgreany, Dunmore and Cloghermore indicates that there was a significant population in these areas that may still have been buried according to rites not easily reconcilable with Christian beliefs of the period.

The possible inclusion of pagan Scandinavian burials in sites that were being used by local populations during the ninth and tenth centuries may provide an explanation for the finding of artefacts of Scandinavian character in places such as caves. More importantly, however, it would provide clear evidence of Scandinavian settlement of areas of Ireland well outside the urban centres and accepted areas of Scandinavian control.

## 3.2 THE ENCLOSURE

Enclosures with a D-shape, as identified in Cloghermore, are somewhat unusual in the Irish archaeological record; a number of these have been recorded, and some have been identified as Hiberno-Scandinavian camps.

At a site at Athlunkard, Co. Clare, a placename originally rendered 'longford' in the seventeenth century, a D-shaped enclosure abutting the River Shannon has recently been identified (Kelly and O'Donovan 1998). The site is surrounded by marsh and enclosed by a curved earthen bank forming an enclosure measuring 75m by 30m. The authors suggest that the site represents the remains of a Viking *longphort* founded between AD 840 and AD 930 and compare it to sites at Dunrally, Co. Laois—identified in recent years as Longphort Rothlaoibh, the destruction of which is recorded in the annals in AD 862—and Annagassan, Co. Louth, where an oval enclosure called Lisnarann, overlooking a D-shaped island, may be the site of the *longphort* recorded in the annals in AD 841 (Kelly and Maas 1999, 137–43).

Similar, though larger, enclosures have been identified in England and linked to the Scandinavian settlement of that country (Dyer 1972). Dyer records the presence of a number of D-shaped enclosures on the boundary of the Danelaw and divides them into two main types: those that are sited on flat land beside rivers or navigable streams and contain a number of acres; and those that are sited on small islands surrounded by fenland or marsh, the islands providing a good view across the surrounding countryside.

The larger, riverside sites are exemplified at the Hillings, Eaton Socon, in Huntingdonshire, at Wimblington in Cambridgeshire, and at Bolnhurst in Bedfordshire, and the generally smaller, island sites occur at Stonea Island, Huntingdonshire, and particularly at Woodmer End, Shillington. At Woodmer End there is a D-shaped earthwork known locally as Church Spanel. Rising 15 feet (*c.* 4.7m) above meadows once liable to floods is an artificially fortified gravel island with a stream on one side, a strong D-shaped outer bank with a wet inner ditch, and a slight inner bank. The site measures 550 feet by 350 feet (*c.* 168m by *c.* 107m). Dyer suggests that these sites may represent frontier forts of the Danelaw and may have been constructed soon after it was established.

At Repton, Derbyshire, excavation has revealed evidence suggesting that a D-shaped enclosure was constructed as a winter camp for the Viking army of AD 873–4. The River Trent forms one side, and the rest of the site is surrounded by a bank and ditch, in which the pre-existing monastic church is incorporated as a gatehouse (Biddle and Kjølbye-Biddle 1992).

Interestingly, the limestone reef at Cloghermore meets many of the criteria of Dyer's island sites: the reef is in effect a stone island situated in land that is marshy and prone to flooding. The nearest watercourse to the site is 500m to the south-south-east, a river known as the Little River Maine, which flows generally south-eastward to join the River Maine in the townland of Springmount, 5.2km away. The River Maine, having flowed through Castleisland and been joined by the Brown Flesk flowing from the east, flows west from here to enter the sea at Castlemaine Harbour. The River Lee, 1.2km to the north-east of Cloghermore, flows west to enter Tralee Bay at Blennerville.

However, although the form of the enclosure at Cloghermore can be paralleled in Ireland and Britain, the Cloghermore enclosure is unlikely to be defensive, given its small size. The enclosure may well be part of a wider complex of monuments on the surface of the limestone reef, as suggested by the presence of cairns, meandering banks and at least two other enclosures higher up the limestone reef. However, only an extensive programme of excavation could confirm that these structures are coeval with the use of the cave and the D-shaped enclosure.

# 4 THE BURIAL RITES

Two basic burial rites are recorded within Cloghermore Cave: articulated burial, noted in Area W and Area U (partially articulated remains of a child), and disarticulated burial, noted elsewhere in the cave. However, these basic rites are complicated by the inclusion of cremated and unburnt animal remains, including horse, suggesting more specific burial rites. Given the dating evidence, it is clear that the earlier burials are of native Irish; however, the later burials, and in particular those associated with rites involving animal bone, both burnt and unburnt, horse burial and grave-goods, must, given the date, be seen as representing a Scandinavian or Hiberno-Scandinavian group.

It was obvious during the excavation and has subsequently been confirmed by analysis of the human remains that a full selection of bones was not being recovered from the cave. Even the articulated burial in Area W had been disturbed and was missing a number of bones, most noticeably the skull. As a total weight, less than half of the bone that should be recovered, based on the minimum number of individuals (MNI) in the cave, was retrieved.

## 4.1 THE EARLIER BURIALS

The fact that up to two-thirds of the bones that should be in the cave are missing may be due to the removal of bones by visitors to the cave or animals. However, there is little evidence of animal activity within the cave, and the volume of bone that is missing is too high to have been removed as souvenirs. It is more likely that, in the case of the earlier burials, this lack of bone is due to the form of the burial rites. It is clear that these earlier burials must, given the dating evidence, be native Irish, yet the burials are possibly those of a non-Christian population (Pl. 30). This is suggested by the use of the cave rather than a recognised Christian burial site, the evidence of defleshing of the bodies elsewhere, and the disarticulation of the

PL. 30
*Disarticulated human bone in the Two-Star Temple. Radiocarbon dating suggests that the burials in this area relate to the earlier phase of burial.*

skeletal remains. Some of the artefacts from the cave may be associated with the earlier burials, given their long currency in the archaeological record, although most of the finds fit more comfortably into a tenth-century context.

The earlier, native Irish burials are characterised by a general lack of finds and the recovery of only partial skeletal remains, as evidenced in the Two-Star Temple. Given the volume of bone missing from these burials, it can be stated that only certain bones were placed in the cave. Analysis of the bone material has shown that there are very few bones from the hands and feet among the earlier burials. These are among the smallest bones in the body and are the most likely to be lost if a body is moved after decomposition. Clearly, the bodies were interred elsewhere, and certain skeletal elements were brought to the cave after full decomposition. Such an exercise may have been carried out at set times of the year as part of a general religious/ritual festival. There is also the possibility that the bodies were exposed for the purpose of excarnation; however, this would seem the less likely scenario within the wider Christian society of the time.

Interestingly, this lack of bones from the hands and particularly the feet contrasts sharply with the occurrence of bones from the feet of two sub-adults and an adult with a sub-adult torso in the pit in

Area V, which would seem, on the basis of the presence of numerous artefacts and a radiocarbon date, to be one of the later burials. The skeletal elements brought to or left in the cave were placed on stone floors, in clefts and on rock shelf areas before the brown clay was brought in and were meant to be visible. In other words, the cave seems to have been used by this pagan Irish population as an ossuary, being accessed at regular intervals over a period that may extend from the fifth to the ninth century.

## 4.2 BURIAL RITE IN EARLY MEDIEVAL IRELAND

The rite of burial in Ireland in the mid-first millennium AD is still an archaeologically grey area. A variety of burial traditions are in use in the Iron Age, utilising cremation as well as inhumation. In the transition from the Iron Age to the early medieval period little is known of the burial practices in vogue. Inhumation appears to be the favoured rite, though not exclusive, and in barrows cremation continues to be used into the earliest part of the early medieval period.

In the early medieval period extended inhumations were placed in dug graves—stone-lined, slab-lined and lintel graves, the last form probably evolving from the slab-lined graves. This new rite of extended inhumation, which was introduced to Britain in the later second century, appears to have been introduced to Ireland very shortly after (O'Brien 2003, 65).

It is also evident that, in the late seventh and the early eighth century, burial in formal Christian cemeteries was not yet the norm (O'Brien 1992a, 132), although it is suggested that the standard formal burial rite was that of extended supine inhumation oriented east–west (O'Brien 2003, 67).

The first English graves that can confidently be said to contain Christians date to the eighth and ninth centuries, marked by an increase in control by the Church; and by the tenth century several churches were equipped with graveyards (Bassett *et al.* 1992, 4). However, it is not known at what date burial in formally consecrated Christian cemeteries became the standard practice in Ireland (Leigh Fry 1999, 40).

It is likely that there were some Christians in Ireland in the fifth century, perhaps traders and settlers from Roman Britain, and certainly sufficient numbers for Palladius to be sent by Pope Celestine to minister to the 'Irish believers in Christ'. Thomas suggests that by

431 there were communities, or at least an identifiable community, of Christians in Ireland. They could, at least, be called *credentes*, presumably implying baptised and confirmed Christians, and were sufficient in numbers to warrant a bishop (Thomas 1981, 300), whose mission appears to have been concentrated along the eastern coast of Ireland. However, it must be stressed that Ireland was not swiftly converted (Edwards 1990, 99).

It is not until the sixth and seventh centuries, with the growth of monasteries, that a rapid spread of Christianity is seen throughout Ireland, with the resultant assimilation of the Church into Irish society (Edwards 1990, 99). Hughes (1966, 45) suggests that the sixth-century Church in Ireland was not merely legislating against pagan survivals, as it would do for centuries to come, but was also struggling against a pagan environment. It is now realised that almost nothing is known of the Church before the seventh century and that it grew in a more *ad hoc* fashion than was previously thought (Edwards 1990, 100).

However, although a significant amount is now known about the major religious foundations such as Clonmacnoise, which from around AD 900 received political patronage in return for conceding burial rights (Bradley 1998, 42), almost nothing is known of the hold that Christianity had in the more rural and inaccessible areas. In these areas it may have taken considerably longer for a major change in religious beliefs to occur. In spite of the assumption that Christianity was the dominant religion of the island by the sixth century AD, there are no documents from Ireland dating to this period. The non-Christianity of the primitive Church, except insofar as it bore directly on Church affairs, was studiously ignored (Ó Cróinín 1995, 2). In the late seventh century Tírechán refers to a burial of converts: 'and they made a round ditch (*fossam rodundam*) after the manner of a *ferta*, because this is what the heathen Irish used to do, but we call it *relic*' (Bieler 1979, 145). This appears to describe a ring-ditch or barrow and indicates a continued use of such monuments into the early medieval period. Yet the term *relic* is used, from which stems the Irish word *reilig*, meaning a cemetery (O'Brien 1992a, 133). Interestingly, the *ferta* was then made over to Patrick, and he is described as making an earthen church in that place (Bieler 1979, 145). Various inducements are offered in the early eighth-century sources to encourage Christian burials to be separate from pagan ones, which indicates that burial in non-Christian tribal or family cemeteries was still being practised in Ireland in this period (O'Brien 1992a, 136).

The closest excavated early medieval religious foundations to Cloghermore are at Ardfert and Reask, at the western end of the Dingle Peninsula, Illaunloughan and Church Island, Valentia. The early medieval site at Reask, Co. Kerry, was excavated in the 1970s, its earliest date, from a sample taken from a hearth, being sometime between the third and the seventh century. It is unclear whether this determination pre-dates the use of the site as a cemetery and indeed whether the earlier phases of the site were lay or monastic. A total of 42 lintel graves were excavated, all of which contained a fill of loose soil with a red/orange staining but no bone. It is clear that soil conditions on the site did not favour the preservation of bone (Fanning 1981, 81). The stone church at Reask may date from the eighth century or perhaps slightly later (*ibid.*, 98).

At Illaunloughan, Co. Kerry, several graves, some of which were lintelled, were excavated, and an early medieval date is postulated (Marshall and Walsh 1998, 106; 2005, 84–5). In comparison, a radiocarbon date from skeletal material from a lintel grave from Moyne graveyard, Shrule, Co. Mayo, returned a determination of AD 860–1020 (Manning 1987, 58).

It is unfortunate that definite dating is not available for the burials at Illaunloughan and Reask, as this would enlighten us on when Christian-style burial was adopted in Ireland. It has been suggested that 'lintel' graves' are of post-seventh-century date (O'Brien 2003, 67), but this is not certain. Recently, a large oval enclosure containing the remains of eighteen individuals was excavated in the townland of Clogher, Lixnaw, Co. Kerry. All but one of the burials were aligned east–west, with the exception of a partially crouched burial that was aligned north–south. Two of these east–west burials were radiocarbon dated to AD 450–670 (Beta-194915) and AD 530–650 (Beta-194916). No trace of any structure that may have indicated the presence of a church was noted on the site (Coyne 2004; Collins and Coyne, forthcoming).

Leigh Fry (1999, 42–3) suggests that, given the various laws and decrees that were made in an effort to standardise Christian burial, and the continuing resistance that they encountered in continental Europe in the ninth century, it would be unwise to presume that burial in traditional, non-Christian sites and non-Christian burial practices could not have survived in Ireland to some extent into the tenth century and later. Therefore, there is no reason why the disarticulation and placement of selected remains within the cave at Cloghermore cannot be explained by the continuing adherence to earlier practices, such as the veneration of ancestral remains and the ritual placement of selected bones in sites such as caves and megalithic tombs, as discussed in a Neolithic context by Cooney (2000, 86–94). Indeed, in discussing the pagan Iron Age, Raftery (1994, 189) has stated that the burials of Iron Age Ireland are of decidedly local character, reflecting a long continuity of funerary practices extending back to 'remote antiquity'. There would clearly be a case for suggesting a continuity of certain aspects of burial ritual into the early medieval period, within a possibly pagan milieu, as may be the case at Cloghermore.

### 4.3 THE LATER BURIALS

The articulated burial in Area W offers the clearest picture of the events that may have led to the disarticulation and removal of bone material from the later burials interred according to rites of probable Scandinavian origin. There is clear evidence that the skull of this individual had been pulled from the body and his right foot had been placed over his left knee when the body was in an advanced state of decomposition but before the flesh had completely decayed. The disturbance of the leg/foot may well be accidental, but the removal of the skull is most certainly not The removal of the skull before the complete decomposition of the flesh, tendons etc. would not have been a pleasant task and would go against the more usual practice of allowing complete decomposition before disarticulation of the skeleton. Any attempt at full disarticulation of a partially decomposed body would require the limbs etc. to be severed from one another, thus leading to cut-marks on the bone, none of which were noted.

The removal of the skull from the body in Area W and the disturbance of the leg/foot may point to a deliberate desecration of the burial. Similarly, the partially articulated remains of a child in Area U again suggest disturbance rather than deliberate disarticulation. The burial in Area W is of Scandinavian or Hiberno-Scandinavian character, and this desecration may have been perpetrated by the native Irish population that had been using the cave before the occurrence of the later burials in the tenth century, after its abandonment by a Scandinavian or Hiberno-Scandinavian group. Indeed, this suggestion is substantiated by the finding of a number of bones in the Graveyard that displayed evidence of peri-mortem breaks. In her analysis of the bone material, Lynch states that the severity of some of the breaks clearly indicates that they occurred when the bones were defleshed or partially defleshed but still fresh. She also suggests that the breaks are evidence of deliberate damage (Appendix 2). Yet there is also the possibility that the skull, and perhaps bones from other burials within the cave, was removed by a departing group for reburial elsewhere, in their Scandinavian homeland or in the more secure hinterlands of the Scandinavian towns such as Limerick or Cork.

Interestingly, analysis of the human bones indicates that there are a few burials within the cave for which there are more complete skeletal remains than the others. This suggests a clear difference in burial rite and a probable temporal division between the two groups of burial. The burials for which there are more complete skeletal remains are a prime adult male and an adult female in the Graveyard (Quadrants C and D), and a child aged 1–3 years and a neonate in the Entrance Gallery (Areas U and X respectively). Clearly, these burials are different from the rest in that all skeletal elements are represented.

It is likely that these burials were interred in a similar articulated manner to the prime adult male in Area W but were later disturbed, either as a deliberate act of desecration or by later general disturbance of the site. However, given the evidence of disturbance of the burial in Area W shortly after interment and the breaking of fresh bones noted above, a deliberate act of desecration seems the most likely scenario.

Indeed, such an act may also explain the obvious problems with the complete lack of identifiable human bone from the cremation deposit within the stone setting in the Graveyard. As already stated, it is highly unlikely that such an elaborate ritual was undertaken solely to cremate animals or that artefacts such as the cremated spindle-whorl and amber beads are associated solely with an animal cremation. One must assume that a body was cremated as part of this ritual and that the cremated remains were possibly placed in a container within the stone setting. The artefacts associated with the burial suggest that it was of a female of some status, and the fact that any presumed container has been removed may well be explained by a deliberate act of desecration or by removal for burial elsewhere upon abandonment of the site.

In light of this suggestion, the recovery of bones that exhibit evidence of charring from the arm and hand of a female in Area U is interesting. Lynch suggests that this burning took place when the bones were defleshed but articulated. Given the elaborate nature of the probable cremation burial—possibly the construction of the post-and-wall structure on the surface, the subsequent dismantling of this structure and the construction of a pyre—it is not unreasonable to suggest that this may have been the primary burial of the later phase of use. The unusual collection of human remains and artefacts in the pit in Area V must also be seen as part of this highly ritualised method of burial and, from radiocarbon dating evidence and the artefact assemblage, clearly dates to the late ninth century. Indeed, given the highly ritualistic treatment of the burial in the pit, it is possible that this was associated with the cremation burial in some way.

There appears to be a total of four adults that relate to the later phase of burial in the late ninth and the early tenth century: the articulated male in Area W, the prime adult male and female in the Graveyard, and the presumed cremated female. Three sub-adult burials also appear to belong to this group: the child aged 1–3 years in Area U, the neonate in Area X and the child aged 1–3 represented only by a torso in the pit in Area V. The presence of foot bones from other children and an adult is hard to explain but must surely represent a ritualistic treatment of the main child burial.

One of these later interments was associated with the placing of parts of a horse (a single mandible was recovered from the Graveyard and Area U), comprising mainly the head and limbs, in the cave, a rite that, given the date, must surely be seen as Scandinavian in origin. It is difficult to associate the horse with any particular burial. It may be associated with the prime adult male from the Graveyard, although the finding of some unburnt horse bone around the stone setting and an unburnt horse tooth within the cremation deposit may associate it with the suggested cremation burial. The male burial in Area W, the only burial still articulated, given its location so close to the entrance, may well be the last burial inserted in the cave but again clearly belongs to this later phase of burial.

## 4.4 THE DEMOGRAPHICS WITHIN THE CAVE

In looking at the division of the cave burials into native Irish and possible Scandinavian or Hiberno-Scandinavian groups, it is worth considering the demographics and artefacts from the main excavated area of the cave: the Two-Star Temple, the Graveyard (including Areas Z and T) and the Entrance Gallery (including Areas U, V, W and X and the entrance shaft). It is unlikely that looking at the more discrete excavated areas, apart from the articulated burial in Area W and the pit in Area V, would be of any worth, given the high probability of bone material from one area having been mixed with that of another. In Areas W and V this probability is removed by clearly defined boundaries to the area of burial: the pit in Area V and the grave-cut for the articulated burial in Area W.

## The Entrance Gallery

Analysis of the bone material showed that five adults were recovered from this area: one young female, one prime female, two prime males (including the articulated burial in Area W) and an old adult of indeterminate sex. Three sub-adults were also recovered: two children aged 1–3 years and a neonate.

The artefact assemblage from the fill of the entrance shaft included two bone pins (2 and 3), a whetstone (7), a copper-alloy fragment (9) and decorated bone comb fragments (60:1–4), as well as iron fragments.

It is difficult to assess the human bone found at the base of the entrance shaft, as it may have been either a deliberate deposition before sealing the shaft or the result of later disturbance. However, it may be that, similar to the suggestion by Lynch for the fragmentary remains of a second male with the articulated skeleton in Area W, these bones were deliberately included in the base of the shaft and should be viewed as part of the ritual sealing of the shaft. As such, they may date to the second phase of use or may have been chosen from the disarticulated remains already within the cave.

Area U, a dead-end offshoot passage on the eastern side of the long, sloping entrance gallery (Area X), was one of the most productive areas of the cave. It is noteworthy that the bone analysis notes the relatively complete skeletal remains of a child aged 1–3 years from Area U and that some of these bones were partially articulated.

The artefact assemblage from Area U included the unusual decorated bone handle (132), a bone gaming-piece (151), an iron bucket handle (137), a stone spindle-whorl (138), part of a draw knife (139:1), a pendant whetstone (141), a blue glass bead with yellow enamel decoration (143), the shaft of a copper-alloy pin (152) and an iron stud (153), as well as other, unidentified iron and copper-alloy fragments.

In Area X there was also one burial of note—that of a neonate—as, again, a relatively complete but disarticulated selection of bones was recovered. In discussing these bones, the analysis notes that 'none of these bones were damaged post-mortem in comparison with virtually all of the other skeletal remains recovered from this area and indeed the cave in general'. It is also suggested that, given the excellent preservation of these bones, they may have been among the last to have been deposited in the cave.

Finds recovered from Area X include an antler pin-beater (14), burnt hazelnut shells (16 and 23), part of the upper stone of a rotary quern (25), a whetstone (32), a stone disc bead (104), an amber bead (110), bone comb fragments (111:1–4), a perforated straw stalactite (112), iron shears (128:1–8) and an iron knife blade (131), as well as numerous other blade and iron fragments.

## Area V

Area V is essentially a large pit cut into the sterile cave sediments that underlay the brown clay. The pit is situated immediately inside the base of the entrance shaft and west of Area W. Clear evidence of *in situ* burning was uncovered on top of the fill of this pit.

The pit contained the remains of one adult—represented only by bones from the foot—and three sub-adults—represented by the torso of a young child and the metatarsals of two further children. This pit produced the highest density of artefacts from anywhere in the cave, including an antler spindle-whorl (120), fragments of double-sided comb teeth-plates (123 and 124), a bone point and bone pin (125 and 126), a bone gaming-piece with intact peg (135), a decorated double-sided antler comb (136), part of a small iron shears (163), and a fragment of red jasper (204), as well as other iron fragments.

The deposits in this pit were clearly sealed and must be viewed as a very deliberate deposition. These deposits and those within the stone setting in the Graveyard are clearly highly ritualistic. Charcoal recovered from the base of the pit provided a radiocarbon date of 1140±60 BP (Beta-150537), clearly placing the deposits in the early tenth century.

## Area W

Area W produced the only articulated burial from the cave (Pl. 31), which is described as follows by the on-site osteoarchaeologist, Linda Lynch.

The skeleton was lying in an extended supine position with the left leg slightly flexed to the right. The left forearm and hand, the right

PL. 31
*The articulated burial in Area W.*

upper arm, the pelvis, the upper left leg and the right leg and foot were not recovered *in situ*. The cranium, mandible and hyoid were noted as absent during excavation. The remainder of the skeleton was articulated. The bones were in an excellent state of preservation, with minimal post-depositional erosion or fragmentation.

The skeletal remains were those of a male aged between 30 and 40 years at the time of death. The preservation of complete long bones facilitated an estimation of stature of *c.* 167.9cm. There was evidence of a well-healed break to the wrist, but no other pathological lesions and/or processes or traumatic incidences were noted on the preserved bones.

As mentioned, the cranium, mandible and hyoid were absent. The first and second cervical vertebrae were recovered lying articulated, 6cm superior to the third cervical vertebra. An examination of the uppermost cervical vertebrae revealed no evidence of trauma.

If this male had been decapitated, cut-marks would have been present on the preserved neck vertebrae. The absence of the cranium, mandible and hyoid, with the displacement of the upper two vertebrae, suggests that the entire skull had been lifted sometime soon after death.

The evidence also suggests that the flesh had not completely decayed at this time: the mandible and hyoid would still have been attached to the cranium, and as the skull was pulled away the upper two vertebrae were displaced from the remaining vertebrae while still partially articulated.

There is further evidence of the disturbance of the corpse relatively soon after burial: the articulated metatarsals and a number of phalanges of the right foot were recovered lying in a prone position (that is, with the sole facing upward) to the lateral side of the left knee. Unless the right leg had been badly broken, it is physically impossible to place the right foot in such a position. It seems likely that the partially decomposed foot was disturbed, possibly accidentally, by the individuals who took the skull.

The soil above and around this articulated burial produced the fragmentary remains of a single adult male, as well as five fragments of bone representing two sub-adults. Lynch suggests that the deposition of the fragmentary remains of this second male may have been part of the ritual for the interment of the articulated burial (Appendix 2) (Pls 32 and 33). Radiocarbon dates were taken from bone and charcoal recovered from Area W; however, the bone sent for dating was not from the articulated burial but from the fragmentary remains of the second male and produced a date of 1180±40 BP (Beta-150538). The charcoal was recovered from the base of the shallow grave-cut in which the burial lay and produced a date of 1150±60 BP (Beta-150536). This suggests that the articulated burial dates to the late ninth or early tenth century but that bone from the earlier burial was disturbed and mixed in with the soil covering the burial during its interment or was deliberately included as part of the burial ritual, as suggested by Lynch.

Area W produced a number of artefacts associated directly with the articulated burial: two copper-alloy pins, probably used to hold a shroud closed over the body (96 and 122), a small iron knife (94), a small carved stone vessel or crucible (100), a copper-alloy button (105), a water-rolled pebble of red jasper (107), a copper-alloy ringed pin (115), a boat-shaped whetstone (116) and fragments of an iron shield boss (145:1–3). Fragments of a copper-alloy buckle tang (119) were found in the soil immediately over the burial, as were numerous other iron fragments.

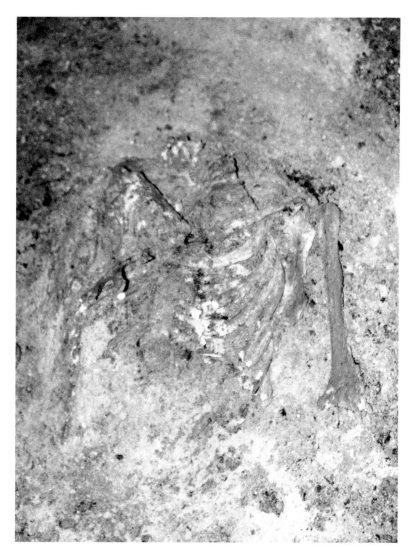

PL. 32
*The torso of the
articulated burial in
Area W.*

PL. 33
*Reconstruction of the
articulated skeleton in
Area W, after
excavation.*

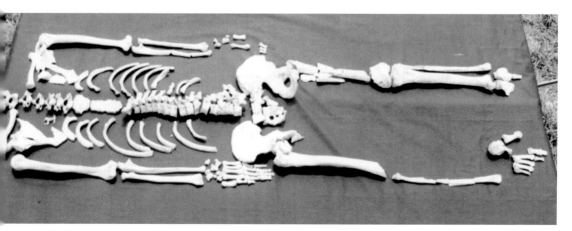

## The Graveyard

As discussed earlier, the Graveyard was identical to the Two-Star Temple before the brown soil was brought in, with a stone floor, clefts and alcoves. It is therefore most probable that disarticulated burials similar to those recorded in the Two-Star Temple had been placed here also and that they were subsequently covered by or mixed into the brown soil. The radiocarbon dates from the Graveyard substantiate this thesis as human bone from this area gave dates ranging from 1550±50 BP (Beta-137052) to 1140±40 BP (Beta-137046), suggesting a calibrated date range of AD 430–910.

The greatest depth of soil within the Graveyard was found on the eastern side of the chamber; by contrast, the western side had only pockets of the soil deposited between and in some cases under roof-collapsed boulders. Similar to the Two-Star Temple, the chamber was initially divided into four quadrants, designated A–D (clockwise from the north-east corner), for the purpose of assessing the surface bone in 1999. However, these arbitrary divisions are unsuitable for interpreting burial within the chamber.

The Graveyard produced the remains of seven adults: three young adults, including a male, a female and one of indeterminate sex, two prime female adults, a prime adult male and an old adult. Seven sub-adults were also recovered: one infant, one child aged 1–3 years, two children aged 2–3 years, one child aged 4–5 years, one child aged 7–8 years and one child aged 8–9 years.

The bone analysis shows the presence of the relatively complete but disarticulated skeletons of a prime adult male and female in Quadrants C and D on the western side of the Graveyard chamber. This raised area was composed of roof-collapsed boulders with pockets of the brown clay between the stones. The bone was recovered lying on and between the stones, and the artefacts from this half of the chamber included a bone comb (83), a gaming-piece (84), the decorated walrus ivory item (91), and numerous iron and copper-alloy fragments. In discussing these remains, the bone analysis notes that the bones of the male and female were very different in appearance. Those of the female were clean and well preserved, and those of the male were discoloured, with a very distinctive 'dark brown mottled deposit with tinges of green and grey' (Appendix 2).

It is important to remember that the Graveyard also contained the subcircular stone setting filled with cremated animal bone, ash and charcoal. Indeed, it would have to be suggested that a burial, probably also cremated, was associated with this deposit, even though analysis of the cremated material did not identify any human bone. Yet it seems unlikely that only animal bone and a bone spindle-whorl were cremated, and the amber beads (41, 44, 48, 64 and 69) are clearly associated with the deposition of the cremation. The artefacts in particular suggest that the cremation deposit relates to a burial. This may be explained by the common practice in Scandinavia of placing cremated human remains in a container inside these stone settings (see, for example, Ramskou 1976; Gräslund 1980, 53; Sander 1997, 49–50). Perhaps this was also the case at Cloghermore, but the container and its contents were removed from the cave at some point. Interestingly, unburnt horse bone was found around the setting, including a single unburnt horse tooth within the stone setting.

Other artefacts from the Graveyard were an iron axehead (1), a copper-alloy pin fragment (42), an iron spearhead ferrule with a fragment of iron blade fused to its side (45 and 46), the silver hoard consisting of hack-silver broad-band armlets and ingots (61, 66, 72:1–2, 73 and 74), an iron barrel padlock mechanism (51) and a bone bead (68), as well as copper-alloy fragments and numerous iron fragments.

Area T, on the boundary between the Entrance Gallery and the Graveyard, produced artefacts that included two iron rings (195 and 200) and a fragmentary link (207)—which probably represent the remains of a horse-bit—a hone-stone (197), a saddle-type quernstone and rubber (198 and 199), as well as numerous other iron fragments.

Area Z was a narrow, curving offshoot passage at the northern end of the Graveyard. It was partially blocked from the Graveyard by a large boulder that had the appearance of having been lifted during a period of disturbance and propped across the entrance to this narrow passage. The basal layer in most of the passage was a shallow layer of the cream-coloured sandy sediment found in Area X. However, as the brown clay occurred over a small area just inside the entrance to the passage from the Graveyard, it probably slipped into the passage from the larger chamber or was pushed in during the disturbance that moved the large boulder. The artefact assemblage from Area Z again came from this brown soil and included fragments of a bone comb (75 and 76), a bone disc bead or spacer (79), two small spherical glass beads (80 and 81) and a well-preserved plain-ringed, loop-headed copper-alloy pin (82), as well as numerous iron fragments, many with wood accretions.

## The Two-Star Temple

To facilitate the assessment and collection of the bone in this

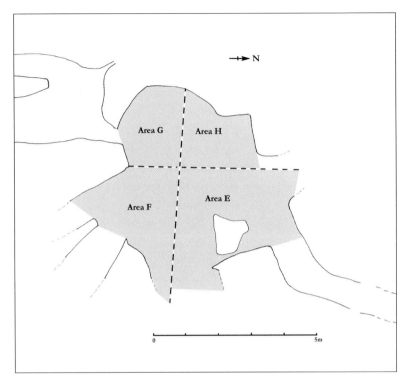

FIG. 15
*Plan of the Two-Star Temple (Areas E, F, G and H).*

chamber, it was initially divided into four quadrants, designated E–H (clockwise from the north-east corner), during the 1999 season of excavation (Fig. 15).

The Two-Star Temple produced the remains of three adults, of which one was female and one male. Four sub-adults were also recovered: one neonate, one child aged 4–6 years, one child aged 6–7 years and one child aged 9–10 years.

Finds from this area were minimal and were confined to a small deposit of the brown clay soil situated immediately inside the entrance from the passage connecting this chamber to the Graveyard. The artefacts comprised an iron arrowhead (53), a stone spindle-whorl (52), a quartz crystal (54) and iron fragments (55:1–3).

The small deposit of the brown clay soil in the Two-Star Temple may well be a result of disturbance caused by natural processes within the cave or the activities of visitors to the cave. Therefore, the presence of the artefacts within this soil is not truly representative of the burial rite within the chamber. Indeed, the vast majority of the bones from this chamber were recovered from other areas, where no artefacts were noted.

## 4.5 THE EARLIER BURIALS: IRISH PARALLELS

The use of caves for burial in Ireland has been discussed above in dealing with caves that have produced human remains and artefacts comparable to those from Cloghermore. However, a full analysis of the bone material from sites such as Dunmore Cave may illustrate a similar pattern of burial to that at Cloghermore, with the cave serving as an ossuary for the deposition of bones after interment elsewhere.

## 4.6 THE EARLIER BURIALS: FOREIGN PARALLELS

The use of caves for burial is common over a wide area of Europe over a long period of time. Caves such as Abric Romani in Catalonia, Spain, were used as paupers' cemeteries up until recent times. The cave at Vieligal in northern Portugal, which produced both burnt and unburnt remains, appears to have been used from the Neolithic to the present (Straus 1997). In certain parts of the Caucasus Mountains small natural caves were used as family burial vaults, and vast grottos were used as burial-grounds (Lubin 1997, 146). In the Crimea, Ukraine, a large cave near Menar-Khanym-Chokrak consisted of three chambers, each containing human bone. The site is interpreted as an ossuary, with the bones of the dead placed on the cave floor and subsequently disturbed by visitors to the cave. The site dates to between the first and the third century AD (Burov 1997, 133).

## 4.7 THE LATER BURIALS: IRISH PARALLELS

As discussed above, the presence of quantities of disarticulated human bone is recorded at Kilgreany Cave, Co. Waterford, Dunmore Cave, Co. Kilkenny, and caves in County Clare. It has also been suggested that this is evidence of the use of these sites as places of burial by local populations, possibly according to a pagan burial rite. Yet at all of these sites there is at least the possibility, as discussed above, of subsequent use by Scandinavian or Hiberno-Scandinavian groups. This suggestion offers a possible explanation for the occurrence of animal bone intermixed with the burials, a well-attested part of Scandinavian burial rites, and the presence of certain artefacts.

In the case of Cloghermore the majority of the disarticulated burials within the cave are, based on radiocarbon dating, related to the first phase of burial and pre-date recorded Scandinavian settlement in Ireland.

Evidence of Scandinavian burial in Ireland comes mainly from the cemeteries of Islandbridge and Kilmainham in Dublin. At Kilmainham the majority of the burials came to light between 1850 and 1870 (Edwards 1990, 180). However, the main part of the cemetery was destroyed by this time, and probably a great part of the grave-goods passed unnoticed by the workers (Bøe 1940, 11). It has also been suggested two native Irish cemeteries already existed at these locations, into which the pagan Vikings inserted their dead in the ninth century (O'Brien 1998a, 221). Interestingly, Ó Floinn (1998, 137) suggests that there were at least four separate cemeteries over a much greater area than previously thought.

It was only in 1910 that it was realised that a proper cemetery had been uncovered; thus we have little idea of the orientation or layout of the graves, and we are almost entirely dependent on the grave-goods, which can seldom be linked to specific graves (Edwards 1990, 180–1). The burial customs indicate that the Viking population of ninth-century Dublin was pagan, although the cemetery was sited not far from a monastery at Kilmainham (ibid., 181). The origins of this cemetery probably lie in its association with this Early Christian monastery at Cell Maigenn, established before the ninth century (O'Brien 1998a, 217). The cemeteries at Dublin contained variations in burial rite, including inhumation, cremation and burial in flat graves (Ó Floinn 1998, 137). Notwithstanding the almost total absence of find associations, it appears that both men and women were afforded pagan burial (ibid., 138).

From the early excavations a reliable inventory is given in only one instance, a grave containing a skeleton accompanied by a sword, a spear, an axe and the iron handles and nails of a wooden casket. As a rule the graves were interments, and in one case where the arrangement was noticed the skeleton was extended with the head to the south. Cremation may have occurred in exceptional cases, as a sword and some of the spearheads must have been intentionally bent before burial, a custom that in Norway was strictly confined to cremation burials. The cemeteries of Kilmainham and Islandbridge certainly represent the most important Norse burial-place in Ireland and Britain. The importance of Dublin is further emphasised by other finds from within the boundaries of the city. Male graves with weapons have been discovered in College Green, Bride Street and Palace Row (Bøe 1940, 65–7).

The cemeteries at Islandbridge and Kilmainham almost certainly contain residents of the Dublin longphort, which was in existence until AD 902. The majority of the graves at Islandbridge and

Kilmainham were occupied by males accompanied by weapons and, to a lesser extent, the paraphernalia of trade (Batey and Sheehan 2000, 129). The burials from Islandbridge and Kilmainham do not, at first glance, provide convincing parallels for the burials at Cloghermore, except for the articulated skeleton in its shallow grave-cut in Area W. Yet it must be remembered that a small number of other bodies seem to have been interred in a similar style but later disturbed, as discussed above.

However, there are other aspects of the burial rite recorded at Cloghermore that can be paralleled, to some degree, in Ireland, in particular the presence of large quantities of unburnt animal bone and the horse burial. In reassessing Sir William Frazer's account of the levelling of a mound at Donnybrook in 1879, Hall (1978) questions Frazer's theory that the remains found in the mound resulted from 'a piratical incursion by Vikings who left their victims and one of their own number to be buried by the Irish'. Hall sees the mass grave as representing native Irish alone rather than the mixed casualties of a battle between the Irish and the Vikings. He suggests that Frazer's theory disregards the possibility that the Viking warrior was buried according to Scandinavian tradition but equally notes the possibility that the Viking burial may have been inserted in an existing mass grave. However, he suggests that the evidence indicates that all of the occupants of the mound were laid to rest at one time and under 'Scandinavian supervision' (ibid.). Indeed, Frazer's description indicates that the warrior burial and the mass burial were inserted at the same time, while the use of a mound is suggestive of non-Christian origin. Hall also suggests that aspects of the mound are paralleled in Viking Age burials in Scandinavia and on the Isle of Man.

Of most interest, as a parallel for the rite at Cloghermore, is Hall's interpretation of the middle layer of the mound. This layer, containing charcoal, animal bones (horse, cow, sheep, pig, dog and possibly wolf) and burnt stones, is seen as part of the funerary ritual rather than evidence that the mound was constructed from clay filled with settlement debris. This layer contained a similar mix of material to that recorded throughout the excavated areas of Cloghermore Cave, and the presence of a mass grave at the site is also relevant in the context of Cloghermore. Interestingly, Hall (ibid., 74–5) also suggests that the two burials described as female, at the feet of the warrior, may represent the ritual killing of these individuals to accompany the warrior in death (74–5), a practice that also may explain the presence of female remains close to the articulated male burial in Area W at Cloghermore. O'Brien (1992b, 173) suggests that the warrior burial, possibly accompanied by two females who had no grave-goods, was inserted in an existing, native, secular or familial cemetery of the Early Christian period. Yet, as Hall noted, the use of a mound and the informal nature of the burials within it are not suggestive of a Christian origin and tend to support a non-native interpretation of the site and burial rite.

## 4.8 THE LATER BURIALS: FOREIGN PARALLELS

During the years AD 921–2 the Arab Ibn Fadlan served as secretary of an embassy from the Khalif of Baghdad to the Bulgars of the middle Volga. About one-fifth of his account of his journey, the *Risala*, relates to the Rus (Scandinavians) that he met at the camp and trading post, later the town of Bulgar. His account of a Rus funeral is the most celebrated part of the *Risala*, and a number of aspects of the description he gives are paralleled at Cloghermore.

> At last I was told of the death of one of their outstanding men. They placed him in a grave and put a roof over it for ten days while they cut and sewed garments for him...Then they brought a dog, which they cut in two and put in the ship. Then they brought his weapons and placed them by his side. Then they took two horses, ran them until they sweated, then cut them to pieces with a sword and put them into the ship. They took two cows, which they likewise cut to pieces and put in the ship. Next they killed a rooster and a hen and threw them in.

After the final rite of cremation, in which the animals described above, the dead man, a ritually sacrificed slave girl and the ship are all burnt, he describes the final act of the funeral.

> Then they constructed in the place where had been the ship which they had drawn up out of the river something like a small round hill, in the middle of which they erected a great post of birch wood, on which they wrote the name of the man and the name of the Rus king and they departed (Jones 1968, 425–30).

The evidence uncovered on the surface at Cloghermore, immediately to the east-south-east of the entrance to the shaft, clearly suggests that a wooden building or structure was erected in this area, supported on wooden posts. The evidence also suggests that it was partially walled (the slot-trenches) and probably roofed (the internal posts). This structure was, it appears, deliberately taken down after a period of time, and the pyre on which the animals were cremated was constructed in the same place, possibly using the wood from the structure. As seen from the quoted sections of Ibn Fadlan's account, a temporary roofed structure was constructed over the dead warrior, for a period of ten days, while his funeral was being prepared. The structure at Cloghermore may well have served a similar function to that described by Ibn Fadlan, acting as a mortuary house before the funeral.

Similarly, the animals placed in the ship to be cremated with the dead warrior are paralleled in the rite recorded at Cloghermore. Ibn Fadlan describes the cutting up of a dog and two horses after they had been run until they sweated. He also notes the cutting up of two cows and the killing of a rooster and a hen. At Cloghermore the animal bone assemblage includes bones of dog and horse, both burnt and unburnt, as part of the cremation deposit and of the general bone assemblage from the cave. The horse bones consist of parts of the skull and at least one bone from the leg, a tibia, with cut-marks that McCarthy interprets as indicative of dismemberment (Appendix 3), as well as unburnt horse teeth and bone from the cremation deposit.

The fact that the bones represent only parts of a horse suggests that the horse had been dismembered before being placed in the cave. The Ibn Fadlan account clearly shows that such dismemberment was part of the burial rite, although the difficulty of bringing a whole horse into the cave may also have dictated the inclusion of only parts of the animal at Cloghermore.

Large quantities of cattle bone were recovered from Cloghermore; however, in the light of Ibn Fadlan's account, it is interesting that at the base of the entrance shaft to the cave, immediately inside the entrance, there was a crushed but intact cattle skull and the fragmentary remains of a second. The skulls were placed on the western side of the entrance, facing out from the cave, and the presence here of only the skulls is suggestive of dismemberment. Analysis of the animal bones also identified the mid-line splitting of carcasses, including cattle, and the axial chopping of pig skulls, suggested as a method of gaining access to the brain (Appendix 3).

Domestic fowl, as recorded in Ibn Fadlan's account, were not recovered from Cloghermore Cave; however, it is noteworthy that the bones from five species of wild bird were recovered from the base of the entrance shaft, the same area as the cattle skulls above and the remains of a dog. The species represented were stonechat, fieldfare, greenfinch, starling and plover.

Finally, Ibn Fadlan describes the construction of a mound on the spot where the ship was burnt and the erection of a wooden post on the top of the mound. No mound was constructed at Cloghermore, but the cave is situated beneath a very large Waulsortian reef/ outcrop that has the profile of an upturned boat. These facts may have dictated the choice of the cave as a burial site. Indeed, there was a marked tendency in Scandinavian Scotland to use pre-existing mounds, and Graham-Campbell and Batey (1998, 146) interpret this as a device used to ensure the identification of the burial in the landscape. Surely there was no better way to ensure the identification of the Cloghermore burials in the landscape than to place them under one of the largest limestone outcrops in the area, a natural, pre-existing 'mound' in the broadest sense.

The final erection of a wooden post carved with the name of the dead man and that of the Rus king is probably also paralleled at Cloghermore, where the very large post-hole (16) and a stone socket (2B) were uncovered in Trench 3, close to the entrance shaft. These features do not seem to have been part of any structure, and the post-hole (16) may represent the last activity on the site. The post-hole may have contained a memorial post similar to that described by Ibn Fadlan, and the socket, containing packing-stones, may have contained a stone pillar.

The funeral rites described by Bersu and Wilson (1966) for the burials at Balladoole and Ballateare on the Isle of Man have similarities with both the rite that Hall (1978) has suggested for the mound at Donnybrook, Dublin, and that at Cloghermore. At Balladoole the burial mound was capped with a heap of stones in turn covered by a layer of cremated bone including horse, ox, pig, sheep/goat, dog and cat (Bersu and Wilson 1966, 10). However, the mound was not interpreted as the site of the cremation, nor was any trace of the pyre site noted elsewhere in the immediate area. Small bits of cremated animal bone, mixed with blackened soil, charcoal and ash, were also noted in the centre of the mound, which the excavator took as evidence that the mound had been constructed on the pyre site, using the remains/debris of the fire in the construction (*ibid.*)

At Ballateare the main burial was that of a male; it was noted that he had a small knife placed on his chest, an arrangement paralleled in

Area W at Cloghermore. In the upper levels of the mound a thin layer of cremated animal bone was noted under the modern humus and a layer of the mound soil. This material also provided the filling for a post-hole, 0.70m in diameter, in the centre of the mound. The layer also covered, and partly included, the very decayed bones of a skeleton (Bersu and Wilson 1966, 47). Bersu and Wilson interpreted this as evidence of a wooden platform on which the body of a female had been laid, as a sacrifice. Near the centre of the platform a hole had been dug for the insertion of a wooden post, the whole area finally being covered with a layer of cremated animal bone mixed with black soil and charcoal. The bones of ox, dog and sheep were identified from the layer (*ibid.*).

Interestingly, this interpretation identifies the presence of a wooden platform on which the body was lain, and such a purpose may also explain some of the post-holes found on the surface outside the cave at Cloghermore. Perhaps excarnation or temporary exposure was part of the burial rite at both Ballateare and Cloghermore. The presence of posts at both Ballateare and Balladoole is very much in keeping with the rite described by Ibn Fadlan and with the evidence from Cloghermore. Indeed, the posts at both Ballateare and Balladoole were held in place with packing-stones, similar to the arrangement noted in the large socket close to the entrance shaft at Cloghermore. Wilson suggests that the post-holes at Ballateare and Balladoole may have contained wooden or stone memorial slabs and notes the recorded presence of 'standing stones' at three Scottish sites and the common occurrence of such stone or wooden posts in Scandinavia.

The presence of cremated animal bone at both of these sites on the Isle of Man is a very important link with Cloghermore. Wilson (Bersu and Wilson 1966, 89) suggests that the presence of cremated animal bone with an inhumation burial is a partial reflection of the tradition of full cremation burial as seen in Scandinavia.

In Scandinavia further aspects of the rite identified at Cloghermore can also be paralleled. Although a small number of nails and clench-bolts were recovered from Cloghermore, no timbers were, and it is probably safe to assume that none of the burials was placed in a coffin. Two small copper-alloy pins were recovered from Area W around the articulated skeleton; these small pins, one of them bent/curved, possibly held a shroud closed around the body.

The wrapping of a body in a shroud is not unknown in the burial record of Scandinavia, and, in assessing the burial customs at Birka,

Gräslund (1980, 12–13) stated that it is likely that the body was often wrapped in some kind of shroud and placed directly in the grave-pit. She also noted that the grave-pits are usually of an irregularly rectangular shape. The short sides of the pits are usually straight, although a curved or rounded outline, similar to the shallow pit in which the burial in Area W at Cloghermore was placed, also occurs. Coffinless graves had a wide distribution in Viking Age and early medieval Scandinavia. Many finds from other parts of Scandinavia suggest that, especially in coffinless graves, the dead were either wrapped in a shroud or placed under a cover of cloth or some other organic material (Gräslund 1980, 15).

Similarly, the orientation of the burial in Area W, with the head to the north-east, is not unknown. Of the graves that Gräslund studied on Bjorko, the dominant orientation is with the head to the west, but nine coffinless and twelve coffin burials are oriented with the head in a generally north-eastward direction.

The stone setting uncovered in the Graveyard is also not unknown in Scandinavia and is usually associated with cremation burials. At Birka, stone settings represent only a small proportion of the graves, but where the diameter of these settings are known they vary from 1.4m to 2.7m (ibid.), similar in size to that from Cloghermore.

Of the graves excavated by Sander (1996, 53) at Helgö Cemetery 116, 39 were of a type composed of circular or roughly circular stone settings, and, although many of these had kerbs and were far larger than the setting at Cloghermore, eleven were less than 3m in diameter. Indeed, graves such as A51, A68 and A72 are similar in size and form to the stone setting in the Graveyard at Cloghermore. These burials at Helgö contained cremation layers and a bone container, with both the container and the cremation deposit containing human and animal bones. Although the cemetery at Helgö contained graves of more than one period, Sander regards the three graves noted above and many of the other smaller graves as being Viking Age.

Cremated animal bones occurred in 35 of the 48 excavated graves at Helgö 116, or 73 per cent. Nine different animal species were identified: horse, cattle, sheep/goat, pig, dog, cat, bear, bird (mostly domestic fowl) and deer. Dog and sheep/goat were the most common cremated remains. Seven was the largest number of animal species recorded from a single grave; another grave contained six; and three graves contained five (Sander 1997, 94, table 12). Unburnt animal bones were also recovered from within and underneath the graves. Cattle were the most common, followed by sheep/goat, pig and horse. There were also bones from dogs, hares and birds.

The most recent work on burial traditions and rituals in south-east Scania (Svanberg 2003, 15–150) shows that, although cremations occur, inhumation is the dominant rite in this area between AD 800 and AD 1000. Indeed, Svanberg has suggested, on the basis of the available evidence, that in certain regions, such as south-west Scania and Bornholm, inhumation was the burial tradition (*ibid.*). Svanberg's analysis of burials in this area illustrates many comparisons with Cloghermore. The range of artefacts from many cemeteries is comparable, as is the inclusion of significant numbers of child burials. Indeed, he suggests that at the cemeteries of Öland and Möre the gender of the children was stressed by giving them equipment specific to one of the adult sexes. This is interesting when one considers the predominantly domestic equipment deposited in the pit in Area V with the remains of two children, suggesting possibly that they were female.

Svanberg's analysis also suggests that human sacrifice was a component of the burial ritual, such as in south-west Scania, where it was suggested by the presence of more than one individual in a grave in such a manner as to indicate a difference in status (Svanberg 2003, 93). Given the deposition of bones from two children and an adult in the pit in Area V and the presence of some bones of a second individual in Area W, with the only articulated burial, clearly human sacrifice may be an explanation.

The occurrence of animals in the burials of south-east Scandinavia is quite common; the dominant position of horse and dog at cemeteries like Öland and Igelösa is interesting, although other animals such as sheep, goat and pig occur. From the point of view of the cremated animal bone deposit at Cloghermore, Svanberg's comments on the cemetery at Vätteryd are interesting. He suggests that animal bones were regularly deposited along with the remains of humans in cremation pits and that it is probable that the sacrifice of animals was common in the burial rituals of the cemetery (Svanberg 2003, 111). Clearly, this opens the question of whether cremated human bone was part of the cremation deposit at Cloghermore, possibly in a ceramic container. The container may have been removed from the cave intact as part of the suggested desecration of the site or by a departing Scandinavian group for reburial elsewhere, as has been suggested for the missing skulls from the site.

## 4.9 HORSE BURIAL

The practice of horse burial or horse sacrifice has a long history and is usually connected with influences from Turkish and Altai-Siberian equestrian nomadic tribes (Klindt-Jensen 1968, 143–9). Klindt-Jensen has demonstrated that the custom was practised by the Hittites as early as 1400–1300 BC and in south Russia between 1700 BC and 1000 BC. Thereafter, the custom continued in south Russia and presumably spread to northern Europe during the Early Iron Age. A selection of horse bones—the skull and bones from the extremities—often occurs in association with sacrifice and burials in the Roman Iron Age in northern and central Europe. The custom was also practised by the Magyars and other tribes in the Danube area at the end of the fourth and in the fifth century (ibid.).

It has been proposed that the purpose of the horse, like that of a ship, was to carry the dead to the afterlife. However, the horse would have been a most valued possession, and its slaughter may be seen as the ritual destruction of wealth to express social status, as well as to show cultural allegiance or religious belief (Sikora 2000, 17). The horse is associated with two Scandinavian gods, Freyr and Odin. The animal is a prominent symbol of fertility in Scandinavian mythology, associated with the god Freyr, and horse sacrifice is often linked to a fertility cult (Ellis Davidson 1964, 25; Turville-Petré 1975, 56). Indeed, recent work on the tapestries from the burial chamber at Oseberg, Norway, has interpreted them, coupled with the presence of beheaded horses, as evidence of a connection between the burial and the fertility cult of Freyja (Ingstad 1995). Iceland has particularly strong evidence of horse cults, with horse fighting being banned only in the sixteenth century (Kavanagh 1988, 96). The most famous image of the horse is Odin's eight-legged grey horse Sleipnir, which appears on many memorial stones, especially in Gotland. Odin is the god of war but also figures largely in death, particularly death by violence (Turville-Petré 1975, 56).

However, the possibility that the horse should be viewed as a type of grave-good rather than a sacrificial offering has been raised by Horning (1993) through his analysis of the horse burials from the Late Saxon period cemetery at Rullstorf in northern Germany.

### Horse burial in Ireland

Only three possible horse burials are known from Ireland—at Athlumney, Co. Meath, between Newbridge and Miltown, Co.

Kildare, and at Islandbridge, Co. Dublin—however, records of the structure of the graves are negligible, and all three are in effect antiquarian finds.

The site of the burial at Athlumney, Co. Meath (identified as Navan by Kavanagh (1988, 98)), was found during the construction of the Dublin–Drogheda railway line. The site is referred to as a 'battle pit', and the presence of charcoal is noted. The evidence suggests that this was a multiple burial; 'the human bodies do not appear to have been placed in any order' (Wilde 1861, 573–4), with the only recorded grave-goods being a horse harness and a bridle bit. Here the horse skull and bone were interspersed with the human remains. The lack of weapons in the assemblage is noteworthy, and for this reason Kavanagh (1988, 103) suggested that it may have been the burial of 'a Viking settled in the area', pointing to the fact that Annagassan, where a *longphort* was established in AD 841, is a short distance away.

The record of the possible grave with a horse near Newbridge, Co. Kildare, notes that it was found in a field and that the remains of a horse were found interred with a man, giving the impression that the horse was buried whole. The grave also produced a spearhead and a bone pin (Kavanagh 1988), suggesting a ninth- or tenth-century date.

The grave at Islandbridge, Co. Dublin, was probably flat and produced only a single horse tooth and that of an ox (Sikora 2000, 52). The burial probably dates to the ninth or tenth century (Ó Floinn 1998, 137–8), although Raftery expressed some doubt about this being a Scandinavian grave owing to the lack of grave-goods (Bøe 1940, 60).

The burial from Athlumney was dated to the late ninth/early tenth century by Armstrong (1921, 12) on the basis of the decoration of the harness mounts, and this date has more recently been corroborated by Kavanagh's (1988, 101) date of the horse-bit from the grave. However, it has been suggested that Kavanagh's assertion that the presence of the horse in burials 'proves their importance' to the farmer in Viking settlements gives no consideration to the possibility that many Viking Age burials of riding gear and horses represent cavalry/equestrian interments (Randsborg 1980; Roesdahl 1982; Braathen 1989; Sikora 2000, 17).

## Horse burial elsewhere in the Viking world

Evidence of horse burial is known from across Scandinavia. In Norway, horse burials are known from farmsteads, as well as larger settlements, and most are recorded under mounds. The mounds can vary from 80m in diameter to as little as 4.5m, and it has been suggested that there is a correlation between the size of the mound and the number of horses buried (Sikora 2000, 31). Horse remains occur mainly with inhumations but are also known from cremation burials, both male and female. Interestingly, in at least ten cases horse teeth or parts of a horse skull/jaw are the only remains present. Dog bones are found in association with the horse in a number of graves, and cattle bone is also known; indeed, one grave at Oseberg, Norway, contained both cow and dog (Sikora 2000, 99).

In Denmark, flat graves are more common, and horse remains are almost exclusively associated with inhumation burials; in a number of cases only horse bone or teeth are recorded. The bones of other animals are also recorded from graves containing horse remains, with dog being the most common, followed by pig, cow, sheep and bird. Interestingly, in the burial from Stengade the horse was inhumed but the pig, cow, gosling and calf bone were burnt and placed on top of the burial. Sikora (2000, 45) suggests that this indicates different relationships between human and horse and the other animals. Horse equipment (bits, stirrups and/or spurs, harnesses, mounts) is far more common in the horse graves of Denmark than Norway. This supports the picture of heavy cavalry graves in Denmark as opposed to perhaps the farm horse in Norway, where the bit is the most common piece of equine equipment (Sikora 2000).

Eleven Viking Age graves with horses are known from Scotland. There is much uncertainty about the external morphology of many of the pagan Norse graves in Scotland, but Graham-Campbell and Batey (1998, 134) have concluded that in general these burials seem to have been insertions in previously existing or natural mounds. Indeed, in his discussion of the Haithabu ship grave Wamers (1995, 154) argues that the construction of a mound is a clear indication of paganism in the burial ritual. Sikora (2000, 71) notes that the lack of grave mounds in Ireland and Scotland is a defining feature; however, the location of the cave at Cloghermore under a large rock 'mound' may have been an important feature in its choice as a burial site. All of the recorded graves in Scotland were inhumations, with both the human and the animal remains being unburnt. Like in Norway, the bit is the most common equestrian artefact from the graves, but there is only one example of the burial of another animal with the horse in the grave, at Pierowall, where 'part of a dog skeleton' is recorded (Graham-Campbell and Batey 1998).

Horse burial is more common in Iceland than anywhere else in the Viking world: of 300 burials in Viking Age Iceland, 111 are horse graves (Sikora 2000, 61). The character of horse graves in Iceland is distinctive: most contain a complete horse placed at the feet of the interred or in a separate grave a few metres away. The horses are sometimes beheaded, with the head placed near the stomach of the horse. However, in 36 cases only horse bone or teeth, not full horse remains, are mentioned, while in thirteen cases the horse was definitely cut up before being placed in the grave (*ibid.*). In one unusual case, at Miklibær, parts of a horse were placed at the head of the grave and have therefore been interpreted as food offerings rather than horse sacrifice. The most common piece of equestrian equipment is the strap-buckle, and the spearhead is the most common weapon, with knives and whetstones also occurring quite often. Dog remains are known from nine graves, cow from one, and pig bone from one. However, at Kápa the male interment included bones of a dog, sheep, cow and pig, as well as the horse.

In a Swedish context it is interesting that the burial of parts of horses does not occur at Birka, although it is known from some Swedish Viking Age cremation burials (Gräslund 1965, 141f). The combination of parts of the skull and the bones of the lower extremities of horses occasionally occurs in Viking Age cremation burials in eastern Sweden in circumstances that suggest horse sacrifice. Such an assemblage of bone is very similar to that recovered from Cloghermore, which may also be suggestive of sacrifice.

However, unburnt animal bone occurs at Birka in the cremation deposits, on top of them and in the filling of the mounds (Gräslund 1980, 60). Unburnt and scorched bones found in or on top of cremation deposits are interpreted as the remains of funeral feasts relating to the building of the mound. Horse teeth also occur in cremation deposits, burnt, unburnt and scorched. These too are associated with funeral feasts and bring to mind Ibn Fadlan's description of the burial rites of the Oguze in the 920s. Horses were slaughtered, and while the meat was eaten by the guests at the funeral the hides were mounted on stakes (Klindt-Jensen 1957, 85).

In summary, although cremation of the human remains is quite a common characteristic of Norwegian horse burials, horse graves in the Viking west are exclusively inhumations, where the horse is buried whole or in part. The Scandinavian evidence shows the skull to be the commonest body part included in the grave (Sikora 2000, 74). Sikora also suggests that the fact that the Irish, Scottish and

Icelandic horse graves are not of a strictly cavalry type argues for a more Norwegian character for these burials, while acknowledging that these areas were settled before the equestrian grave tradition became popular in Scandinavia. However, the Swedish evidence of the presence of animal bone, including horse, on top of and around cremation deposits and the interpretation of this as evidence of funeral feasting are interesting from the point of view of the Cloghermore evidence.

### 4.10 ANIMALS, BURIAL RITUAL AND CULTIC PRACTICE

Almost 17,000 animal bones were recovered from the excavations at Cloghermore (Appendix 3). The bones were retrieved from all areas of the cave; however, the sample from the Two-Star Temple was very small, totalling only 157 fragments of bone representing the three main livestock animals, sheep, cattle and pig. The assemblages from Trenches 1 and 4 were also quite small, and no bone was recovered from Trench 2. The small sample from the Two-Star Temple is to be expected, given that the animal bone, similar to the artefacts, is almost certainly associated with the later phase of burial and the brown clay soil that had been brought into the cave. Similarly, small samples were recovered from Areas Y and Z, where there were minimal amounts of the brown soil.

The largest samples were recovered from the Graveyard (4829 bones), Area U (2433 bones), the entrance shaft (1890 bones) and Area V (1786). In all areas cattle and sheep accounted for most of the bone, with pig ranking third. As with the human bone, the animal bone was scattered throughout the cave and had suffered much breakage and disturbance, both as part of the suggested desecration of the site and subsequently. Therefore, it is difficult to associate specific bones, artefacts and burials (although the iron horse-bit is clearly associated with the horse remains) or to interpret the animal remains by area. However, the samples from three areas are worthy of special comment, as they are isolated samples and were deliberately deposited: Area V, Area W and the cremation deposit within the stone setting in the Graveyard.

It has already been suggested that the treatment of the human remains in the pit in Area V—the torso of a child and bones from the feet of an adult and of two further sub-adults—is probably ritualistic. Analysis of the animal bone has shown that the pit contained 1786 animal bones, representing mainly sheep and cattle, with pig again third. Interestingly, McCarthy noted that most of the cattle and sheep bones came from young individuals, including two neonatal lambs, and the pig bones also suggested the slaughtering of young individuals. There was also evidence, in the form of mid-line splitting, of the halving of carcasses. The sample also contained the remains of a juvenile dog and a single bone each from a horse and a cat. The presence of so many young animals in a pit with sub-adult human bones is clearly of some ritual significance, although it is impossible to interpret the presence of adult foot bones.

Area W is the location of the only articulated burial from the cave, that of an adult male, and McCarthy suggests that the remains of sheep from this area represent complete carcasses. Although dismemberment is not in evidence, the deposition of complete carcasses at this location is surely significant.

The cremation deposit contained burnt bone from the three main domesticates, sheep, cattle and pig, in that order. However, it also contained a small sample of unburnt bone, including two teeth and part of the mandible of a horse and the only bone of hare from the excavation. The inclusion of only parts of the horse and the presence of unburnt teeth in a cremation deposit are very similar to finds recorded by Gräslund (1980, 60) from parts of Sweden.

In general terms McCarthy regards the animal bone assemblage from Cloghermore as different from other assemblages of the period from Ireland. It shows sheep (rather than cattle) as the most common animal, followed by cattle, but with low values for pig. It also shows that the slaughter of young animals, particularly lambs and piglets, was common practice. McCarthy notes that the slaughtering of such young animals makes little economic sense and suggests that the animal remains derive from ritual activity. She suggests that the slaughter and butchering of the animals took place nearby, probably on the surface, and meat provisioning was clearly significant. The fact that a significant amount of animal bone was recovered from the cobble sealing layer, the charcoal-rich black soil that underlay this layer, and the fill of a number of the features in Trench 3 (see Appendix 3, Table 4) suggests that the slaughtering of the animals may have taken place here.

There is no doubt that a large proportion of the animal remains represents food refuse, possibly consumed as part of ritual feasting before the insertion of burials in the cave. However, there is also the strong possibility that some of the bones represent food offerings placed in the cave with the dead.

There are also the remains of a number of species outside the three main domesticates, which are clearly indicative of ritual activity and possibly of the worship of specific deities or adherence to particular cults in the pagan religious beliefs of Scandinavia. The most obvious of these is the horse, and aspects of the significance of the horse in relation to burial have been discussed previously. Only unburnt horse bone was recovered at Cloghermore, although some of the remains were clearly associated with the deposit of cremated animal bone. The bones were dispersed throughout the cave, but this is to be expected given the disturbance of the site, and McCarthy interprets them as the remains of a single individual.

At least three dogs were recovered from Cloghermore. The largest assemblage of bones, representing a mature individual about the size of a modern sheepdog, came from the base of the entrance shaft—interestingly, the same location as the crushed cattle skulls. The deposition of a dog or parts of a dog at this location would surely be of some ritual significance as a final act before sealing the shaft. Dog bone was also recovered from Area U, the pit in Area V and the Graveyard.

In Scandinavian mythology horses and dogs have strong links to death and the journey to the otherworld, and this is an important aspect of their link to Freyja, in her capacity as a welcomer of the slain, as outlined in the Edda poem *Grímnismál*, where she is said to have half of those who died in battle while the other half belonged to Odin (Ellis Davidson 1964, 39, 176). Freyja was also associated with a form of magic called *seiðr*, which could include harmful magic such as dealing out death to its victims. This aspect of *seiðr* is found in conjunction with a horse cult more than once in the sagas (Ellis Davidson 1964, 121–2). The Valkyries sent by Odin to escort heroic kings and heroes to Valhalla are described as dignified figures on horseback, and wall hangings from the Oseberg ship burial show a royal funeral procession dominated by horses. One scene shows a woman in a hood on a red horse, and it has been suggested that this may be the goddess Freyja (Ingstad *et al.* 1992, 242). It is noteworthy that dogs, as well as horses, were among the animals sacrificed at the Oseberg funeral.

Freyr was Freyja's twin brother, and, while Freyja was seen as helping in affairs of the heart and having some powers over the dead, Freyr was represented as a sovereign deity of increase and prosperity. His image in the temple at Uppsala, according to Adam of Bremen, was a phallic one (Ellis Davidson 1964, 96, 121–2). Freyr was closely associated with the horse cult, and sacred horses were kept in his sanctuary at Thrandheim, Norway; the sagas also refer to horses kept near Freyr's temples in Iceland. Indeed, Ellis Davidson suggests that the horse fights so popular in Iceland were originally associated with the cult of Freyr.

Boar was represented at Cloghermore by tusks and vertebrae from at least one individual, recovered from the Graveyard. Unfortunately, this bone was mixed with other faunal material from the area, but McCarthy has noted that the tusks are sufficiently large to have come from a wild boar. Both Freyr and Freyja are associated with the boar. Freyr is said by Snorri to own the boar Gullinbursti, made by the dwarfs, whose coat shone in the dark and who could outrun any steed. Freyja also had a boar, called Hildisvín. Ellis Davidson (1964, 98) notes that the association of the boar with deities of fertility is likely to be very old. One of Freyja's names as recounted by Snorri was sýr, or 'sow', and the wall hangings at the Oseberg ship burial depict figures with swine heads, which have been taken to be Freyja (Ingstad *et al.* 1992). Ellis Davidson (1964, 149) also notes that the heroes in Valhalla are described as feasting on pork and mead, which, in conjunction with the practice of funeral feasting, may explain the quantities of pig bones recovered from the site at Cloghermore.

Freyja is also closely associated with cats, the bones of which were recovered from a number of locations within the cave. The most obvious link is Freyja's chariot, which is said to have been drawn by cats (Ellis Davidson 1995, 108; 1998). The links between Freyja and cats have, according to Ellis Davidson, not been explained satisfactorily, but she notes that cats were among the animal spirits that helped in divination by a witch, or *volva*, associated with the cult of Freyja. This ritual, according to extant accounts, involved the wearing of a costume of animal skins including boots of calf skin and gloves of cat skin (Ellis Davidson 1964, 117–20). The cremated bones of cats were recovered at four graves excavated by Sander (1997, 93) at Helgö Cemetery 116, and all four were of Viking Age date. In writing on prehistoric cremations in Västmanland, Sweden, Iregren (1983) states that cat bones are something of a 'diagnostic fossil' for the Viking Age.

Grave A6 at Helgö Cemetery 116 is interesting from the point of view of the Cloghermore evidence. The grave contained no human bone, but a small quantity of cremated cat bone lay in a pottery vessel in a thin cremation layer. The grave-goods consisted of six rock-crystal and carnelian beads and seventeen monochrome glass beads. There were also a few unburnt sheep/goat bones in the fill (Sander 1997, 95). Sander notes that the grave did not differ in any way from the others, except in its lack of human bone. She suggests that the cat had not been buried for its own sake but may have been a 'replacement' for a dead human being, where the corpse could not be buried (*ibid*.). Grave 50 from Helgö Cemetery 150, dated to the first half of the ninth century, contained the cremated bones of a woman together with cat bones, pig teeth and pieces of antler, the cat being the primary animal in the grave (Lamm 1970).

In the context of burial ritual and possible connections to the cults of certain deities, it is also noteworthy that the lightly charred fragments of hazelnut shells (16 and 23) were recovered from the interface of Areas X and U at Cloghermore. Ellis Davidson (1995, 111) suggests that nuts are symbols of fertility and thus linked to Freyja, and presumably Freyr, and Gräslund (2000, 59) has suggested that the occurrence of hazelnuts in graves is symbolic of rebirth.

There is also the presence of red jasper, a stone again associated with Freyja, in the cave at Cloghermore. Two of the pieces are clearly fragments (204 and 222) and may derive from the use of jasper with iron strike-a-lights. However, the presence of the water-rolled pebble with the articulated burial in Area W and the placement of the two fragments in the obviously ritual context of the pit in Area V suggest a more ritualistic significance.

Clearly, there is a ritual significance to the presence of these animals, the nut shells and the jasper in the cave at Cloghermore, and the evidence suggests that there may be a link between these ritual deposits and the cults of the sibling deities Freyr and Freyja. Indeed, the lack of identifiable human bone within the stone setting at Cloghermore may be explained in a similar fashion to that at Grave A6 at Helgö, with one of the cremated animals acting as a substitute for the dead human. Surely it is more than coincidence that the finds from Grave A6 consisted only of beads, the same as the stone setting at Cloghermore. The importance of this evidence is in the familiarity with the cults of these deities and the rituals associated with them that it suggests, as this indicates that the cultural context of the later burials is Scandinavian rather than Hiberno-Scandinavian.

# 5  ARTEFACT DISCUSSION

Artefacts were recovered from all of the excavated areas inside the cave, including the Two-Star Temple, where there was very minimal soil cover, and the passage that linked the Graveyard and the Two-Star Temple (Area Y). On the surface, all excavated areas again produced artefacts. The artefacts were fairly evenly distributed throughout the various areas, with the greatest number coming from Trench 3, on the surface, although the greatest density came from the pit in Area V, immediately inside the cave. When groups of fragments, particularly iron, which is often so badly broken and corroded that it cannot be fitted together in any coherent fashion, are taken into account, the cave produced over 350 individual items. The artefacts are made of stone, bone, antler, ivory, amber, glass, copper alloy and iron.

Iron objects dominate the assemblage from the cave. Unfortunately, the iron is generally in very poor condition owing to the annual flooding of the cave and the presence of a bat colony during the winter. The resulting mixture of bat faeces and water produced very acidic conditions, which undoubtedly hastened the corrosion of the iron. A number of the iron objects can be identified, although complete objects of iron are rare from the cave. Objects of copper alloy also seem to have fared badly in this environment, as only a few small fragments, apart from the two ringed pins (81 and 115), were recovered. The other artefacts from the cave did not suffer too much damage from the natural process within the system, although a number of the amber beads were very brittle upon discovery and subsequently broke. This brittleness appears to have been caused by exposure to fire/heat.

Given the disturbed nature of the cave, owing to the annual flooding, digging and the visits of cavers, coupled with the fact that all of the burials, except that in Area W, were disarticulated, it is difficult to associate most of the material with specific burials. However, a clear case can be made for viewing the material from around the single articulated burial in Area W and the pit in Area V as discrete assemblages associated with a specific group of bones. This is possible as these assemblages are separated from the rest of the material by artificial boundaries: the shallow grave-cut for the articulated burial in Area W and the pit in Area V. In these areas it is possible to associate the artefacts with a defined portion of the skeletal material from the cave and, indeed, to associate the bones of various individuals with one another to some degree.

In the other areas of the cave the picture is less clear. The material recovered from Area X, the sloping gallery from the entrance shaft to the Graveyard, has seen much disturbance owing to slippage and collapse, as well as visitors to the cave. Bone and artefacts were scattered throughout the soil that rested on the sterile cave sediments. However, there may also be a possibility that the assemblages from more peripheral areas of the system, separated from the main galleries by natural boundaries, can be interpreted as relating to specific incidents of burial rather being than scattered randomly. This may be the case with the material from the offshoot passages/alcoves of Areas T, U and Z, which may have been the location of articulated burials subsequently disturbed.

In the Graveyard itself, most of the bone was recovered from Quadrants A and B, where there was a substantial depth of soil and loose stone. This area of the chamber was also the location of the stone setting containing the cremated animal bone, and it is possible to associate a number of artefacts, particularly the amber beads, with the cremation deposit. The silver hoard (61, 66, 72:1–2, 73 and 74) was also recovered from this area (Quadrant B), but it was at the very base of the excavated material in a hollow created by earlier roof collapse and the action of flowstone, and so it is impossible to associate the hoard with any particular burial or group of bones.

The western side of the Graveyard chamber (Quadrants C and D) was in effect a raised area created by massive boulders and roof-collapsed stone. The artefacts from this area were recovered from pockets of soil in between the stones, and this area and Area Y produced the least amount of skeletal material. The artefacts from Area Y were also recovered from pockets of soil at the interface of two boulder-strewn slopes of collapse in the passage between the Graveyard and the Two-Star Temple.

As already noted, all of the artefacts and the skeletal material were associated with a single soil layer, the brown clay, making it impossible to create any stratigraphical matrix for the assemblage.

## 5.1 IRON ARTEFACTS

The iron artefacts fall into two main categories: those that can be identified as specific objects or parts of larger objects and those collections of small fragment that cannot be identified at all.

Of the identifiable material, blades or portions of blades, from knives, shears and a possible sword or spearhead, are the most common items recovered. Weapons are represented in the assemblage by an arrowhead (53), a spearhead ferrule with a blade fragment attached (45 and 46), an axe (1) and fragments of a shield boss (145:1–3).

### Axehead

The iron axehead (1; Fig. 16) was the first find from the cave and was

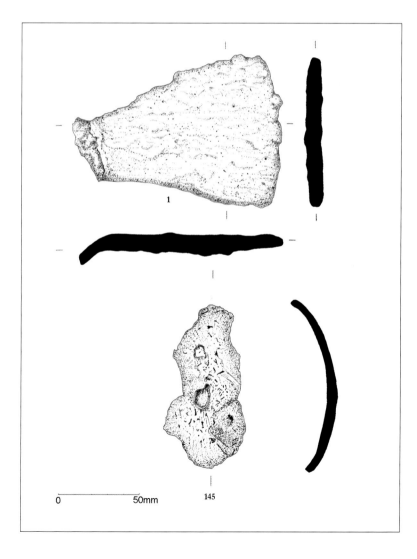

0      50mm

1

145

**FIG. 16**
*Iron axehead (1) and fragmentary shield boss (145).*

recovered by cavers from the general region of Areas W and V at the southern end of the sloping gallery, Area X. The axe is now in the possession of the National Museum of Ireland. It is corroded, covered in accretions and broken across the original socket.

The remaining portion of the axe suggests that the socket was formed by curving the butt end of the axe around to form a suitable hole for the handle. Whether the curved butt was subsequently welded back to the axe blade is not clear, but, given that the remaining portion of the axe is badly corroded, the possibility that the socket was cast cannot be completely ruled out .

The axe is, in shape and form, unlike the axes recovered from Cahercommaun (Hencken 1938, 50, fig. 31, no. 336), Carraig Aille (Ó Ríordáin 1949, 76, fig. 12, no. 514) or Lagore (Hencken 1950, 107–8, fig. 40, A–D). However, it is very similar in blade shape and size to axes recovered from Viking period graves in Iceland, such as those at Sílastaðir, Glæsibæjarhreppur, and Kroppur, Hrafnagilshreppur (Eldjárn 1956, 178, pl. 83, 185–6, pl. 92). Similar axes have also been noted in assemblages from graves on Gotland, Sweden, such as that at Hablingbo, Havor (Thunmark-Nylén 1995, 8, abb. 103b). Only two other axes are known from Scandinavian burials in Ireland: both are from Kilmainham and were found in 1845 (Harrison 2001, 70).

## Spearhead

The ferrule (45) is probably from a spearhead, and the blade fragment (46) fused to it may be from a sword or the blade of the spear itself (Fig. 17). The lozenge shape of the blade in section would be more in keeping with that of spear blades of the Viking period than the normally 'fullered' sword blades (Graham-Campbell 1980, 67–8). However, the width of the blade is more indicative of a sword, although broad-bladed spears are known, while there is the slightest hint of a central 'fuller' on one side of the blade, which may have become filled with iron oxides as the blade corroded.

All of the spearheads recovered from Dublin were socketed, and some of the sockets, similar to that from Cloghermore, have perforations for attaching nails (Wallace 1998, 218). An iron spearhead from Garryduff (O'Kelly 1963, 45, fig. 5, no. 136) has a sub-square socket, similar to the example from Cloghermore, and a relatively broad blade, and an example from a grave at Karlsnes, Landmannahreppur, Iceland, has a similar ferrule (Eldjárn 1956, 66–7, pl. 14).

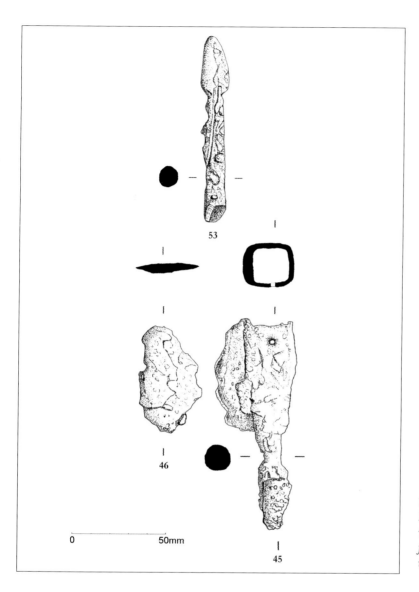

FIG. 17
*Iron spearhead (45)
with attached blade
fragment (46) and
iron arrowhead (53).*

## Shield boss

Three very corroded curved iron fragments of similar thickness (3mm)
and with fragments of wood accreted to the iron were recovered from
Area W (145:1–3; Fig. 16). Two of the fragments fit together and form
part of what was originally a rounded or domed object; the third piece
is undoubtedly from the same object. The fragments are probably the
remains of an iron shield boss, although it is difficult to make a definite
identification of the boss type, as the collar area and flange are missing.
However, it is clear that the boss would have been of a domed type
rather than a conical type or other variant.

Similar domed bosses are known from Irish contexts, such as Lagore (Hencken 1950, 99, fig. 33, nos 98–9), and Viking contexts in Ireland, such as the burial from Eyrephort, Co. Galway, where a fragmentary boss with traces of wood adhering to it was interpreted as being of a Scandinavian type (Sheehan 1987, 65). Interestingly, the Eyrephort boss is the same thickness as the Cloghermore fragments. In Scandinavia itself, Rygh's (1885, figs 562–4) classification of iron bosses of the Viking period includes three types (R562–4) with the same domed/curved form suggested by the fragments from Cloghermore. Graham-Campbell (1980, 68, nos 269–70) also notes that the majority of Viking period shield bosses belong to two simple hemispherical forms: a high-domed type with a neck and a low-domed type that gradually replaced it.

## Arrowhead

The arrowhead from Cloghermore (53) is socketed, with a flat, rounded head, suggestive of a military type rather than a hunting arrowhead (Fig. 17). Wallace (1998, 218) noted that most of the arrowheads from the Dublin excavations were socketed, although some appear to have been tanged, and similarly interprets this as evidence of military use rather than hunting.

The arrowhead from Cloghermore is very closely paralleled by a broken example from Grave A68 at the Helgö Cemetery (Sander 1997, 42, fig. 2:49). The Helgö arrowhead was recovered from a cremation deposit inside a stone setting very similar in size to that uncovered in the Graveyard chamber at Cloghermore. The Helgö arrowhead is socketed, with a head very similar to that from Cloghermore, and is 101mm long, compared with 97mm for the Cloghermore example. Sander (1997, 66) compares the Helgö arrowhead to an example from the Vendel period mound A70 at Lunda Cemetery and gives a calibrated radiocarbon date of 787±107 for Helgö Grave A68.

Like axeheads, arrowheads are rare from Scandinavian burial contexts in Ireland, and a minimum of two graves, both again at Kilmainham, contained them (Harrison 2001, 70). It is also noteworthy that most of the arrowheads from Irish contexts such as Lagore and Carraig Aille are tanged rather than socketed.

## Knives

There are only two intact knives from Cloghermore: 94, associated with the articulated burial in Area W, and 160:3, from the Graveyard.

Both are small, the blade on 160:3 being only 20mm long. The site also produced a number of blade fragments that may be from knives or possibly shears, which include 93:2, 93:3, 109:1, 109:2 and 165:1–2 (Fig. 18).

A number of knives from Carraig Aille have the same general form as the small knife (94; Fig. 18) found with the articulated burial in Area W at Cloghermore, particularly the similarly small example, no. 177 (Ó Ríordáin 1949, 75, fig. 11). Knives of this small type, with a straight back curving to the tip and a rectangular-sectioned tang narrowing from the blade, are also known from graves at Birka (Arbman 1943, 182–3, nos 6 and 9) and from settlement areas at Helgö (Holmqvist and Arrhenius 1964, pl. 38). Similar knives are also known from Coppergate, York, where they are classified as Back Form A1 (Ottaway 1992, 580).

Knife 160:3 is more difficult to parallel and appears to have more in common with small craft knives of the pivoting or folding type

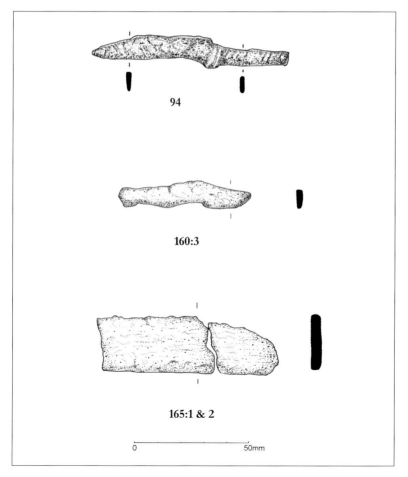

94

160:3

165:1 & 2

0                    50mm

FIG. 18
*Iron knives (94, 160:3 and 165:1–2).*

than with the more conventional knife forms.

The site also produced fragments from a draw knife, including an intact end (139:1–3). A fragment very similar to the intact end was found at Cahercommaun (Hencken 1938, 210, fig. 28). Both have a similarly small perforation. Broadly similar knives, but with ends of differing form and larger end perforations, were recovered at Carraig Aille II (Ó Ríordáin 1949, 74, fig. 11, nos 145 and 440). Such knives are best interpreted as draw knives.

### Horse-bit and harness fittings

The two iron rings (195 and 200) and the curved fragment (207) are probably best interpreted as the remains of a horse-bit (Fig. 19). The curved toggle-like piece (95) and the small, extremely corroded ring

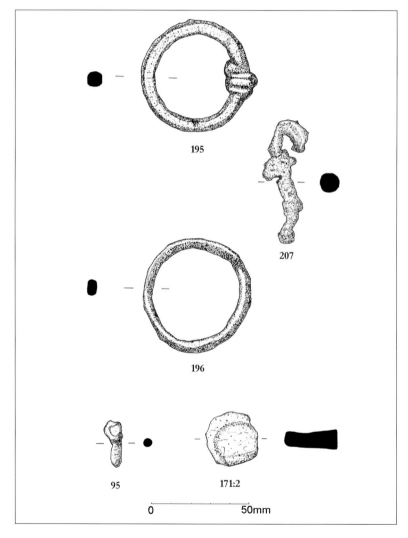

FIG. 19
*Horse harness
fittings (195, 196,
207, 95 and 171:2).*

(171:2) may also belong to this group of artefacts (Fig. 19).

Similar rings are known from Ireland; Carraig Aille produced six iron rings, complete and broken, with diameters of 85–40mm, which were interpreted as horse harness fittings (Ó Ríordáin 1949, 76, 79, fig. 12, no. 447). The horse-bit from Carraig Aille I (96, 97, fig. 21, no. 121) has rings of similar size to Cloghermore, and the links are of the same type as link fragment 207. Indeed, one of the three fragmentary links from Carraig Aille (75, fig. 11, no. 475) is identical to this link fragment from Cloghermore. A horse-bit from Lagore (Hencken 1950, 103, fig. 37, C) has terminal rings of similar size to those from Cloghermore; however, the links are of a different form from fragment 207 and the links from Carraig Aille, being of flat section rather than rounded. Six slightly smaller rings, with diameters of 10–40mm, were recovered from Garryduff (O'Kelly 1963, 62, fig. 7). Interestingly, most of the rings from Irish contexts, noted above, are of rounded section rather that the rounded square to rectangular section of the Cloghermore rings.

The Cloghermore rings are almost identical in size and form to the terminal rings of a two-link horse-bit from a rich male Viking Age cremation, including horse bones, from Zaljuščik, near St Petersburg (Leningrad) in Russia. The rings of this bit are 46mm in diameter and are rounded square to rounded rectangular in section. The grave is dated to somewhere between the late ninth and the second half of the tenth century (Graham-Campbell 1980, 81, 286). Petersen (1951, 10f) describes this type of bit as the simplest and most numerous type of Viking period horse-bit.

An even closer parallel for one of the Cloghermore rings, particularly 200, is from the very rich burial at Broa, Halla, Gotland, in Sweden, dated to c. AD 800. The rings here are again part of a two-link horse-bit, but both have a moulding or corroded smaller ring interlocking the larger ring (Salin 1922). This feature is identical to that on ring 200 from Cloghermore. Rings of similar form and size are known from two-link horse-bits in Iceland, where the occurrence of a smaller ring interlocking the larger ring is relatively common (Eldjárn 1956, 312–14, figs 142–5).

## Bucket/vessel handle

The iron handle (137; Fig. 20) was recovered in four parts that were fitted together during conservation and is clearly, with its flattened hand grip, from a bucket or other such vessel. Wallace (1998) has stated that most of the stave-built buckets and containers from

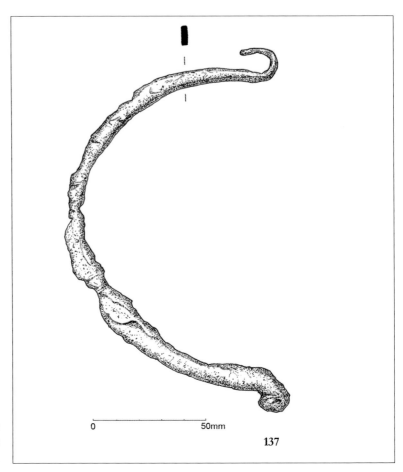

FIG. 20
*Iron bucket handle*
*(137).*

0                                          50mm

137

Dublin did not appear to have had iron handles. However, blade handles of copper alloy were used for small, possibly decorated, stave buckets, and some of the iron wire handles from Dublin had flattened hand-grips (*ibid.*, 211).

A similar type of iron handle with hook terminals and a flattened hand-grip was found at Cahercommaun (Hencken 1938, 51–2, fig. 32), although it is much larger, with a flatter/shallower curve than that from Cloghermore. Hencken notes that handles of the type from Cahercommaun are found on Irish buckets of the Christian period and buckets of Irish origin in Scandinavian museums. He also states that similar handles in the north (Scandinavia) are as old as the Roman Iron Age and Merovingian period.

The small size of the handle from Cloghermore suggests that it was the handle of a small stave-built bucket, such as those with copper-alloy handles from the Dublin excavations. Indeed, an almost identical iron bucket handle is recorded from a grave at Lindholm Høje, Norway (Ramskou 1976, fig. 178). Handles similar to the Cloghermore example have been recovered from other Viking Age burials. A male burial from Ballinbay, Islay, Scotland, which contained a range of artefacts—sword, axe, adze and shield boss—included what is described as a 'cauldron handle', very similar to that from Cloghermore, with bow shape and simple, hooked terminals (Graham-Campbell and Batey 1998, 122–4, pl. 7.5).

## Shears

Cloghermore produced parts of four definite shears (128, 129, 131 and 163) and a fragment of a shears bow (103.2), as well as fragments from iron blades where it is difficult to suggest whether they are from knife or shears blades (Figs 21 and 22). The bow fragment and the partial shears, 128, 129 and 131, were recovered close together near the side

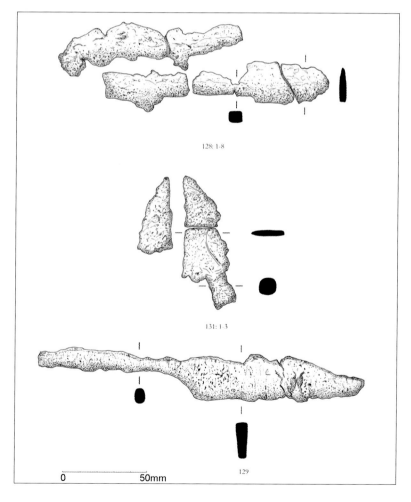

128: 1-8

131: 1-3

129

0          50mm

FIG. 21
*Iron shears and fragments (128:1–8, 129, 131:1–3).*

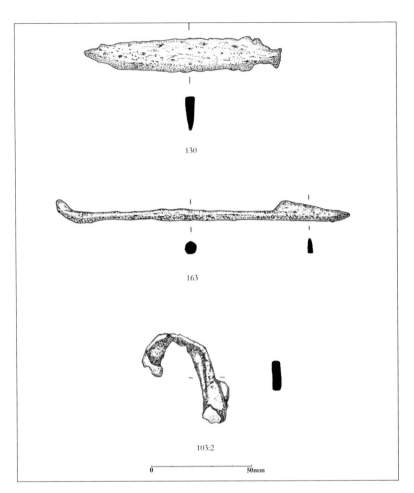

FIG. 22
*Iron shears and
fragments (163, 103:2
and 130).*

wall of the cave at the southern end of Area X. A blade (130) that was found associated with them may represent another shears.

The other definite partial shears (163) was recovered from the large pit designated Area V, inside the base of the entrance shaft, where it was associated with, among other things, a double-sided antler comb (136), a gaming-piece (135), a bone pin (126) and a piece of jasper (204). This was the smallest shears from the site, comprising one complete side of the shears and part of the U-shaped bow; it was only 143mm in overall length, and the blade was only 33mm long.

Shears 129 was more than 189mm long, with a blade of 104mm, and shears 128 appears to be of a similar size, given the length of the remaining stem from blade top to bow. The surviving bows are all of simple, U-shaped type—no example of the looped bow was found— and the surviving stems are both circular sectioned (129 and 163) and rectangular sectioned (128).

A number of iron shears were recovered from Carraig Aille (Ó Ríordáin 1949, 76–7, fig. 12, no. 398). However, Ó Ríordáin points out that this simple type of shears, similar to those from Cloghermore, had a long history, beginning in the Early Iron Age and continuing into medieval times. Similar shears were also recovered from Garryduff, with both bow forms represented (O'Kelly 1962, 44, fig. 5); the period of occupation suggested by the excavator for the two-phase occupation of Garryduff I was AD 650–750/800. A fragmentary shears from Garryduff has a blade only 33mm long, the same length as 163 from Cloghermore. The smallest complete shears from Garryduff (376) is only 110mm long, and the largest (479) is 214mm in overall length (ibid.). Shears with both bow types were also recovered at Cahercommaun, where example 599 had a blade just 36mm long (Hencken 1938, 47, fig. 29). Similar shears are also known from Norway, where a shears from a grave at Tinghausen, Ytre Arne, was only 156mm long with a blade of only 40mm long (Shetelig 1912, 197, fig. 459). The excavations at 16–22 Coppergate, York, produced shears with only looped bows, although both rounded and rectangular stem sections were represented (Ottaway 1992, 548, fig. 219). None of the Coppergate shears was as large as 128 and 129 or as small as 163.

## Barrel padlocks

The iron mechanism of a barrel padlock (51) and a possible barrel padlock (194) were recovered from Quadrant D in the Graveyard and Area Y, midway along the passage linking the Graveyard and Two-Star Temple (Fig. 23).

Barrel padlocks are known from Viking times and continued in use throughout the medieval period in Ireland and Britain. They would have been used, according to size, for securing items of furniture such as chests, caskets, doors and handles. The padlock mechanism (51) is quite corroded and may be tentatively compared to the innards of a Type D padlock from Winchester. This type was in use in England before the Norman conquest, for securing human or animal limbs (Goodall 1990, 1001–4). The possible padlock (194) is more unusual in that it is formed of an iron core with two end-plates of tin. The puzzling aspect of this artefact is the fact that the barrel is quite short, and X-rays revealed the strengthening bar to be placed across the end-plate and not along the barrel as would have been expected. The cavity also appears to be empty, with no trace of the mechanism, if one existed, surviving. It is broadly similar to a Type A padlock from Winchester, which dates from the tenth century

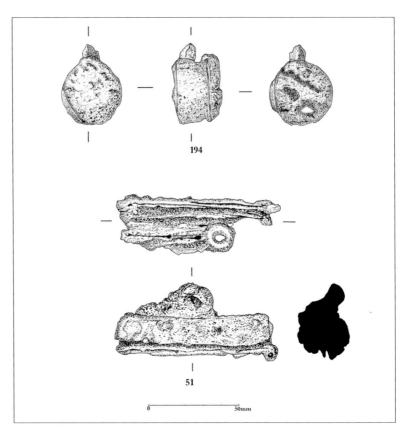

FIG. 23
*Barrel padlocks (51
and 194).*

(Goodall 1990, 1009), although the barrel is approximately half the normal size. This piece may have been a purely decorative casket mount, styled on the padlocks of the period, rather than a functional example of the type.

## Anvil

An iron anvil (170; Fig. 24) was recovered from Trench 3 and is one of the more readily identifiable iron objects from the site, in that it is closely paralleled by one of the anvils from the toolbox found at Mästermyr, Gotland, Sweden (Arwidsson and Berg 1983, 15, pls 9, 21:72.). The Mästermyr example is slightly bigger than that from Cloghermore, but they are of the same general size and shape, with a slightly concave striking surface and a generally square shape. The Mästermyr anvil is from a Viking Age wooden toolbox containing many other iron tools and finished products, some of which can be dated generally to the ninth and tenth centuries (*ibid.*, 38).

A similarly small anvil from a Norwegian Viking Age grave, with a convex working face, is illustrated by Rygh (1885, no. 392), and the

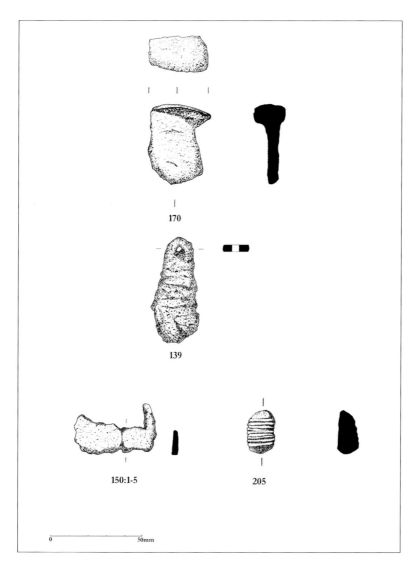

FIG. 24
*Iron anvil (170), draw knife (139), saw (150:1–5) and spool (205).*

more common L-shaped or beaked anvils are known from much of the Viking world, including York (Ottaway 1992, 513–14).

## Saw

A number of fragments recovered from Area U (150:1–5; Fig. 24) appear to be from a single object best interpreted as a small saw. Fragments of what Ó Ríordáin describes as saws (1949, 96, fig. 21, no. 148, 76, fig. 11, no. 34) from Carraig Aille are very similar. He notes that similar saws were recovered from the excavations at Garryduff (O'Kelly 1963). Though fragmentary, the Cloghermore saw appears to have been quite small and may have been used in the process of comb making or other such light work.

## Augur bit

A small C-sectioned iron fragment (70), which tapers from its broken end to a rounded tip, appears to be the tip from an augur or spoon bit, similar to those recovered from Coppergate, York (Ottaway 1992, fig. 208). The shape and size of the Cloghermore fragment are most closely paralleled by no. 2266 from Coppergate, which Ottaway parallels with examples from Norway (Rygh 1885, no. 418), and one from the toolbox recovered at Mästermyr, Gotland, Sweden (Arwidsson and Berg 1983, pl. 28).

## Dibblers

Carraig Aille produced three socketed, pointed iron objects similar to examples 159 and 178:2 from Cloghermore (Fig. 25), which it was

FIG. 25
*Dibblers (159 and 178:2), vessel handle (221), strips (146 and 147) and bar (88:2).*

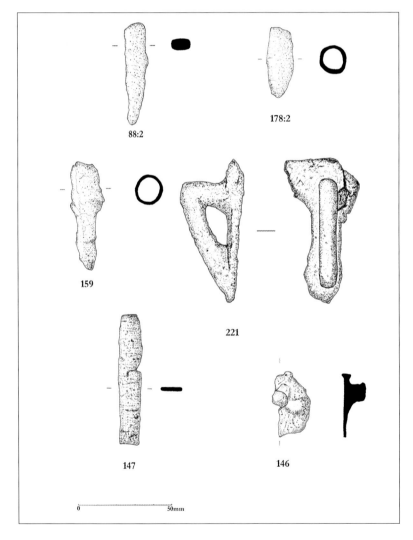

suggested possibly belonged to spearheads (Ó Ríordáin 1949, 72, fig. 10, nos 505, 524). Objects of this type have recently been interpreted by Wallace (1998, 207) as 'dibblers', which he suggests are more likely to have been for planting stouter wall posts.

Wallace describes 'dibblers' as iron cones with a single seam. They probably had long wooden handles; one of the examples from Cloghermore (159) still has wood in its socket. At least three different sizes were recorded from the Dublin excavations: the largest is almost conical with an obvious seam and a wide top; the medium is a reduced version with a rivet-hole below the rim; and the smallest has a blunter point resembling what has been interpreted elsewhere as armour-piercing arrowheads. Dibblers are described by Ottaway (1992, 654, fig. 279) as ferrules.

## Strips and bars

Cloghermore produced a number of iron fragments, which, in the case of the iron from Coppergate, York, have been classified as strips and bars (Ottaway 1992, 492–500). Examples of bars are 29, 70, 88:2 (Fig. 25), 89:3, 109:5, 127:1, 157, 160:1, 178:1 and 220, and iron strips include 62:2, 93:5, 146 and 147 (Fig. 26).

Ottaway notes that some of this material is identifiable as parts of objects or unfinished objects and compares the material to that from a workshop site at Helgö, Sweden (Hallinder and Tomtlund 1978). He also notes the occurrence of a small number of similar items in the Viking Age toolbox from Mästermyr, Gotland (Arwidsson and Berg 1983, 18–19, pls 25, 30), and suggests that it is clear evidence of ironworking. However, in the case of a burial site such as Cloghermore, these items are more likely to represent the remains of larger items now corroded rather than scrap for reprocessing. Yet, given the finding of a small anvil (170), there is a possibility that some ironworking was taking place nearby or that one of the people interred in the cave was a smith.

## Nails, staples and clench-bolt

Cloghermore also produced a number of iron nails and probable nails with three different head types: flat (190), slightly domed (109:2), and domed and solid (103) (Fig. 27). Similar nails have been recovered from Coppergate, York, which Ottaway (1992, 608–14) notes may be from a wide range of sources, the most relevant from the perspective of Cloghermore being coffins and small chests or boxes.

Of the clearly identifiable, complete staples from Cloghermore,

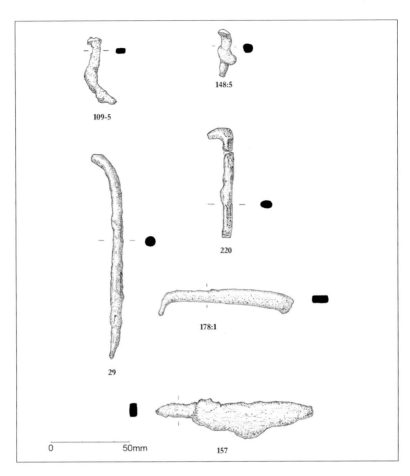

**FIG. 26**
*Iron bars (29, 109:5, 148:5, 157, 178:1 and 220).*

six are U-shaped (62, 86, 109:4, 168, 173:2 and 196) and a single small example (63) is rectangular (Fig. 27). In four of the U-shaped staples the arms come together either by having one arm curved in toward the other (86, 168 and 196) or by having the arms pinched together (173:2). Four of the Cloghermore examples are small: 63 is 10mm long; 196 is 20mm long; 168 is 27mm long; and 62 is 30mm long. The three remaining examples are larger: 109:4 is 40mm long; 173:2 is 49mm long; and 86 is 52mm long.

Unlike the small number of U-shaped staples from Coppergate (Ottaway 1992, 619–22), most of which have rectangular cross-sections, the Cloghermore examples all have generally circular cross-sections; the D-shaped to rectangular cross-section of the rectangular staple is paralleled on most of the Coppergate examples. Ottaway suggests that smaller staples, such as 62, 63, 168 and 196, were usually associated with wooden boxes/chests or repair work and that larger examples are more likely to have been used for structural purposes.

In Scandinavia small U-shaped staples were found securing

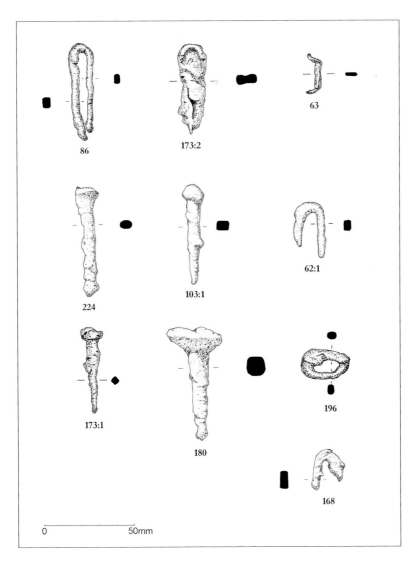

FIG. 27
*Nails (103:1, 173:1
and 224), staples
(62:1, 63, 86, 168,
173:2 and 196) and
clench-bolt (180).*

fittings to chests at Fyrkat, Denmark (Roesdahl 1977, 122, figs 197–8),
Sønder Onsild, Denmark (Roesdahl 1976, figs 10d, 11c), and Kaupang,
Norway (Blindheim *et al.* 1981, 209, fig. 38, no. 19f, pl. 39).

There is also a single clench-bolt from Cloghermore (180; Fig.
27), which could have been used for any number of wood-joining
purposes; however, such bolts are often associated with shipbuilding
and repair. The bolt from Cloghermore is very similar in size and
form to a group of bolts from the Balladoole ship, Isle of Man (Bersu
and Wilson 1966, pl. 3).

The presence of nails, staples and the clench-bolt, together with
the small barrel padlock (194), and the occurrence of iron straps, plates
and bars that may all be fittings suggest that a wooden chest had been

placed in the cave. A number of badly corroded iron fragments from the cave still have wood accreting to them. Indeed, when one considers the presence of an augur bit (70), a saw (150) and an anvil (170) from the site, as well as the volume of unidentifiable iron, it is possible that the chest may have been a toolbox of some sort.

## Iron vessel handle

A triangular iron handle with part of the wall of an iron vessel still attached (221; Fig. 25) was recovered from the topsoil in Trench 2; this is very similar to the handles of three-legged iron pots/skillets that were still in use in Ireland in the nineteenth century and is therefore likely to be modern intrusion.

## Miscellaneous iron

Various miscellaneous iron fragments were recovered during the excavations (Fig. 28).

FIG. 28
*Miscellaneous iron (93:2, 145:2, 190, 148:1 and 148:6).*

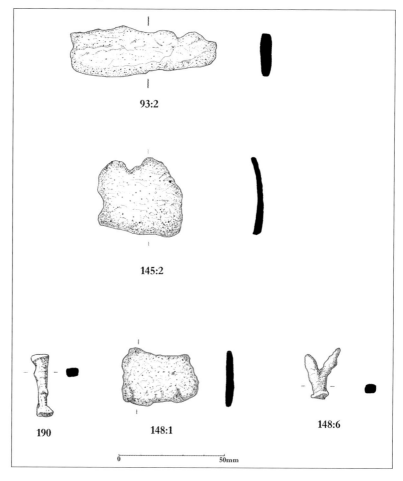

93:2

145:2

190    148:1    148:6

0    50mm

## 5.2 COPPER-ALLOY ARTEFACTS

### The ringed pins and pin fragments (Pl. 34)

The ringed pin 82 is of the plain-ringed, loop-headed type; the pin 115 and the heads of the two broken pins (42 and 201) are also loop-headed, although 201 is unusual in that it is the only one made from iron. There is also part of the shaft of a pin (152) (Fig. 29).

There is a considerable body of evidence on the plain-ringed loop-headed pin and the broadly contemporaneous spiral-ringed baluster-headed pin in Ireland in the period immediately preceding the Viking incursions, with the plain-ringed loop-headed type being the popular form during the eighth and ninth centuries (Fanning 1994, 52–3). The type is known from fifth/sixth-century levels at Rathinaun crannog and Back of the Hill ringfort, near Ardagh (*ibid.*). This type was also recovered during excavations at Carraig Aille II (Ó Ríordáin 1949, 72, fig. 10), Lagore (Hencken 1950, 71, fig. 14, no. 1117) and Garryduff (O'Kelly 1963, fig. 6). Fanning suggests that this

PL. 34

*The complete ringed pins 115 (left) and 82 (right).*

0    50mm

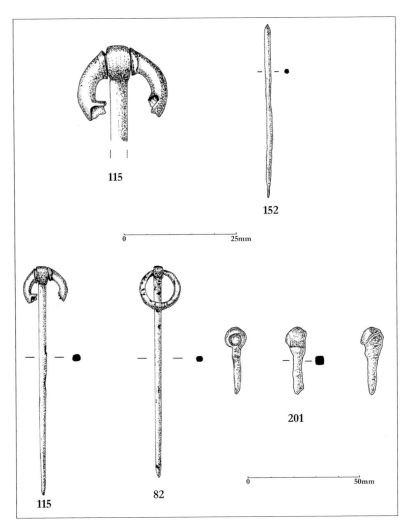

FIG. 29
*Ringed pins and*
*fragments (82, 115, 152*
*and 201).*

evidence places the plain-ringed loop-headed pin type at the head of the ringed pin series.

The occurrence of this pin type in Viking contexts in Ireland has a distinct bias in that only a handful are known from graves—Larne (Fanning 1970, 75, fig. 2) and possibly Donnybrook (Frazer 1879, 50)—while 60 are known from Viking occupation levels in Dublin. Apart from the Larne find, none of the dozen or so Irish Scandinavian graves outside Dublin has produced a ringed pin, although a plain-ringed loop-headed pin from Kinnegar, Co. Donegal, may be from a Viking burial, given the old accounts of 'cists' at the location (Fanning 1994, 17). In contrast, Kelly (1986, 179) states that after their arrival the Vikings adopted the fashion of both wearing ringed pins and using them as 'shroud pins for burials'.

The two pins of this type—one of copper alloy and the other of iron—from Dunmore Cave, Co. Kilkenny, may also have Scandinavian associations, given the massacre recorded there in 929 and the coin hoard of 920–5 found in the cave (Dolley 1975). The pins were recovered separately (Monks 1946–7), but the copper-alloy example was recorded as having been associated with some bones and two bobbin-shaped wooden objects of a type recorded in Viking burial contexts such as Birka (Arbman 1943, object B, 750).

The decorated pin from the Early Christian settlement on Dalkey Island, Co. Dublin, may also have Scandinavian associations, given De Paor's (1976, 31) suggestion that the island was used as a 'piratical lair' in the late ninth and the early tenth century. The most significant group of pins of this type from within Dublin is the 32 examples recorded from Fishamble Street—seven of copper alloy and the remainder of iron—where the tenth- and eleventh-century building levels are clearly identified (Wallace 1992). Fanning suggests that the clustering of the datable pins between 925 and 975 indicates a *floruit* for this pin form, which was adopted by the Norse settlers during the ninth century.

Outside Ireland, examples of this pin type are known from Peel Castle, Isle of Man (Freke 1986), and the three examples from Meols in Cheshire are old finds. Only one of the English examples, an iron pin from All Saints Pavement, York (Hall 1976, 19), comes from an excavated context. Sixteen pins of this type are recorded from Scotland (Fanning 1983, 334–6), of which seven are from Viking burials—both male and female; the distribution of the pins reflects the Viking settlement of the Western Isles. In Scandinavia there are numerous examples recorded from Viking graves in Norway (Petersen 1928, 192), with specimens known also from Danish graves (Brøndsted 1936, 200; Fanning 1991) and an important group from Birka in Sweden (Arbman 1943, fig. 44). Examples are also known from settlement sites such as Aggersborg in Denmark, Kaupang in Norway and Haithabu in northern Germany, where they are datable to the ninth century (Fanning 1994, 129–30). Petersen (1928, 197) records that the pins in Norway occur in both male and female graves, the female graves belonging mainly to the ninth century and the male graves to the ninth and tenth centuries. An interesting parallel for this pin, as well as the broken pendant whetstone (141), is provided by a female burial at Kneep (Cnip), Lewis. The burial contained oval brooches, a string of forty beads, a comb and a sickle, as well as a plain-ringed loop-headed pin and a small perforated whetstone (Graham-Campbell and Batey 1998, 74, pl. 5.3).

The pin 115 is unusual because of the unusual ring, which has more in common with the ring of a pseudo-penannular ring-brooch than the ringed pins classified by Fanning (1994, 5), who describes the type as being fitted with a 'loose ring or hoop of a pseudo-penannular form, often embellished with enamelling, interlace or zoomorphic ornament'. Examples are known from native Irish contexts such as Lagore (Hencken 1950, 71–7), and similar or related forms have been found among the Insular material in Viking graves in Norway (Petersen 1928, fig. 216; 1940, figs 160–3). No examples have been recovered from any of the Dublin settlement sites, although there are some antiquarian finds from the vicinity of the Islandbridge/ Kilmainham cemeteries (Wallace and Ó Floinn 1988, nos 5 and 6). Fanning suggests that this type of fastener was in vogue during the second half of the eighth century and the early part of the ninth century (ibid.).

However, two pins from County Louth, in particular that from Cortial, have rings similar to the pin from Cloghermore (Kelly 1986). Kelly describes the Cortial pin as having a plain ring 'flared on either side of the loop'. He goes on to point out that this form is found in Viking graves of the ninth century, as well as in ninth-century levels in the crannog at Ballinderry II (Hencken 1942, 73, fig. 18) and in the Norse settlement at the Brough of Birsay in Scotland (Curle 1982, 62, fig. 39:422). Interestingly, Kelly (1986) notes that the Cortial pin would fit easily into a Viking assemblage and suggests that it is the lost property of Scandinavians rather than native Irish and could therefore be interpreted as evidence of the activities of Vikings in County Louth.

A pin from Cush (Ó Ríordáin 1940, 149, fig. 35, no. 319) appears to have a flared ring and a loop-headed pin similar to Cloghermore. There is a setting for a stud at the lower side of the ring, to which is attached an animal head projection. The ring is marked with parallel incised lines.

One of the ring pins recovered from Carraig Aille (Ó Ríordáin 1949, 65, fig. 8, no. 136) also has similar flared ends to the ring on the Cloghermore pin where it locks into the looped head of its short pin. Of gilt bronze, the ring is 32mm in diameter and the pin is 66mm long. Ó Ríordáin describes the pin as having decorated bosses and interlaced panels at its base. He suggests a date in the eighth or the early ninth century for the pin while noting that some of the artefacts, including the silver hoard, date to the tenth century.

In Scandinavia, a loop-headed ringed pin with a fixed ring, the flared ring ends locking around the looped pin head, from a coffin burial at Birka (Birka I, Grave 1007), Sweden, is described by Graham-Campbell (1980, 204, 58, fig. 377.1, pl. 44.1) as 'a well developed and preserved Scandinavian variant of the insular ringed pin'. He dates the pin to his Middle Viking period: the late ninth century to the second half of the tenth century. Similar pins are recorded from other graves at Birka (Arbman 1940, 44).

Most of the remaining copper-alloy fragments from the cave are extremely small and, in most cases, unidentifiable as part of a larger object. However, the fragment 40 may well be from the rim of a vessel, and 108A–B appear to be part of a rivet.

## Copper pins

Two small flat-headed copper pins (96 and 122; Fig. 30) were recovered from Area W, associated with the articulated burial. Pins are a common find from medieval and post-medieval periods. They have been used for a variety of purposes, including dressmaking, fastening veils and as shroud-pins (Hayden and Walsh 1997, 136), and have a long period of use. Biddle (1990, 552) suggests that dress pins are an early medieval phenomenon. The pin 121 is a simple pin with a flattened head. It can be paralleled with a copper-alloy pin from the Viking site at Freswick Links, Caithness (Batey 1987, 423). The pin 152 is broken at the head, which may indicate that the head was formed separately. However, the bent pin 96 has a slightly domed, hemispherical head with a lightly incised circle on the surface of the head. This pin and 121 are possibly from a shroud or winding cloth or may have held a cloak closed around the articulated burial in Area W.

## Iron stud and copper-alloy button

Tanged studs with similarities to both the iron stud and the copper-alloy button from Cloghermore (153 and 105; Fig. 30) were recovered from the excavations at Lagore (Hencken 1950, 83, fig. 21). Hencken noted that these studs have appeared at Cahercommaun (seventh–ninth century), Creevykeel (eighth–ninth century), Garranes (fifth–sixth century) and Cush, although the Cush example (Ó Ríordáin 1940, 147, fig. 35, no. 305) is of a very different type.

Four examples were recovered from Lagore; those bearing the closest resemblance to the Cloghermore example are 689 and 968, even though both are decorated. Hencken noted that the only parallels he

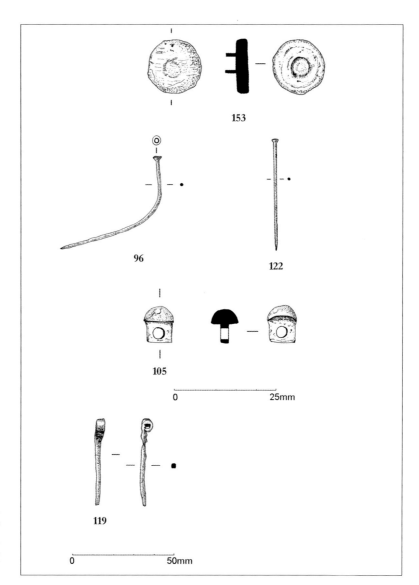

had found were from the Roman period in western Germany (*ibid.*).

However, although there are similarities between these studs and the iron example from Cloghermore (153), the copper-alloy object (105) is substantially different and is more likely to be a button. A close parallel for the iron stud from Cloghermore, with its broken cylindrical fixing at the rear, is a copper-alloy example from York (Mainman and Rogers 2000, fig. 1251, no. 10682). The closest parallels for the copper-alloy button (105), with its solid head and perforated tang, are a series of buttons from graves at Birka, particularly those from grave 1074 (Arbman 1943, 93, fig. 19).

## 5.3 BONE, ANTLER AND IVORY ARTEFACTS

### Pin-beater

The antler object 14 appears to be a so-called pin-beater (Pl. 35; Fig. 31). Rogers (1999, 1967–8) divides this artefact type into three forms: the cigar-shaped form with two working ends, the flat single-ended form, and a form that he describes as being longer than the others (155–167mm), with a rounder cross-section and a roughly chopped, unfinished butt. The object from Cloghermore is 183mm long, with a rounded cross-section and the characteristic unfinished butt, and is therefore clearly related to the third form. Nine examples of Rogers' Type 3 are recorded from Coppergate, York, ranging in date from Period 4B, c. AD 930–975, to the twelfth century. Four of the Coppergate examples were unfinished, but in the others the wear was concentrated toward the tip. Types 2 and 3 are described by Rogers as single-ended pin-beaters associated with the use of the two-beam vertical loom, which seems to have emerged in English towns in the tenth century (*ibid.*).

PL. 35
*Triangular bone plaque (99), antler pin-beater (14) and decorated bone handle (132).*

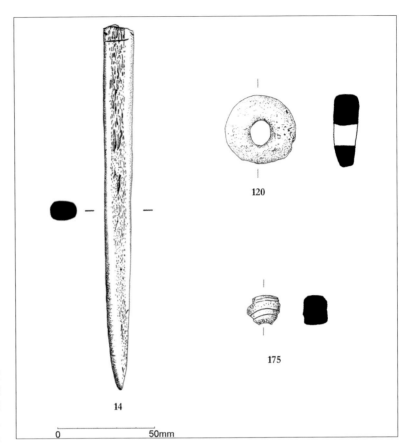

FIG. 31
*Antler pin-beater (14)
and spindle-whorl
(120) and fragmentary,
burnt bone whorl (175).*

## Gaming-pieces

Four bone objects recovered from Carraig Aille (Ó Ríordáin 1949, 82,
fig. 14, nos 58.1, 407, 339, 349) and described as 'beads or ferrules' are
identical to the small, barrel-shaped, perforated bone objects
recovered from Cloghermore, one with intact, removable peg (135,
with peg, and 151; Fig. 32; Pl. 36). The decoration of concentric incised
lines on the Carraig Aille examples is also similar.

Hencken records the recovery of six cylindrical, lathe-turned
bone beads from Lagore (1950, 196, fig. 106, no. 1116), the illustrated
example being similar to those from Cloghermore and Carraig Aille.
However, the presence of a removable peg in one of the
Cloghermore examples (135) suggests that these were gaming-pieces,
for use with a board similar to that from Ballinderry I, rather than
beads or ferrules.

An interesting group of bone artefacts associated with an
inhumation burial (no. 10) at Knowth, Co. Meath (Eogan 1974, 76, fig.

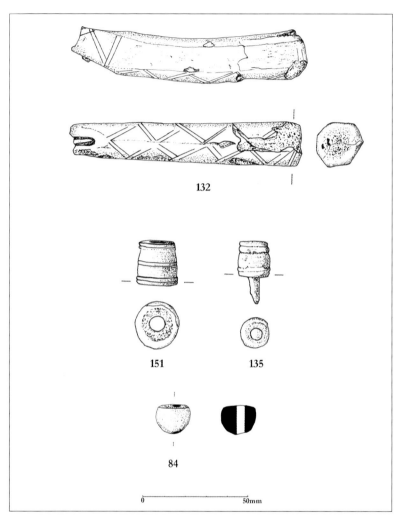

FIG. 32
*Bone gaming-pieces (84, 151 and 135 (with peg) and decorated handle (132).*

PL. 36
*The perforated walrus ivory ball (91) and bone gaming-pieces (151 and 135).*

31), provides a close parallel for another of the bone artefacts from the cave (84; Fig. 32). Eogan interprets the thirteen objects found with this burial as gaming-pieces and describes them as consisting of a rounded head, 16–18mm in diameter, with a peg, averaging 24mm long, inserted through the central hole in the head. The peg was missing from some examples, and Eogan suggested that it had become detached in antiquity. He notes that it is difficult to cite parallels for the 'gaming-pieces' but parallels a bone die from the associated burial No. 11 with an example from Lagore, Co. Meath. This bone object from Cloghermore is also very similar two four gaming-pieces illustrated on Plunkett Table 46, showing Viking artefacts in the collections of the Royal Irish Academy (Harrison 2001, fig. 3).

## Bone handle

This unusual handle (132; Fig. 32) is clearly not from a knife, as a bone peg holding part of the broken bone object attached to the handle is still in place; however, clear parallels for the handle are not obvious. Hencken (1950, 187–8) describes one of the objects recovered from Lagore as 'part of a comb with a handle at the end'. The illustration of the find (188, fig. 99, no. 608) is accompanied by an illustration of a more intact example from the River Thames at Wandsworth, which, though not very similar to the handle from Cloghermore, may offer a function for the handle. Hencken notes that similar combs have been found at Dorestad (AD 750–900) in the Netherlands and at Birka (ninth–tenth century), where Arbman (1937, 238) considered them to be Frisian in origin. However, the curved nature of the Cloghermore handle makes it unusual for a comb. It is also possible that the handle held something used in weaving, such as a small weaving sword.

## Pig fibula bone pins

Cloghermore produced eight bone pins or parts thereof, of which all are probably made from the fibulae of pigs (Figs 33 and 34). None of the examples was fully intact: they were broken across the perforation of the head (2, 126, 156, 176 and 187), missing the shaft or the tip of the shaft (3 and 134) or had the appearance of being unfinished (125 and 176), even though it may never have been the intention to work the bone any further. Similar bone pins have been recovered at Irish sites such as Cahercommaun, of which Hencken (1938, 38, fig. 23) states that 'such pins are common in Ireland during the Christian period and material from sites of this time in the National Museum nearly always

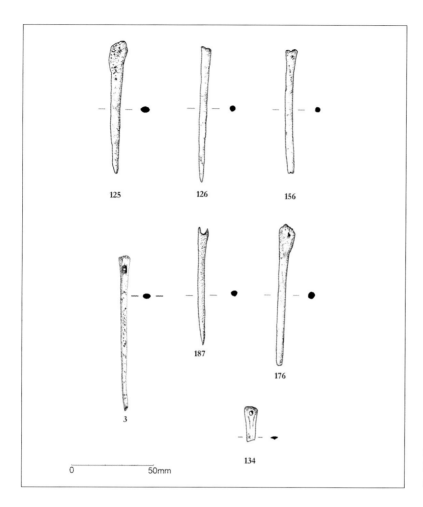

125 126 156

187

176

3

134

FIG. 33
*Bone pins (3, 125, 126,
134, 156, 176 and 187).*

0        50mm

includes them'. Such pins are also known from Scandinavia, with examples being recorded in graves at Kirchof on Gotland, Sweden (Thunmark-Nylén 1995, abb. 452 and 453).

## Triangular bone plaque

This thin bone plaque (99; Fig. 35) was one of a small number of artefacts recovered from Area Y, midway along the passage that linked the Graveyard and the Two-Star Temple. It has two circular perforations and a slot near its base; though bearing some similarities with the more usually square weaving plaques common on sites of the period, it is best interpreted as a strap-end from a belt or possibly a leather harness.

## Spindle-whorls

Cloghermore produced one spindle-whorl of antler (120; Fig. 31) and

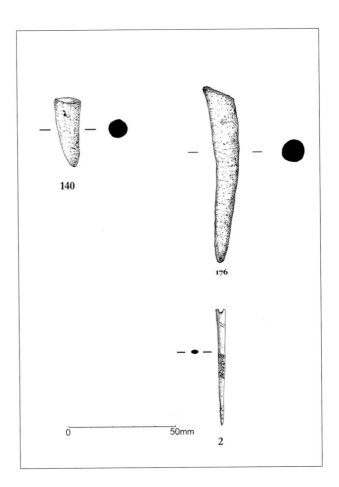

FIG. 34
*Bone pin (2) and antler
tines (140 and 176).*

FIG. 35
*Bone plaque (99) and
perforated ivory ball
(91).*

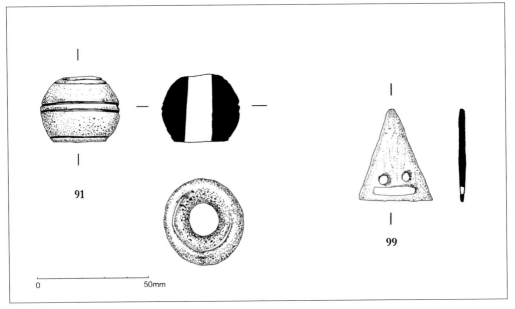

part of a bone whorl (175; Fig. 31) decorated with two concentric incised arcs around the central perforation. The antler whorl is badly eroded and, as with the stone examples, is not particularly diagnostic regarding date. The partial bone whorl, however, has been burnt and was recovered from the site of the cremation pyre in Trench 3, clearly suggesting that at least some personal objects were cremated along with the animal remains. These are discussed in more detail with the stone spindle-whorls, below.

## Ivory ball

This perforated, spherical object (91; Fig. 35) is made from ivory, and it has been suggested that it is made from the base of a walrus tusk (A. MacGregor, pers. comm.). It is decorated with a series of incised concentric lines running around its body. No convincing parallel for this unusual object has been found. However, it is an exotic find, given that walrus ivory cannot be obtained south of the Arctic Circle; indeed, Sawyer (1982, 71) suggests that, before the colonisation of Greenland, walrus ivory could be obtained only from northern Norway. The ivory itself must therefore be seen as an import; however, the object may have been manufactured in Ireland, possibly in Dublin, where it is known that walrus ivory was imported and worked (Roesdahl 1995, 26).

## Combs

Cloghermore produced evidence of at least six combs (60, 75, 83, 98, 136 and 181; Figs 36–8), of which the most complete is the double-sided comb 136 (Pl. 37; Fig. 37). The site also produced numerous teeth-plate and side-plate fragments.

The fragmentary comb side-plates 60 and 75 appear to come from combs of Dunlevy's Class F (1988, 362–7), which is broken into three major sub-classes. The partial comb 83 is also probably of this class, as are the teeth-plates 67 and 76; however, the teeth-plate 76 may be part of the curved comb 75. The class is described as consisting of single-edged composite combs with an arched spine. Class F1 combs are distinguished by relatively deep, quite flat or thin, C-shaped side-plates when viewed in cross-section. Class F2 are strong, heavy, well-polished combs with rounded, thick, usually C-shaped side-plates. Class F3 combs are lighter, with side-plates of bevelled or trapezoidal shape.

Dunlevy states that the type seems to have developed through the narrowing and lengthening of Roman high-backed, single-edged

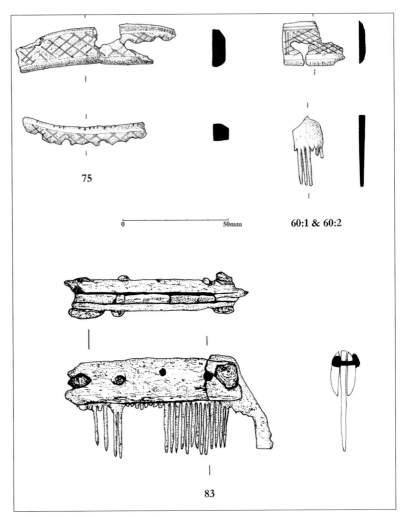

FIG. 36
*Bone combs (60:1–2, 75, 83).*

FIG. 37
*Antler comb (136).*

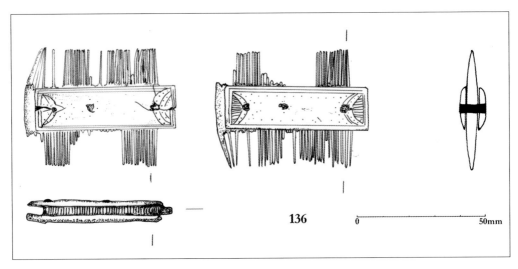

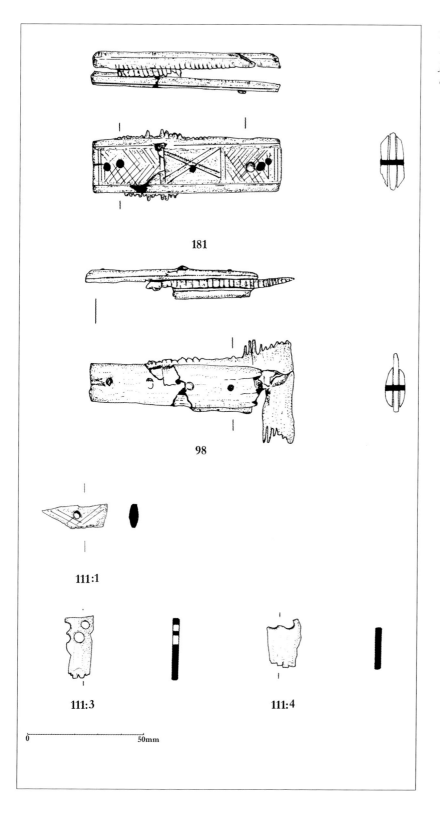

FIG. 38
*Bone comb and
fragments (98, 181
and 111:1, 3, 4).*

181

98

111:1

111:3            111:4

0                    50mm

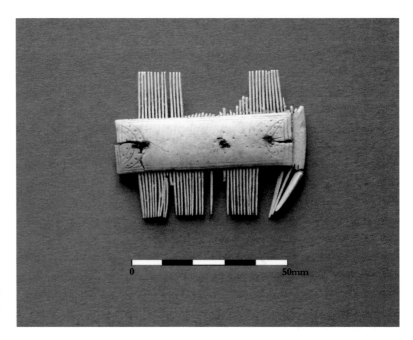

combs; by the seventh century recognisable Class F combs had
evolved.

Dunlevy (1988, 362–7) notes that combs closely related in shape
to the varieties of Irish Class F are found, particularly in Norway
(Grieg 1933, 223–7), Sweden (Arbman 1943, figs 156–66; Andersen 1968,
25–30; Märtensson 1976, 317–21; Stenberger 1961, abb. 73, grab. 133),
Schleswig, northern Germany (Tempel 1970, 34–41), Frisia (the North
Sea coast of Germany and The Netherlands) (Roes 1963, 19–21, pl.
XXIV; Düwel and Tempel 1970, 353–62), Scotland (Hamilton 1956, 124,
134, pl. XXII, fig. 69, nos 11, 12; Grieg 1940) and England (Waterman
1959, 87–90).

Dunlevy states that Class F combs are generally decorated with
incised linear motifs in the form of cross-hatching, saltire, herring-
bone, zig-zag and bands of vertical or horizontal lines. Other
decorative features include the projection of the teeth-plates above
the side-plates to form a crest and the perforation of the side-plates
with T- or cross-shapes. Functional additions include a handle or a
second row of teeth.

The curved base and spine of the remaining fragments of side-
plate 75 are best paralleled by the comb from Knowth (Dunlevy 1988,
413, fig. 7, no. 1), which is assigned to Class F2; however, the bevelled
and trapezoidal shape of the side-plate, in section, is more indicative
of Class F3. It is also clear that the Cloghermore comb was not very

long, little more than 60mm, given the dimensions and curvature of the remains of the side-plates.

The partial comb 83 is also probably best assigned to Class F2, given its strong, thick, C-sectioned side-plates, although it is impossible to suggest an original length for the comb or whether it was decorated (even though the surviving portion is undecorated). However, the real difficulty with this comb is the unusual gabled end-plate that has survived. Dunlevy does not record any similar end-plate on the Irish combs included in her study. Indeed, the closest identified parallel for this gabled end-plate is on a comb from a burial at Hemse, Färgerigaten, Gotland, Sweden (Thunmark-Nylén 1995).

Dunlevy notes that there are short and long versions of the F2 combs; the main concentration of the short combs is from Dublin, with only two from elsewhere. In Dublin the long and short types seem to be contemporaneous and have been found in contexts dating from the late ninth–tenth century to the late tenth–early twelfth century.

Combs of Class F2 occur in such quantities in Scandinavia that they have been subdivided, but there seems to be general agreement that this comb shape was in general use in late ninth–tenth century (K. Ambrosiani 1981, 23–32).

The majority of combs of Class F3 have also come from Dublin, where they have two types of end-plates and are frequently decorated with panels of incised parallel line ornamentation, often in a chequered style (Dunlevy 1988, 366).

The teeth-plates 67 and 76 from Cloghermore are from single-sided combs, but the tops of both are triangular and perforated (Figs 39, 40). Dunlevy notes of Class F1 combs that 'apart from a short, functional, perforated projection above the spine...which occurs occasionally on combs in Ireland and other countries, the crest feature occurs quite regularly on combs in Ireland' (Dunlevy 1988, 364). These two teeth-plates appear to be examples of this perforated projection.

Dunlevy notes that the distribution pattern suggests that this was the style of comb favoured in Dublin in the tenth–twelfth centuries and that the uniform nature of the combs and the regular use of antler might support an argument for a mass-production centre of this comb in Dublin.

The finely made double-sided antler comb from Cloghermore (136; Fig. 37; Pl. 37) is an example of Dunlevy's Class B, which she describes as being usually of bone, with three to five teeth-plates, and secured by three to five rivets, usually of metal. The combs may have straight, convex, angular or ornately shaped ends or ends with

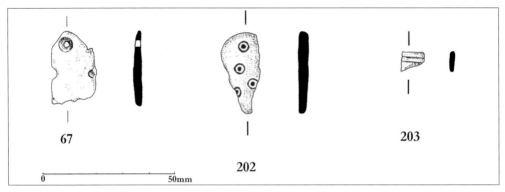

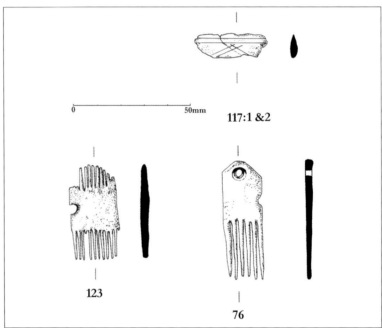

FIG. 39
Bone comb fragments
(67, 202 and 203).

FIG. 40
Bone comb fragments
(117:1–2, 76 and 123).

ornately shaped end-teeth. The side-plates are flat or C-shaped and occasionally trapezoidal in cross-section. They are usually well decorated, with the tops of the rivet-heads incorporated in the design. The main decorative motif is dot-and-circle. The combs vary in length from 50mm to 100mm and in depth from 30mm to 70mm (Dunlevy 1988, 353).

Combs of this class with convex ends similar to 136 from Cloghermore have been recovered from stratified deposits at Lagore and Dooey, where Dunlevy notes that all of the combs appear to belong to the later phases of occupation, the seventh to mid-ninth century. Combs of this class have also been found at Cahercommaun (Hencken 1938, 42, fig. 26, no. 717). Dunlevy (1988, 356) suggests that Class B combs have a long currency, dating to anywhere between the third and the ninth/early tenth century. The only combs from outside Ireland that can be compared closely with the Irish Class B are examples from Scotland, which Dunlevy describes as being so similar in style, shape and decoration as to be almost indistinguishable. She cites examples from Scotland dated to between the seventh and the ninth century.

The fragmentary comb 98 belongs to Dunlevy's Class D1 or D2, and the fragmentary comb 181 seems to belong to this Class D, although there are no end-plates remaining to enable a definite identification. Class D combs are described as double-edged composite combs with wide end-teeth, straight ends and trapezoidal side-plates when viewed in cross-section. Frequent teeth cutting marks and a highly polished finish are common. Class D combs are subdivided into three forms (Dunlevy 1988, 358).

Comb 98 is undecorated and has the straight end of D1 combs but the C-sectioned side-plates of D2 combs, and the fragmentary end-teeth appear to be wide on one side but not on the other. Overall, the evidence favours an identification of Class D1. Combs of this type have been recovered from Carraig Aille, Cush (Ó Ríordáin 1940, 155), Ballinderry 1 (Hencken 1936, 140, fig. 12C no. 216–17) and Cahercommaun (Hencken 1938, 10, 42, fig. 26, no. 10), as well as from High Street in Dublin. Dunlevy (1988, 359) suggests that combs of Class D1 date to between the fifth and the tenth century. Combs of this general double-sided type have also been recovered from Viking period graves on Gotland at Träkumla, Tjängdarve, and at Hablingbo, Havor (Thunmark-Nylén 1995, abb. 294b and abb. 125).

The side-plate no. 78 from Lagore (Hencken 1950, 186, fig. 97) has an incised saltire motif, similar to that on the central panel of comb 181 from Cloghermore. Similarly decorated combs were recorded at Ballinderry I (Hencken 1936, 30, 164, figs 6E, 30D), and the motif also occurs on the side-plate of a comb from Carraig Aille (Ó Ríordáin 1949, fig. 13, nos 71, 234). These combs also exhibit the cross-hatching seen on 181. In general, Dunlevy suggests that the Class D comb form evolved abroad from a Saxon prototype and was introduced as a developed comb type to Ireland, probably from Scandinavia.

The fragment of ring-and-dot-decorated bone from Cloghermore (202) may be from a single-piece decorated comb similar to the example designated A from Lagore (Hencken 1950, 190, fig. 102A), which is classified as Class A2 by Dunlevy (1988, 252–3).

There are a number of fragments of both side- and teeth-plates from the cave, but the only other pieces of interest are two fragments of teeth-plates, III:3–4. The teeth have been broken from both, but they both bear the remains of perforations: two broken perforations on III:3, and two complete and two broken perforations on III:4. It is possible that the fragments come from a comb of Dunlevy's Class E: double-sided composite combs with four side-plates and decorative perforations. However, they may also be evidence of the reuse of broken comb components for the making of small disc beads or bead spacers similar to those recovered from the cave.

### 5.4 STONE ARTEFACTS

## Spindle-whorls

Cloghermore produced three complete spindle-whorls, two of stone (52 and 138; Fig. 41) and one very eroded antler example (120), as well

FIG. 41
*Stone spindle-whorls (52 and 138), stone disc/lid (214) and perforated stalactite (112).*

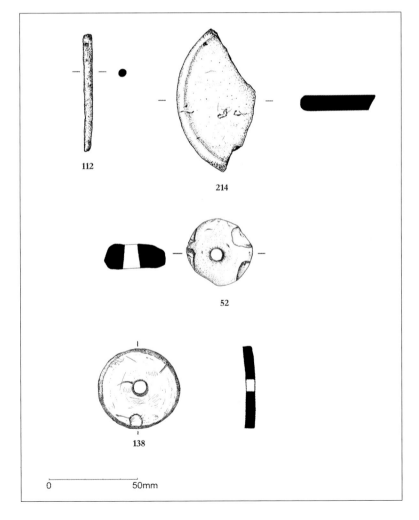

112

214

52

138

0          50mm

as a burnt fragment of a bone spindle-whorl (175). The stone whorls are made from green sandstone (52) and shale/slate (138). The green sandstone whorl is one of only two finds from just inside the entrance to the Two-Star Temple and has a slightly domed profile; the shale whorl is a flat disc. The very eroded antler whorl (A. MacGregor, pers. comm.) was recovered from the upper fill of the pit in Area V. The cremated/burnt fragment was recovered from the pyre site on the surface in Trench 3 and was associated with cremated animal bone fragments.

Eleven bone spindle-whorls and a single antler spindle-whorl were recovered from Carraig Aille I (Ó Ríordáin 1949, 83). Two of the bone whorls (*ibid.*, 82–3, fig. 14, nos 5.1, 6.1) are decorated in a similar fashion to the cremated fragment from Cloghermore, and a roughly made bone whorl (82–3, fig. 14, no. 362) is very similar in style to the antler whorl from Cloghermore. Carraig Aille II produced fourteen perforated stone spindle-whorls made of various types of stone— sandstone and shale being the more usual. The perforation was usually hourglass shaped, and no. 504 (Ó Ríordáin 1949, 88, fig. 17) is very similar to the shale whorl from Cloghermore.

## Stone discs

Cloghermore produced five stone discs, of varying sizes (34, 71, 142, 214 and 223); two have clearly bevelled edges (214 and 223; Fig. 41), and the remaining three all exhibit evidence of working.

A stone disc of similar size and form to 214 was recovered at Lagore (Hencken 1950, 830, fig. 92), which it is suggested may have been used for grinding and mixing colours for use in the craft industries on the site. This does not seem to be a convincing suggestion for the function of the Cloghermore example, which, given its size, may have been a vessel cover or stand.

## Quernstones

Fragments of two upper stones from rotary querns were recovered at Cloghermore: one from inside the cave (25), which was made from red sandstone and had been exposed to fire, and one from Trench 3 (177), which was made from green sandstone. Such querns are common finds on sites of the period, although the example from inside the cave (25) seems to have been refashioned to allow it to be suspended. The cave also produced part of a possible saddle-type quern- or grinding stone and a rubber (198 and 199), both made from red sandstone.

## Whetstones

Eleven worked and shaped whetstones or hone-stones were recovered from Cloghermore, as well as a number of others that may have been used as whetstones. Of the definite whetstones, four were made from red sandstone, three from green sandstone, and one from water-rolled black limestone. The remaining three—a boat-shaped whetstone (116), a pendant whetstone (141) and a rectangular example with rounded ends (30)—are made from what has been identified as a fine-grained mica-bearing siltstone, which is certainly not locally derived (P. Wyse-Jackson, pers. comm.) (Figs 42, 43; Pl. 38).

FIG. 42
*Whetstones (197 and 30).*

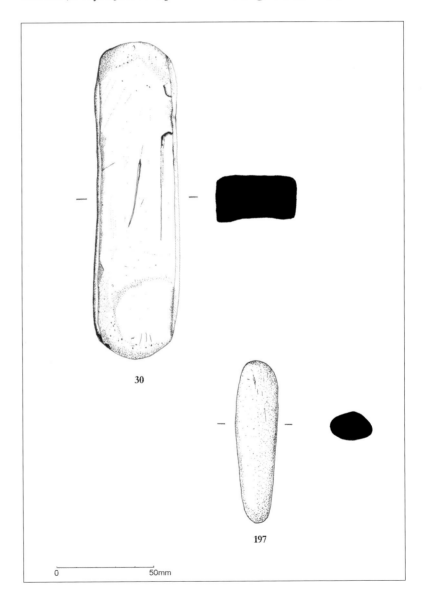

30

197

0          50mm

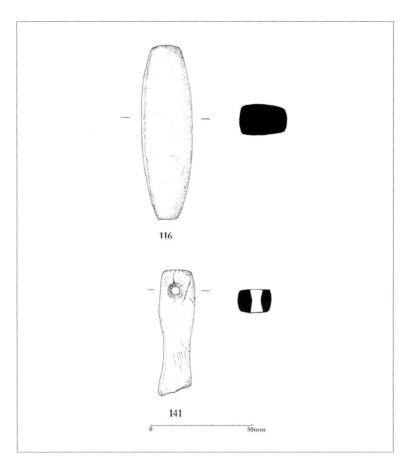

116

141

FIG. 43
*Whetstones (116 and 141).*

PL. 38
*The pendant (141) and boat-shaped (116) whetstones.*

There are no readily identifiable parallels for the small, finely made boat-shaped whetstone (116) recovered with a small iron knife (94) associated with the articulated burial of a male in Area W, and no similar whetstone appears to have been recovered from an Irish site of the period.

Whetstones similar to the small, broken, pendant whetstone (141) have been recovered from Irish sites, including one with the bronze suspension ring still intact from Lagore (Hencken 1950, 177, fig. 92, no. 87) and two small, perforated whetstones from Carraig Aille (Ó Ríordáin 1949, 86, nos 83, 244). Similar pendant whetstones have been recovered from Viking Age graves in Scotland. A male skeleton recovered at Reay in 1926 was accompanied by a plain-ringed loop-headed pin, an axe, a shield boss, a knife, a sickle, a buckle and a small perforated whetstone (Batey 1993, 153, fig. 6.4). A child burial discovered on Kneep Headland, Uig, Lewis, in 1991 contained an amber bead and a stone pendant (Cowie *et al.* 1993); the pendant is similar to the perforated whetstone from Cloghermore.

Of the numerous whetstones recovered from Carraig Aille II, fifteen had deep grooves from the sharpening of pointed objects (e.g. Ó Ríordáin 1949, 85, fig. 16, no. 115.1), similar to the sandstone example (36; Fig. 44) from Cloghermore.

The largest whetstone from Cloghermore is a well-made, deliberately shaped, square-sectioned example of green sandstone (50; Fig. 45), 254mm long. Whetstones of this size and particular form are not common on Irish sites; the longest whetstone from Cush, Co. Limerick (Ó Ríordáin 1940, 160, no. 100) was 305mm long but rough and unshaped. Similar large, square-sectioned whetstones are known from graves at Birka, Sweden, where they date to the early tenth century (Arbman 1943, 187, nos 1 and 4).

The vast majority of whetstones from Irish sites are made from red sandstone and shale, and, interestingly, the largest of the hone/ whetstones recovered during the excavations of Anglo-Scandinavian York were also made of red sandstone (Mainman and Rogers 2000, 2492). Indeed, with reference to the York hones, MacGregor has suggested that the coarser-grained, more local sandstone may have been used for initial sharpening, with final honing done with finer-grained examples. A similar situation may be represented by the presence of both sandstone whetstones and finer examples of mica-bearing siltstone in the assemblage from Cloghermore.

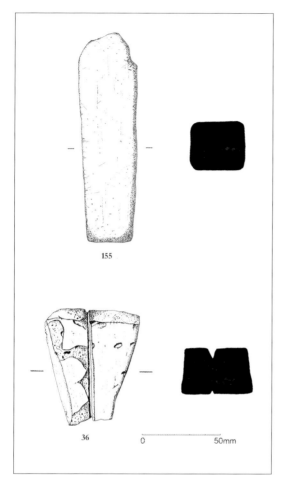

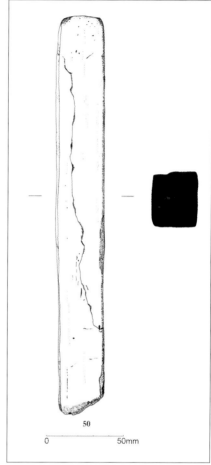

FIG. 44
*Whetstones (36
155).*

FIG. 45
*Whetstone (50).*

## Stone balls

Four medium-sized stone balls were recovered from the excavations at Cloghermore (92, 121, 216 and 219; Fig. 46), from Area W, Area X, Area V and Trench 3 respectively. These stones, which may be what are usually described as potboilers, are of red sandstone (121 and 219), green sandstone (92) and probably granite (216). These potboilers were placed in a large cauldron when it was boiled, in order to prevent the build-up of calcerous accretions on the inside of the vessel (Hurley 1997, 113). They are found on Irish sites from the early medieval period onward. The possible pecking on one example (121) may be the result of wear from constant reuse breaking down the surface of the sandstone. However, the placement of one (216) in the pit in Area V, particularly one that is either of granite or possibly of quartz, may indicate a ritual purpose for this stone.

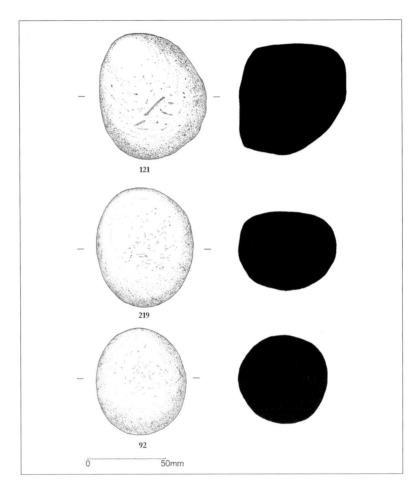

FIG. 46
*Stone balls or
potboilers (92, 121
and 219).*

## Stone axe

The bladed half of a broken siltstone axehead was recovered from
Trench 3 at Cloghermore (179; Fig. 47). This object is undoubtedly in
a secondary context and may be evidence of an earlier, prehistoric
presence on the site. However, a similar broken stone axe that was
recovered from Carraig Aille had been reused as a whetstone (Ó
Ríordáin 1949, 86, fig. 16, no. 52). There are very fine scorings on the
surface of the Cloghermore example also, and such a reuse may well
explain its presence.

## Fragments and pebble of red jasper

Cloghermore produced two fragments and a water-rolled pebble of
red jasper (107, 204 and 222; Fig. 47). One of these (107) was associated
with the articulated burial in Area W, and the other two were
recovered from the pit in Area V. As noted above, red jasper occurs in
Old Red Sandstone conglomerates on the Dingle Peninsula and is

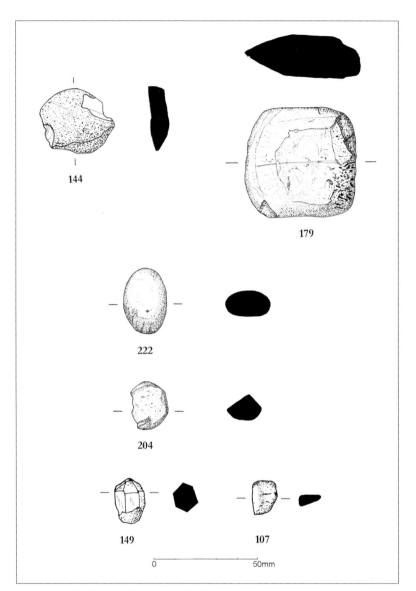

144

179

222

204

149        107

0                    50mm

FIG. 47
Stone axehead
fragment (179), jasper
pebbles (107, 204 and
222), flint strike-a-
light (144) and rock
crystal (149).

frequently found eroded from these rocks, as pebbles found in streambeds. These stones are therefore most likely locally derived. Jasper pieces were recovered from the Viking site at L'Anse Aux Meadows, Newfoundland, Canada. Four 'chippings of red jasper' were found in House F: one from a hearth, two from near a hearth, and one from a midden outside the house. The largest measured 1.9cm and was blunt at one end (Ingstad 1997, 208). Ingstad concludes that 'there can hardly be any doubt that these chippings derive from fire lighting stones'. This offers a possible explanation for the two chips or fragments of red jasper from Cloghermore (107 and 204);

indeed, there was evidence of localised burning on top of the pit in Area V, where 204 was recovered. However, 222 is water rolled and smooth, clearly derived from a streambed, and bears no evidence of having been struck.

## Crucibles

Two objects that may represent metalworking on-site were recovered (Fig. 48). The better example is a small stone vessel (100) made from a split, rounded cobble of greenstone, with a hollowed-out round-bottomed centre. This vessel is best interpreted as a crucible. The second item (97) is a curved fragment of burnt clay with clear evidence of burning and oxidisation on its surface, which is probably part of a clay crucible.

FIG. 48
*Stone crucible (100)
and fragment of a
clay crucible (97).*

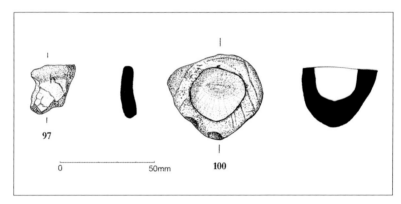

97

0       50mm       100

### 5.5 BEADS

The cave produced thirteen beads: six of amber (41, 43, 48, 64, 69 and 110), three of glass (80, 81 and 143), three small disc beads or spacers of bone (68, 79 and 186), and one small disc bead of stone (104).

## Glass beads (Fig. 49)

The blue glass bead from the cave (143), decorated with yellow enamel cables and bosses, is loosely paralleled by a glass bead from Carraig Aille I (Ó Ríordáin 1949, 90, fig. 19, no. 19.1), which is described as being made of blue glass with applied 'thread' or 'rope' ornament in relief. The threads on the body of the Carraig Aille bead are of pale blue glass, and the collar around one end is of twisted blue and white glass. In the spaces between the crossed blue threads there are small inset knobs of opaque white material, similar in style and shape to the bosses on the Cloghermore bead. However, the Carraig Aille bead is

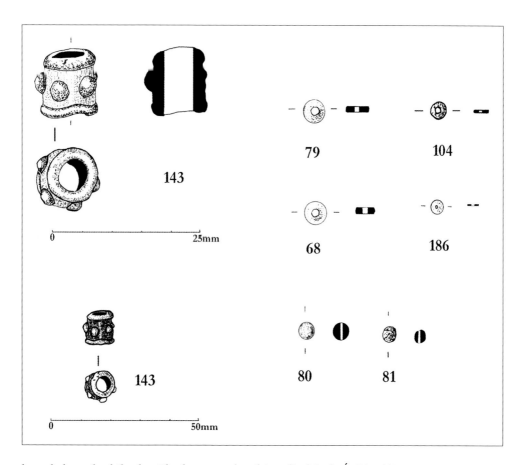

barrel shaped while the Cloghermore bead is cylindrical. Ó Ríordáin (1949, 101–2) states that beads of this type are difficult to date but notes that the only associated find of any value for dating is reported by Armstrong from the Norse cemetery at Islandbridge, Dublin. A blue bead with applied spiral decoration in yellow enamel, like the Cloghermore example, from the settlement site at Kaupang, Norway, has been interpreted as being of Irish origin (Skre *et al.* 2001, fig. 4.7).

The other two glass beads from the site (80 and 81) are spherical, 4.3mm and 5.2mm in diameter, with a 1mm-diameter central perforation. Identical beads were recovered from the excavations at York, almost exclusively from Coppergate, where they have been classified as Type 7 single segment (Mainman and Rogers 2000, 2594–6, fig. 1285, 10313). Mainman and Rogers state that beads of this type appear to be unknown in England outside of York, although they have been found on Norse sites in Scotland such as the Brough of Birsay (Curle 1982, 83) and Jarlshof (Hamilton 1956, 152). A necklace of 44 such beads was recovered from a tenth-century Viking grave at Kneep, Isle

FIG. 49
*Glass beads (143 (blue), 80 and 81); bone and stone spacers (68, 79, 104 and 186).*

of Lewis (Welander *et al.* 1987, 163–5). This type of bead is commonly found in Scandinavia (Callmer 1977, Type E) and was found at the eighth–tenth-century settlement site at Paviken, Gotland, Sweden (Lundström 1981, 9), and the settlement at Hedeby in northern Germany (Dekówna 1990, 34–6). Interestingly, the Cloghermore beads were found in association with a flat bone disc bead/spacer (79), which may have separated the two small glass beads on a string.

## Amber beads

Six amber beads were recovered from Cloghermore (Pl. 39; Fig. 50); all except one (110) were directly associated with the deposition of the cremated animal bone, ash and charcoal in the stone setting within the Graveyard. Five of the beads were uncovered intact (41, 44, 48, 64 and 110), and one was in two pieces and incomplete (69). Bead 110 was found at the base of the sloping gallery, Area X, just as it entered the Graveyard, and, although it was within 0.30m of the cremation deposit, it was not directly associated with it, as were the others.

Two of the beads (41 and 48) broke during retrieval and were repaired during conservation, and all display cracking and discoloration consistent with exposure to heat/fire. The beads are all of generally the same diameter, although they differ in thickness. On all of the beads there is a difference between the thickness of one side and that of the other, most pronounced on 44, and the perforation is placed eccentrically on the beads where there is the greatest difference. This clearly suggests that the beads are all part of the one string, probably from a necklace, the eccentric perforations and sloping/wedge-shaped cross-sections of some of the beads ensuring that they would lie tightly against one another on a curve.

Amber beads of the type from Cloghermore are not well represented on Irish sites of the period. Only two small fragments of a bead of 'poor quality' were recovered from Carraig Aille (Ó Ríordáin 1949, 102); sixteen amber beads were found at Lagore, but only no. 701 bears any resemblance to the Cloghermore beads, although it is flatter (Hencken 1950, 150–1, fig. 74). Amber was also recovered at Garranes (Ó Ríordáin 1942, 121) and Ballycatteen (Ó Ríordáin and Hartnett 1943, 27).

A number of the amber beads from the excavations at York are similar in shape and size to the Cloghermore examples (Mainman and Rogers 2000, fig. 1218, 10782). Graham-Campbell and Batey (1998, 149–50) note that the occurrence of an amber bead in the pagan Norse graves of Scotland is quite common, among both sexes, and suggest that it may have been more than just a fashion, given the reputed amuletic properties of amber. Interestingly, Sander (1997, 71) suggests that the recovery of amber from one of the cremation graves at Cemetery 116 at Helgö is evidence that it was deposited in the grave without having been on the pyre, as amber melts at temperatures above 270°C. A similar situation may have occurred at Cloghermore. However, as noted above, the Cloghermore beads seem to be from a single string, either a necklace or a bracelet, and are therefore more likely to relate to the burial of a female.

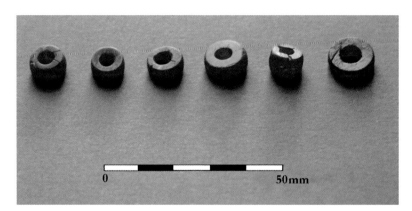

PL. 39
*Amber beads (left to right: 41, 44, 48, 64, 69 and 110).*

FIG. 50
*Amber beads (41, 44, 48, 64, 69 and 110).*

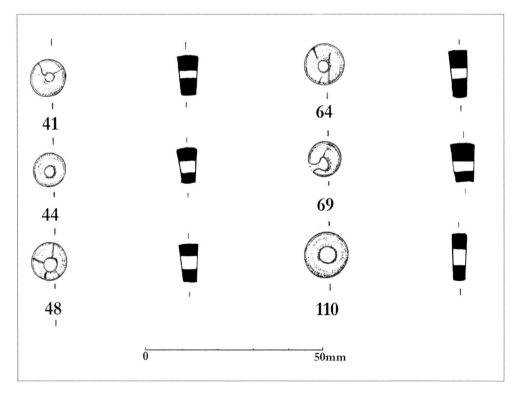

## Bone and stone disc beads/spacers (Fig. 49)

The three bone beads/spacers are of varying sizes: 68 and 79 are 7.5mm and 8mm in diameter, with 2.5mm-diameter central perforations, and 186 is only 4.5mm in diameter, with a 1mm-diameter perforation. The two larger beads were found in association with two spherical glass beads (79) and two amber beads (68), which may suggest that they separated these pairs of beads on a string. The small bead (186) was recovered on the surface in Trench 3. The stone bead (104) is 5.5mm in diameter with a 2mm-diameter central perforation and was not directly associated with any other artefact.

# 6   THE SILVER HOARD

*John Sheehan*

## 6.1 INTRODUCTION

The silver hoard from Cloghermore Cave was found in a small cleft or hollow during the excavation of Quadrant A of the Graveyard. The cleft was formed by a number of roof-collapsed boulders that were welded together by the action of flowstone. It was situated 0.35m below a deposit of the brown clay, only 0.5m from the edge of the stone setting that contained the cremated animal bone deposit. It was filled with the brown clay, and, after the discovery of an ingot and a single piece of hack silver in it, its fill was brought to the surface and sieved through a 2mm wire mesh. This resulted in the discovery of the remainder of the hoard, which comprised a second ingot and three further pieces of hack silver (Pl. 40). No other artefacts were recovered from the fill of the

PL. 40
*The silver hoard.*

cleft, although the area between it and the stone setting produced two amber beads (64, 69:1–2) and a bone disc bead or spacer (68).

## 6.2 DESCRIPTION

The hoard consists of six items: two ingots (61 and 74) and four portions of individual arm-rings (66, 72:1–2 and 73), two of which (72:1–2) are tightly wrapped together.

### Ingots

Ingot 61 is in the form of an oblong bar, of ovoid cross-section, which tapers more to one end than the other (Fig. 52). Both ends are rounded; no nicks or pecks are evident. It is 49mm long, 10mm wide and 7mm high and weighs 25.4g.

Ingot 74 is in the form of a short oblong bar, of ovoid cross-section, with rounded ends (Fig. 52). There is a slight protuberance on one face of the object and a single nick (slice) on the angle of one side. It is 32mm long, 10mm wide and 5mm high and weighs 12.2g.

The two ingots from the Cloghermore hoard are of some interest. Ingots form a significant element of Ireland's Viking Age hoards, functioning as a simple means of storing bullion. Ingots or ingot fragments occur in at least 35 hoards of before AD 1000 from Ireland, fifteen of which also contain coins (see Table 1). All of these are of tenth-century in date, although the large number of ingots in the Cuerdale hoard, deposited in *c.* 905 (Blackburn and Pagan 1986, 294), serves as a reminder that ingots were in circulation in Ireland during the closing years of the ninth century. It is interesting that ingots were generally more popular in Ireland and Denmark than in other parts of the Viking world (Kruse 1993, 188), which emphasises the important links that existed between the silver-working traditions of Ireland and southern Scandinavia during the Viking Age.

Given that Viking Age ingots are generally neither culturally nor regionally diagnostic, it is not possible to state unequivocally that the ingots from Ireland's Viking Age hoards, including the newly discovered examples from Cloghermore, are of Hiberno-Scandinavian manufacture. Nevertheless, there is a strong probability that they are, especially given that broad-band arm-rings—the Hiberno-Scandinavian object type *par excellence*—were simply made by hammering out ingots. Indeed, Hiberno-Scandinavian material forms part of thirteen of the nineteen hoards from Ireland in which ingots are associated with ornaments and/or ornament-derived hack silver. As ingots simply functioned as a means of storing bullion, it is probable that the putative Hiberno-Scandinavian examples, alongside the broad-band arm-rings, played an important role in Ireland's Viking Age metal-weight economy. The nick on one of the Cloghermore ingots, as well as the fact that many ingots in hoards from Ireland are represented in hack-silver form, may be taken as evidence to support this.

| Provenance | Date |
|---|---|
| Millockstown, Co. Louth | After 905–6 |
| Dysart Island (no. 4), Co. Westmeath | c. 907 |
| County Antrim | c. 910? |
| Magheralagan, Co. Down | c. 910 |
| Leggagh, Co. Meath | c. 915 |
| Dunmore Cave (no. 1), Co. Kilkenny | c. 928 |
| County Dublin | c. 935 |
| Monasterboice, Co. Louth | c. 953 |
| Mungret, Co. Limerick | c. 953 |
| Killincoole, Co. Louth | c. 970 |
| Rahan (no. 2), Co. Offaly | c. 970? |
| Dunmore Cave (no. 2), Co. Kilkenny | 970s |
| Ireland (?) | c. 960–90 |
| Marl Valley, Co. Westmeath | c. 986 |
| Ladestown, Co. Westmeath | 990s |

TABLE 1—*Coin-dated hoards from Ireland containing ingots or ingot fragments, of before AD 1000 (after Sheehan 1998a, table 6.1, with additions).*

## Arm-rings

Arm-ring 66 consists of a fragment of a large broad-band arm-ring, tapering in width from one end to the other and bent to form a loop (Fig. 51). One end has been cleanly cut through; the other has been cut twice and snapped. The outer face is ornamented with rows of vertical transverse stamping executed with a bar-stamp with a central row of pellets. No nicks or pecks are evident. It is 21mm wide and 4mm thick at the wider end, measures c. 58mm in extended length and weighs 27.4g.

Arm-ring 72:1 consists of a fragment of a broad-band arm-ring, tapering in width from one end to the other and bent to form a loop

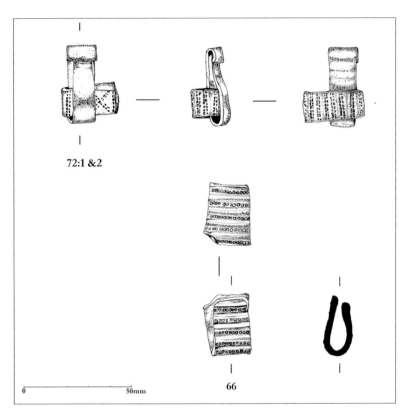

0 ———————————— 50mm

66

FIG. 51
*Hack-silver arm-rings
(66 and 72:1–2).*

(Fig. 51). The wider end has been cut through, in three strokes, from the inner face. The outer face is ornamented with rows of vertical transverse stamping executed with a bar-stamp with a plain centre between serrated edges. A diagonal cross, executed with the same stamp, occurs at the narrower end of the piece. The fragment is interlocked with 72:2, and, although both are ornamented with the same type of stamp, they are not derived from the same ring. No nicks or pecks are evident. It is 14mm wide and 3mm thick at the wider end, measures *c.* 58mm in extended length and weighs 14.5g.

Arm-ring 72:2 consists of a fragment of a rather thin broad-band arm-ring, tapering in width from one end to the other and tightly bent to form a loop (Fig. 51). It has been bent so as to expose the original inner face of the band, and this has largely obscured its decorated outer face. It is clear, nevertheless, that this face is ornamented with rows of vertical transverse stamping executed with a bar-stamp with a plain centre between serrated edges. A diagonal cross, probably executed with the same stamp, occurs at the narrower end of the piece. This end, though obscured, appears to be one of the original terminals of the arm-ring; the wider end has been cut through. The fragment is interlocked with 72:1, and, although both are ornamented with the same type of stamp, they are not derived from the same ring. No nicks or pecks are evident. It is 13mm wide and 2mm thick at the wider end, measures *c.* 81mm in extended length and weighs 11.8g.

Arm-ring 73 consists of a fragment of a small broad-band arm-ring, bent to form a loop. Its expanded mid-portion tapers to severed ends (Fig. 52). The outer face is ornamented with rows of vertical transverse stamping on either side of a central diagonal cross. The ornamentation is executed with a multi-point bar-stamp, the points taking the form of lozenge-shaped dots. No nicks or pecks are evident. It is 10.5mm wide and 2mm thick at the mid-point, measures *c.* 93mm in extended length and weighs 15.55g.

The four Cloghermore ring fragments are classic examples of Hiberno-Scandinavian broad-band arm-rings. Silver arm-rings were

FIG. 52
*Hack-silver arm-ring*
*(73) and ingots (61*
*and 74).*

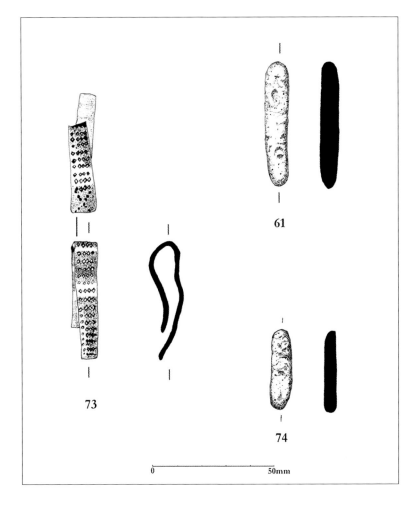

by far the most common products of Ireland's Hiberno-Scandinavian silver-working tradition, which was at its height between *c.* 850 and *c.* 950. Several different classes have been identified, but the most important in numerical terms is the broad-band type (Graham-Campbell 1976, 51–3; Sheehan 1998a, 178–80). Rings of this sort are normally penannular in form and are made from a thick, flat band of silver that tapers in width from the mid-point toward the terminals. Although plain examples occur, these rings are normally decorated with rows of stamped grooves, transversely disposed, which are formed with distinctive bar-shaped punches. The ornamentation, in most cases, features a diagonal cross motif on the expanded central area of the arm-ring.

Over 100 individual examples of broad-band arm-rings are on record from Ireland. They occur, sometimes in hack-silver form, in more than twenty hoards, including the well-known examples from Cushalogurt, Co. Mayo (Hall 1973), Raphoe, Co. Donegal (Graham-Campbell 1988), Dysart (no. 4), Co. Westmeath (Ryan *et al.* 1984, 339–42) and Carraig Aille II, Co. Limerick (Ó Ríordáin 1949, 62–4, fig. 2). These rings have also been noted from at least a dozen finds from Britain and Norway. Classic examples in this regard include that from Cuerdale, Lancashire, in which a substantial portion of the non-numismatic silver is demonstrably of Hiberno-Viking origin (Graham-Campbell 1987, 339–40), and the hoards from Vestre Rom, Osnes and Bøstrand, Norway (Grieg 1929, 239–40, 246, 258–60). The occurrence of broad-band arm-rings alongside coins in a number of hoards from Ireland, Britain and Scandinavia indicates that the type developed during the later ninth century, perhaps *c.* 880, and continued in general circulation until *c.* 930–40 (Sheehan 1990, 125).

The distributional evidence from Ireland suggests that broad-band arm-rings were manufactured there, most probably by the Hiberno-Scandinavians centred on Dublin (Fig. 53). In origin, however, this type of ring is of ninth-century Danish inspiration (Brooks and Graham-Campbell 1986, 97–8; Sheehan 1998a, 194–8). Ultimately, this connection between Viking Age Ireland and southern Scandinavia is due to the primary importance of the southern Scandinavian and Baltic region as a source of the silver used to supply the Hiberno-Scandinavian silver-working tradition. The case for the Danish inspiration for this arm-ring type rests on the occurrence of rings of similar form and ornamentation in several ninth-century hoards from southern Scandinavia. It is likely that these rings, from Denmark and Skåne, are of local manufacture given that

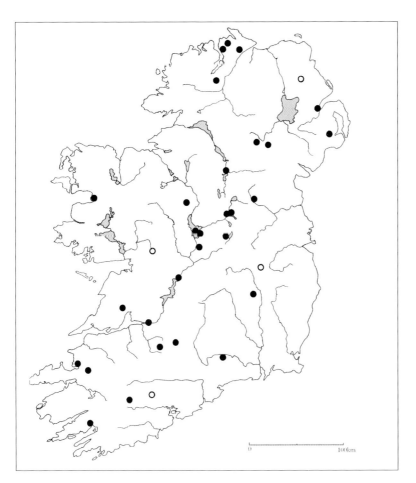

FIG. 53
*Distribution of hoards
containing Hiberno-
Scandinavian broad-
band arm-rings, and
single finds of same, in
Ireland. (Open symbol
indicates a county
provenance only.)*

contemporaneous variants of spiral-rings produced in Denmark feature ornamentation—such as transversely disposed stamped grooves and diagonal crosses—that is closely related to that on the arm-rings. Thus, given its early date, combined with its form and ornamentation, this Danish form of ring may be regarded as the prototype for the Hiberno-Scandinavian broad-band series.

Several individual arm-rings that may be either imported prototype rings from southern Scandinavia or Hiberno-Scandinavian copies of these can be identified in finds from Ireland, and it is also possible to identify close parallels between the motifs and schemes of ornamentation exhibited on Hiberno-Scandinavian broad-band arm-rings and on related material from this part of Scandinavia. These parallels include the use of bar-punches with serrated edges or central rows of pellets, such as were used, for instance, to ornament the rings in the hoard from Kærbyholm, Odense (Munksgaard 1970,

59–60), and arm-rings from many hoards in Ireland, including, indeed, the Cloghermore find. The identification of these types of punch serves to reinforce the proposed links between the Hiberno-Scandinavian silver-working tradition and that of ninth-century southern Scandinavia, as these punches were not commonly used to ornament objects elsewhere in Scandinavia. In fact, they appear to be entirely lacking from Norway, where punches with individual motifs were the preferred fashion. It is interesting that—despite the fact that both the historical and the archaeological evidence indicates that the Norse were much more concerned with Ireland than the Danes were—the archaeological evidence indicates clearly that the southern Scandinavian and Baltic regions were of greater importance than Norway to the development of the silver-working tradition of Viking Age Ireland (Sheehan 2001a, 58–9).

Broad-band arm-rings appear to have been primarily manufactured for the storage and circulation of silver as a form of currency in Ireland's metal-weight economy, but it is very likely that they also served as status objects. The ingots from which they were hammered into ring form, on the basis of the results of preliminary metrological analyses on a sample of complete arm-rings from Britain and Ireland, appear to have been cast to variations on a target weight unit of 26.15g (Sheehan 1984, 57–65). This result is of particular interest as it differs by only 0.45g from the dominant weight unit reflected in the lead scale-weights from tenth-century Dublin (Wallace 1987, 206–7). Although the arm-ring target weight appears to be a valid one, it is also clear that the weights of individual broad-band rings were not intended to be precise multiples or sub-multiples of it, and the weighing of these would have been required during commercial transactions. It is also apparent that the Scandinavians did not always weigh silver accurately elsewhere in the Viking world, and even the lead weights that formed the basis of the metrological system sometimes conformed to the weight standards only very generally. The main weight unit was the *eyrir*, or ounce, and this could be subdivided into thirds or sixths. A value of 24g for the *eyrir* has been proposed, as have others of up to 26.6g, but it is not clear whether these were separate standards or simply a loosely applied single one.

It is not possible to make any definitive statement on the significance of the weights of the arm-ring fragments from the Cloghermore hoard, given that they constitute too small a sample for proper analysis. It is of some interest, however, that the weights of

72:2 (11.8g) and 73 (15.55g) approximate to one-half and two-thirds, respectively, of the value of the lighter *eyrir*. Perhaps significantly, the weight of one of the ingots from the hoard, 74 (12.2g), also approximates to one-half of this value, and that of the second ingot, 61 (25.4g), lies within the range of the heavier *eyrir*.

Silver arm-rings might acquire minor nicks and pecks during commercial transactions, and these represent a characteristic Scandinavian method of assessing silver quality as well as testing for plated forgeries. No such nicks are evident on the Cloghermore rings, although one occurs on one of the ingots (74). The nature of a metal-weight, or *gewichtsgeldwirtschaft*, economy necessitated the reduction of ornaments to hack silver, and examples of broad-band arm-rings reduced to this form occur in many hoards in Ireland, including the Cloghermore find. It is of interest, however, that there appear to be proportionally more complete examples of these rings on record from Britain and Scandinavia. This may be interpreted as indicating the status value attached to Hiberno-Scandinavian arm-rings, particularly once they were removed from the economic milieu in which they were produced (Graham-Campbell and Sheehan 1996, 777).

## 6.3 STRUCTURE

A new classificatory system for Viking Age hoards from Ireland containing non-numismatic material has recently been developed and proposed by the author (Sheehan 2001b, 57–62). The basis for this classification is the composition of the hoards as reflected through the presence, absence or association of the three non-numismatic phenomena that may form part of Viking Age hoards: ornaments, ingots and hack silver. The presence or absence of coins is not deemed to be of particular significance, as coins could be regarded variously as bullion, ornaments or money during the Viking Age. A five-fold division of the hoards is advanced, and the shared characteristics of each of these classes, whether or not they contain coins, are stressed. The non-numismatic components of Class 1 hoards consist of complete ornaments only; those of Class 2 hoards consist of complete ingots only; those of Class 3 hoards consist of a combination of complete ornaments and ingots only; those of Class 4 hoards consist of complete ornaments and/or ingots in association with hack silver; and those of Class 5 hoards consist of hack silver only. The principal classes evident in the material from Ireland are

Classes 1, 2 and 4, which together account for almost 84 per cent of the total number.

The system is capable of accommodating further levels of refinement for the purpose of more detailed analyses. Thus, for example, a hoard that contains hack silver (i.e. a Class 4 or 5 hoard), such as the Cloghermore find, may be sub-classified into one of twelve permutations and combinations on the basis of whether its hack silver is derived from ornaments, from ingots or from both of these, combined with the form of its other non-numismatic contents, if any. This number of potential permutations and combinations is doubled, of course, when coins are also present in the find.

Interestingly, the five principal hoard categories that emerge from the Irish evidence have particular and reasonably discrete distributional patterns (Sheehan 2001b, fig. 9a–f). This may be taken as an indicator that these groupings are not simply creations of the classificatory process and that they reflect a Viking Age reality. Furthermore, when the broad contextual information pertaining to these hoards—such as chronology, distribution and find location—is added to their proposed classifications, it becomes possible to identify and appreciate their social and economic significance more readily. Thus the proposed system facilitates the examination of the various roles that silver hoards and their components played in both Hiberno-Scandinavian and Irish society.

Under the terms of the proposed classificatory system the Cloghermore find is a Class 4 hoard, fulfilling the criteria of being a find consisting of complete ornaments and/or ingots in association with hack silver. There are 21 such hoards on record from Ireland. Nine potential permutations and combinations exist for the compositional structure of the non-numismatic elements of these finds, and seven of these are represented in the hoard data. Thus, there is a good deal of variety evident within the composition of Class 4 hoards. At one end of the range is the find from Raphoe, Co. Donegal, for instance, with its arm-rings, ingots and a solitary large fragment of hack silver (Graham-Campbell 1988). This represents a type of hoard that is clearly at a considerable remove in terms of both composition and nature from the collection of coins, ingots and highly fragmented hack silver contained in the hoard from Dysart Island (no. 4), Co. Westmeath (Ryan et al. 1984, 339–42).

The Class 4 find from Cloghermore may be further categorised as belonging to sub-section 4e of this class, as it contains complete ingots alongside hack silver derived from ornaments. There are only two other Class 4e hoards on record from Ireland. One is from an unknown location in County Dublin and contained a single ingot, two spiral-ring fragments and a collection of Anglo-Saxon coins, as well as some issues of the Vikings of East Anglia and Northumbria (Graham-Campbell 1976, 49, pl. 2); it was deposited in *c.* 935 (Blackburn and Pagan 1986, 295). The other hoard, provenanced only to County Cork, consists of a single ingot and two fragments of broad-band arm-rings (Sheehan 1998b, 162, fig. 15.3). The latter find is of some interest in the context of the Cloghermore hoard, not only because they share a Munster provenance but also because it exclusively contains hack silver derived from broad-band arm-rings in addition to its ingot. It will be discussed below.

All Class 4 hoards may be regarded to some degree as evidence of the use of silver as a means of payment, given that they feature hack silver as an element. Hoards containing hack silver should be viewed as commercially 'active', according to Graham-Campbell (1989, 55), who noted that 'silver bullion will have been so rendered for commercial purposes and not for reasons of status'.

Classic hack-silver hoards are relatively rare in Ireland. In fact, it is noteworthy that few of the Class 4 finds may be classified as 'true' hack-silver hoards in the sense in which this phenomenon is understood in Scandinavia. Typically, however, these Scandinavian hoards are later than the hoards under consideration here, and this may mean that the two bodies of evidence are not directly comparable. The phenomenon of hack silver is usually interpreted as an intermediary form of development between a bullion and a monetary economy, with ornaments and ingots being absorbed into commercial circulation because the available quantity of coined silver was insufficient to meet the needs of a metal-weight economy. In Ireland, however, this does not seem to be the case, and it may have been the retention and use of imported coins, rather than the process of reducing ornaments to hack silver, that resulted in the late tenth-century development of indigenous minting (Sheehan 2001b, 62).

Dublin's mint was established in *c.* 997, after a period of about fifty years during which quantities of Anglo-Saxon coins were being retained and hoarded in Ireland. The clear majority of the coin hoards deposited during this period are from parts of the country focused on Dublin: the north Leinster and central midlands regions. The distributional patterns of hoards with a hack-silver element, however, are largely exclusive to these regions (see Fig. 54). The fact

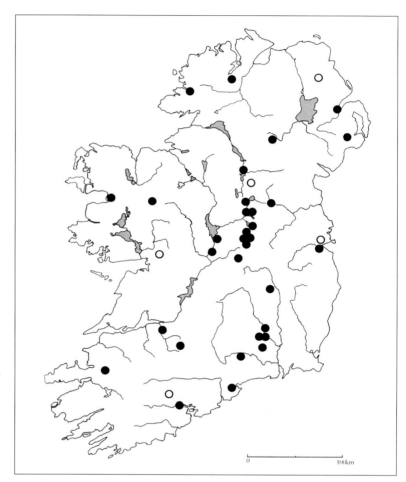

FIG. 54
*Distribution of
hoards containing
hack silver (Classes 4
and 5) in Ireland.
(Open symbol
indicates a county
provenance only.)*

that less than one-third of Class 4 and 5 hoards contain coins, with coins occurring in only four of the 21 Class 4 hoards, serves to distinguish further these finds from the coin hoards and, incidentally, serves to isolate them even further from the Scandinavian hack-silver hoards, which are only rarely found without coins. Thus, it seems unlikely that hack silver played a significant role in the move toward monetarisation that occurred in later tenth-century Ireland.

Nonetheless, it is clear that the Class 4 and 5 hoards served an economic function. This is supported when those finds that are recorded from settlement contexts are considered. The crannóg emerges as the settlement type that is most strongly associated with these types of hoards, although, perhaps not surprisingly given that some of them were developing market functions at this time, ecclesiastical sites also feature. This finding serves as a reminder that crannógs, excavated examples of which have produced impressive quantities of other high-quality metalwork and exotic imports, are often regarded as 'the homesteads of the wealthy and prestigious in early medieval Irish society' (Edwards 1990, 41).

## 6.4 DATE

Given that it has no coin content, the date of the Cloghermore hoard may only be approximated from the evidence of the deposition dates of other related hoards. The presence of fragments of broad-band arm-rings in the find is particularly useful in this regard, for rings of this type occur alongside coins in a number of hoards from Ireland, Britain and Scandinavia. They occur in hack-silver form, for instance, in the finds from Cuerdale, Lancashire, deposited in c. 905, and Dysart Island (no. 4), Co. Westmeath, deposited in c. 907 (Graham-Campbell 1987, 339–40; Ryan et al. 1984, 339–42), demonstrating that the type had already developed during the late ninth century. This is confirmed by the presence of an early variant in the hoard from Croydon, Surrey, deposited in c. 872 (Brooks and Graham-Campbell 1986, 96–7). Other examples from coin-dated hoards from Ireland are present in the County Antrim and Magheralagan, Co. Down, finds, both deposited in c. 910 (Sheehan 2001a, 52–3, fig. 2; Briggs and Graham-Campbell 1986). Later hoards from both Britain and Scandinavia, particularly Norway, also contain broad-band rings, including those from Goldsborough, Yorkshire, deposited in c. 920 (Philpott 1990, 45), from Bangor, Caernarvonshire, deposited in c. 925 (Boon 1986, 92–7), and from Grimestad, Vestfold, and Slemmedal, Aust-Agder, both of which were deposited during the 920s (Blindheim 1981). In overall terms, these and other dates indicate that the broad-band type of arm-ring developed during the later ninth century, perhaps c. 880, and continued in general circulation until c. 930–40 (Sheehan 1990, 125).

Ingots, because of their simple form, are difficult to date. They occur in at least 35 Viking Age hoards from Ireland, fifteen of which also contain coins (see Table 1). All of these latter hoards were deposited in the tenth century, although the large number of ingots in the Cuerdale hoard, deposited in c. 905, serves as a reminder that ingots were also in circulation in Ireland during the closing years of the ninth century.

If the proposed date ranges for the broad-band arm-rings and for the ingots are taken together, a date for the assembly and deposition of the Cloghermore hoard within the period between c. 880 and c.

940 seems likely. However, given that there are no early or prototype forms of broad-band rings in the find, is seems probable that the deposition of the hoard lies in the latter part of this range. A date of c. 910–940 is therefore proposed for the deposition of the hoard.

## 6.5 REGIONAL CONTEXT

With the discovery of the Cloghermore find, there are now fifteen silver hoards containing non-numismatic material on record from the province of Munster. The others comprise those from: Kilbarry, Lohort and Macroom, Co. Cork; Fenit, Co. Kerry; Carraig Aille II and Mungret, Co. Limerick; Rathmooley and Cullen, Co. Tipperary; Kilmacomma and Knockmaon, Co. Waterford; and four hoards with county provenances only, two from Cork and one each from Limerick and Clare (see Sheehan 1998b, 162–3, where selected references are cited). Eight of these fifteen hoards are of Class 1 type, being composed exclusively of complete ornaments, and as such are typical of Viking Age hoards containing non-numismatic material from elsewhere in Ireland; these include the find from Fenit, Co. Kerry, some 7km west-north-west of Cloghermore, which consists of two arm-rings. There is only one Class 2 hoard on record from Munster, from Mungret, Co. Limerick, and its deposition is coin-dated to c. 953 (Blackburn and Pagan 1986, 296). No example of a Class 3 hoard is recorded. Including the Cloghermore find, there are now four Class 4 hoards known from Munster, and there are two Class 5 finds on record (Fig. 54).

The six Class 4 and 5 hoards to which the Cloghermore find belongs share the characteristic of containing hack silver. The Munster examples of Class 4 hoards comprise the finds from Carraig Aille II, Co. Limerick, Kilbarry, Co. Cork, an unlocalised example from County Cork (Pl. 41), and Cloghermore; the Class 5 finds are those from Kilmacomma and Knockmaon, both in County Waterford. In terms of their structure, all of these finds are related, although a number of them may be distanced from the Cloghermore find on other grounds. The Knockmaon find, for instance, is composed of Scoto-Scandinavian 'ring-money' rather than Hiberno-Scandinavian material, and as such is distinctive within the context of Class 4 and 5 hoards from Ireland. In addition, its deposition date of c. 1000 (Blackburn and Pagan 1986, 297) marks it as belonging to a different temporal zone than most of the other hoards. The Kilmacomma find, however, is composed of Hiberno-Scandinavian

PL. 41
*Unlocalised hoard*
*from County Cork.*

material, but its highly fragmented hack-silver content also serves to distinguish it from the other hoards. When these two finds are disregarded, it becomes apparent that the Cloghermore hoard has most in common—structurally, functionally, chronologically and culturally—with the Munster finds from Carraig Aille II, Kilbarry and County Cork.

All of these Class 4 hoards share the characteristic of containing hack silver derived from arm-rings. Two of them, Carraig Aille II and Kilbarry, also contain complete ornaments, and three, Cloghermore, Carraig Aille II and County Cork, feature complete ingots; the Carraig Aille II find also contains an ingot-derived piece of hack silver. All of the culturally diagnostic objects in this group of hoards are of Hiberno-Scandinavian origin and, in the case of the Cloghermore, Carraig Aille II and County Cork finds, consist of hack silver derived from broad-band arm-rings. The contents of the Kilbarry hoard, however, are distinctive in that they consist solely of penannular rod arm-rings and of hack silver derived from these. Although these are of Hiberno-Scandinavian manufacture, it has recently been proposed that they are products of the tenth-century settlement of Cork (Sheehan 1998b, 154–5). This marks the Kilbarry hoard as being different in an important respect from the other three Munster hoards under consideration here, each of which contains broad-band arm-rings of the type manufactured by the Hiberno-Scandinavian silver-working tradition centred on Dublin. In short, it seems possible that the hoards from Cloghermore, Carraig Aille II and County Cork ultimately relate to and derive from Dublin and its economic sphere of influence rather than from the Munster Hiberno-Scandinavian urban settlements. This is of interest given that silver ornaments of the type produced in the Hiberno-Scandinavian tradition centred on Dublin are generally under-represented in the hoards from Munster (Sheehan 1998b, 151–4).

The importance of the Cloghermore hoard, in terms of its proposed connections with the broadly contemporaneous Carraig Aille II and County Cork finds, is that, unlike them, it derives from a well-excavated and culturally defined archaeological context. The cave at Cloghermore has produced a very significant quantity of diagnostically Scandinavian and Hiberno-Scandinavian material, such as some of the glass beads and the ringed pins. It seems obvious, on present evidence, that the range of material culture represented here probably derived from or through Dublin, and the character and contents of the silver hoard support this hypothesis.

## 6.6 SPECIFIC CONTEXT

The physical context of the Cloghermore hoard—a cave—is unusual. There is no detailed information on the find contexts of many Viking Age hoards is Ireland, but it is clear that the majority of those on which there is information derive from settlement contexts. Often these settlements are of native Irish type. In Munster, the hoards from Carraig Aille II, Rathmooley and Kilmacomma were found concealed in ringforts, and the Mungret find derives from an ecclesiastical site. Elsewhere in the country, where crannógs are of more common occurrence, hoards are also found in these contexts (Sheehan 1998a, 175). Hoards are occasionally recorded as being found outside of settlement contexts, and some of these were buried beneath, and were therefore presumably marked by, stones (Ó Floinn 1998, 157). In most cases, however, there is no record of the find contexts of hoards from Ireland.

The only other cave from Ireland in which a Viking Age silver hoard was found is Dunmore Cave, Co. Kilkenny. Discovered in 1973, this consisted of a piece of ingot-derived hack silver accompanied by less than twenty coins. The coins were of Anglo-Saxon type, although Arabic issues, as well as those from the Viking Northumbrian and East Anglian rulers, were also represented. The coins allowed the deposition of the hoard to be dated to c. 928 (Dolley 1975). As was the case at Cloghermore, quantities of human bone were present in Dunmore Cave. Interestingly, a second hoard has recently been found at this location. This also contains ingots and coins, as well as a range of other items that are not usually found in Viking Age hoards, and it has been provisionally assigned a deposition date in the 970s.[1]

It should be noted that two arm-rings were found during excavations in Alice Cave at Edenvale, near Ennis, Co. Clare, in the early twentieth century. One of these was of broad-band type and one of very few gold examples on record, and the other was a copper-alloy example of a coiled arm-ring (Sheehan 2000, 34–6). Both of the Edenvale rings, like those from Cloghermore, are of Hiberno-Scandinavian type. However, unlike the Cloghermore find, they do not constitute a hoard, being found in separate contexts within the cave (*recte* Graham-Campbell 1976, 69). It is interesting, nonetheless, that the method of concealment of the gold ring from Edenvale was quite similar to that used in Cloghermore, it having been placed in a recess of the main chamber of the cave, lying between small stones and covered by a slab (Scharff *et al.* 1906, 67–9). Therefore, even though it constitutes only a single find, it shares with the hoards from Cloghermore and Dunmore the vital characteristic of concealment and should be considered alongside them.

The Cloghermore hoard is therefore quite unusual in terms of its physical context. Along with the Dunmore hoards and the Edenvale finds, it is one of very few Viking Age hoards on record from a cave in Ireland, or indeed elsewhere in the Viking world. It differs somewhat from these other finds, however, in terms of its status and form as a hoard. For example, as noted above, the Edenvale rings constitute only single finds, even if one of them was deliberately concealed. Also, one of the Dunmore finds (no. 2) is so unusual in terms of its contents that it must be regarded as emphatically atypical. Among these finds, therefore, it is only the Dunmore (no. 1) find that provides an appropriate parallel for the Cloghermore find as an actual hoard, in the sense that both of these conform in their characteristics to the range of variables normally represented in the corpus of hoards from Ireland. In this regard, it is worth noting that the deposition date of the Dunmore (no. 1) hoard, *c.* 928, falls well within the date range proposed above for the Cloghermore find.

---

1    The author is grateful to Andy Halpin, National Museum of Ireland, for discussing this find with him. Some details of the hoard are contained in the *Sunday Times Magazine*, 16 July 2000, 46–51.

It is tempting to associate the deposition of a Viking Age silver hoard in a cave with ritual activity, especially when quantities of human bone are also present. There may be some justification for advancing ritual explanations on the basis of the so-called Odin's Law (which is referred to by Snorri Sturluson in *Heimskringla*), which states that men would enjoy in the afterlife the treasures that they had buried in this one. However, despite this prospect, Viking Age silver hoards are only very rarely found in demonstrably ritual contexts, such as graves, and there is no recorded example of the ritual deposition of a hoard in a cave. It seems far more likely that the Cloghermore hoard is a standard deposit, deliberately concealed with the intention of recovery. Whether it was deposited as an emergency hoard or as a savings hoard is impossible to judge, and it may even have served both roles.

### 6.7 OWNERSHIP

It has already been noted that a high proportion of those Viking Age hoards from Ireland on which there is detailed information on their discovery derive from settlement contexts and that these settlements are of native Irish type. This suggests that these hoards were in Irish control and ownership when they were buried, especially when they are from areas that remained in Irish control for all or most of the Viking Age. In the Munster context, for instance, this would clearly have been the case for the hoards from the ringforts at Rathmooley, Co. Tipperary, and Kilmacomma, Co. Waterford, although the Carraig Aille II hoard, also from a ringfort, is less definite in this regard. In the case of this site, other finds of general Scandinavian character are known from the Lough Gur region of County Limerick, in which it is situated, and there is a reference in the Annals of Inisfallen to a Viking base at Lough Gur in 926 (Ó Floinn 1998, 150). In overall terms, however, it appears that most Viking Age silver hoards from Ireland were in native ownership when they were buried. The means by which the Irish acquired this wealth are not fully understood, but it is likely that trade, tribute and gift exchange were involved (Sheehan 1998a, 173–6).

Some of the wealth represented by the hoards, however, must have been owned by Hiberno-Scandinavians. It may safely be assumed, for instance, that at least some of the hoards from the immediate vicinity of Dublin, and from the hinterlands of Hiberno-Scandinavian towns elsewhere, represent local wealth. In the case of

Munster, Bradley (1988, 62–5) has drawn attention to historical and other evidence of the existence and extent of Hiberno-Scandinavian settlement in the rural hinterlands of Limerick, Cork and Waterford. Hoards from these areas include those from Kilbarry and Mungret, near Cork and Limerick respectively, and the late tenth-century find from Knockmaon, near Dungarvan, which derives from an area known to have been controlled by the Hiberno-Scandinavians of Waterford.

It is clear, therefore, that both the geographical and the cultural context of the findspot of a hoard must be examined when attempting to ascribe ownership. In the case the Cloghermore hoard, its geographical context is far removed from the hinterland settlements of Cork or Limerick. It could, consequently, be argued that the hoard is likely to be a native Irish find. Nonetheless, there was a Scandinavian fortified settlement at nearby Castlemaine in 867, according to historical sources (Ó Corráin 1996), and recent archaeological work has shown that not all Hiberno-Scandinavian settlements are alluded to in the historical record (Sheehan et al. 2001). Therefore, there are arguments to be made for a Scandinavian or Hiberno-Scandinavian context for the hoard on geographical grounds. In the case of the cultural context of its findspot, no neat equation with a native settlement site can be made. On the contrary, much of the diagnostic material from Cloghermore is Scandinavian or Hiberno-Scandinavian in its cultural context. In fact, all of the evidence points toward the Cloghermore hoard being in Hiberno-Scandinavian ownership when it was buried.

## 6.8 CONCLUSION

The discovery of the Cloghermore hoard is of particular importance for a number of reasons. Firstly, it is the first find of a hoard of its type on an archaeological excavation in Ireland since 1948, when the Carraig Aille hoard was found during Ó Ríordáin's excavations in the Lough Gur region of County Limerick (Ó Ríordáin 1949, 62–4). Secondly, and more importantly, as it was professionally excavated, its integrity and status as a complete find are beyond doubt. Too often in the past it seems that such finds, which have usually been found by agricultural labourers, might have been only incompletely recovered. The use of a fine-meshed sieve in the excavation process at Cloghermore appears to rule out any possibility that small items, such as coins or highly fragmented hack silver, ever formed part of this deposit. Thirdly, it forms a welcome addition to the relatively few Viking Age silver hoards on record from the province of Munster. And, finally, it is one of very few hoards of its type from Ireland that can be safely regarded as deriving from an unequivocally Scandinavian or Hiberno-Scandinavian cultural context.

In terms of its components, the Cloghermore hoard is quite typical of Viking Age silver hoards from Ireland. When it is considered from the point of view of its structure, however, it is not representative of the majority of hoards from Ireland. In fact, it is one of only three Class 4e hoards on record from the country, although it has important links with other classes of finds, such as the Carraig Aille II hoard. It appears to be representative, in several ways, of the hoards derived from the Hiberno-Scandinavian silver-working tradition that was centred on Dublin, and it does not display the defining characteristics of those hoards that appear to be related to the Hiberno-Scandinavian towns of Munster. As such, it serves as a reminder of the economic primacy of Dublin in Viking Age Ireland.

# 7 SCANDINAVIAN SETTLEMENT

## 7.1 SCANDINAVIAN SETTLEMENT IN IRELAND

Scandinavian settlement in Ireland appears to be very different from that elsewhere in western Europe, a fact noted by Worsaae as early as 1852 (Bradley 1988; Fig. 55). In France, England, Scotland, the Isle of Man, Iceland and Greenland, Scandinavian settlement was essentially rural, with scattered farmsteads the norm, but in Ireland it seems to have been an essentially urban phenomenon.

In discussing this issue, Bradley (1988; 1995) points out that it was normal for emigrant Scandinavians to return to the way of their homelands and become farmers, yet, surrounded by the fertile land of Ireland, they chose to stay in towns and become traders and craftsmen. However, the presence of the urban settlements and the evidence of the Dublin excavations clearly demonstrate a trading relationship between the towns and their hinterlands, with imported and manufactured goods traded for food and farm produce. But this raises the question of whether the population of the rural hinterlands of the towns were native Irish or Scandinavian. In the case of Dublin, Bradley suggests that the view of the town as a stronghold rather than the 'hub of a rurally settled area' has affected the way that the archaeological evidence of Scandinavian settlement in the hinterland has been interpreted. This is seen in the differing explanations offered for the dispersal of Viking Age silver hoards in Scotland and Ireland, with the Irish hoards explained as having been dispersed by trade, and the Scottish material seen as evidence of the dispersed nature of Scandinavian settlement there. Indeed, Bradley suggests that there is a clear case for interpreting those hoards found in Scandinavian-controlled areas of Ireland as indicators of rural settlement.

Such an approach has been taken by Johnson (1999) in her recent

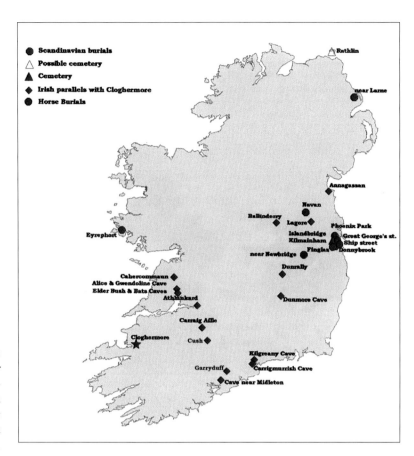

FIG. 55
Map showing major
Scandinavian, Hiberno-
Scandinavian and Irish
sites exhibiting parallels
with material from
Cloghermore.

reassessment of Ballinderry crannóg no. 1. She suggests that there are eight diagnostically Scandinavian artefacts from the site, as well as seven artefacts of Hiberno-Scandinavian character, including the gaming-board. Although she notes that the presence of these artefacts may be due to trade or activities such as tribute or pillage, she suggests that 'there remains a slight possibility that the population at the site was a Viking or mixed Hiberno-Scandinavian group'.

Bradley also points to a number of less clearly Scandinavian areas in Ireland where the archaeological evidence suggests the possibility of Scandinavian settlement. These include the area around the *longphort* at Annagassan, Co. Louth; the settlements established around the harbours of Antrim and Down, in particular Larne, from where there is a well-known burial; the area around another burial from Eyrephort, Co. Galway; and Beginish, Co. Kerry. In the light of Bradley's suggested locations for Scandinavian rural settlement, it is interesting to note the recent excavations in the townland of Truska,

Connemara, Co. Galway, close to the site of the Eyrephort burial. Work here has uncovered the remains of a small, sunken, subrectangular house, as well as burials (Keeley Gibbons and Kelly 2003). The authors conclude that the site is further evidence of an extensive Scandinavian presence in the area and that it may represent a settlement such as described by Bradley. In the case of Beginish, Co. Kerry, excavated by O'Kelly (1956), Bradley suggests that it should be interpreted as a Hiberno-Scandinavian settlement and cites the location of such a settlement as a possible explanation for the placename 'Smerwick' on the Dingle Peninsula. Bradley sees the presence of such settlements along the west coast as being likely, as 'way-stations' would have been needed along the sea route from Limerick to Cork and to the Continent.

## 7.2 SCANDINAVIAN ACTIVITY IN COUNTY KERRY

A recent reassessment of O'Kelly's excavation of Beginish has affirmed much of what Bradley suggested regarding the possibility that the island was a maritime haven or 'way-station' and the potential for the existence of other such way-stations around the coast (Sheehan *et al.* 2001) (Fig. 56). These writers reinterpret O'Kelly's House I (1956) as a derivative of the *grubenhaus* tradition of the Scandinavian, Germanic, Slavic and Anglo-Saxon worlds and support this assertion through a reassessment of a number of finds from the island, both those from the excavation and those found since. Indeed, they suggest that the cultural context of O'Kelly's Phase II of the Beginish settlement is of 'Scandinavian or Hiberno-Scandinavian character'. They concur with Bradley's identification of Beginish as one of a number of 'way-stations' that would have been necessary on the sea route from Hiberno-Scandinavian Limerick to Cork and suggest, on the basis of literary and toponomastic evidence, a number of potential locations for similar havens along the route.

Of interest from the point of view of Cloghermore are the suggested locations for such sites in and around County Kerry. One of these is Scattery Island, Co. Clare, situated in the Shannon Estuary between counties Clare and Kerry, for which there are many annalistic associations with the Hiberno-Scandinavians of Limerick (O'Donovan 1848–51, vol. 2, 698; Mac Airt 1951, 160) and for which the authors offer the translation *skattr-øy*, meaning the island where tribute is collected or the island subject to tribute (*skattr*: Old Norse for tribute; *øy*: island). Another potential way-station suggested by

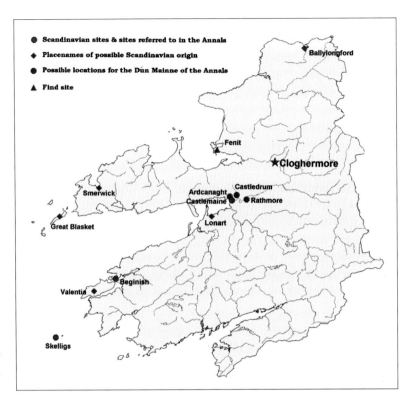

FIG. 56
*Map showing evidence
for Scandinavian
activity in Kerry.*

Sheehan *et al.* (2001) is Smerwick, on the tip of the Dingle Peninsula, for which Oftedal (1976, 132) offered the translation *Smjör-uik*, or 'butter bay'. A third is Castlemaine, where, on the northern bank of the River Maine, on the borders of Ciarraige Luachra, the annals record a Scandinavian fortified base at Dún Mainne. The base was destroyed by the Ciarraige Luachra, the Eóganacht Locha Léin and the Uí Fidgeinte in *c.* AD 867, and the annals record the taking of women prisoners, which suggests that Dún Mainne was a settlement rather than a raiding base (Ó Corráin 1996). In this context it is interesting that Doherty (1998, 325) has suggested that the use of the term *dún*, as opposed to *dúnad* or *longphort*, may be indicative of a permanent settlement rather than a temporary base or raiding camp. Indeed, Sheehan *et al.* (2001) raise the question of whether, given their proximity, Dún Mainne and Cloghermore are connected, and it is interesting that the Little River Maine is only 3km south-east of Cloghermore. Another potential way-station is the Great Blasket, which, according to the authors, appears to have the termination *øy* (Old Norse: island). They also suggest that the termination *-i-* in the forms of the Aran Islands (Arini) and Valentia (Draueri) in portolan and later maps may be due to the adding of the Old Norse *øy* to the original Irish names, indicating 'considerable Viking activity on the southwestern coastline'. Dursey, for which Oftedal (1976, 132) offered the translation *Dyárs-øy*, 'deers' island', is also identified as a possible indicator of a way-station situated on the mainland rather than the island itself.

To these I would add the village and bay of Ballylongford, on the Shannon Estuary in north Kerry—which clearly preserve the term *longphort*, coupled with the Irish *baile*, translated as town/village— and, more importantly, the townland of Lonart on the south shore of Castlemaine Harbour, between Glenbeigh and Killorglin. The Ordnance Survey Name Books note that this townland name preserves the term *longphort*. Indeed, it is worthy of note that a recorded monument in this townland (KE056-048, described as 'fortification') is situated on a small, ragged, subcircular peninsular headland and consists of what is effectively a D-shaped enclosure.

However, evidence of Scandinavian activity in the Kerry area is not restricted to placenames. The annals record that the territory of the Eóganacht Locha Léin was attacked as early as AD 812, and the monastic settlement on the Skelligs was raided in AD 821 (Ó Corráin 2001, 17–18). Cusack (1871, 71) in her *History of the kingdom of Kerry* noted that:

> The Danes, both Black and White, had by this time discovered the value of the treasures in sepulchral caves, dating from long distant ages, and having no particular scruples about or respect for the departed, they did not fail to make use of the knowledge. In 867, a Scandinavian chieftain named Baraid, with Amlaff's son and the Dublin Danes, set out on a marauding expedition, 'until they reached Ciarraighe [Kerry], and they left not a cave there under ground that they did not explore; and they left nothing from Luimneach [Limerick] to Corcach [Cork] that they did not ravage'.

This appears to be an interpretation of an entry from the Annals of Inisfallen, but for the year AD 873 and not AD 867, which states:

> Bárid with a great fleet from Áth Cliath went westward and he plundered the Ciarraighe Luachra under ground.

It is also noted that Bárid was accompanied by 'Amlaib's son with the fleet of Áth Cliath'. Interestingly, the annalistic entry regarding Dún

Mainne referred to above (Ó Corráin 1996) is for the year AD 867.

There is also the evidence of a silver hoard of Early Viking Age date, consisting of an arm-ring and a neck-ring, from Fenit (Sheehan 1998a, 199), 16.5km west of Cloghermore. Although the exact findspot and context of the find are not clear, the presence of another hoard close to Cloghermore is surely indicative of, at least, Scandinavian or Hiberno-Scandinavian influences in this area of County Kerry.

# 8 DATING, SYNTHESIS AND CONCLUSION

## 8.1 DATING

Nineteen radiocarbon dates were taken from the Cloghermore site: two from the trenches opened on the surface, and seventeen from the interior of the cave. Of the dates from inside the cave, thirteen were AMS (accelerated mass spectroscopy) dates taken from unburnt human bone, one was taken from a cremated fragment of animal bone, and three were radiometric dates taken from charcoal.

The samples from the surface trenches (Nos 11 and 15) were taken from charcoal recovered from the base of a truncated post-hole on the outer bank of the enclosure in Trench 1 and from charcoal recovered from the fill of the large post-hole or stone socket, immediately south-south-east of the entrance shaft, in Trench 3. The dates obtained were 1130±60 BP (Beta-137054) and 1160±60 BP (Beta-150535) respectively and were calibrated to AD 785–1025 and AD 710–1000. The dates are broadly similar and suggest that the enclosure and the activity in its interior date to the late ninth or the early tenth century.

The sample from cremated animal bone (No. 13) was taken from a long-bone fragment recovered from the cremation deposit inside the circular stone setting in the Graveyard. The date obtained was 1170±60 BP (Beta-137056), calibrated to AD 765–1010. This date is broadly similar to the dates from the surface trenches and suggests that the activity within the enclosure and the deposition of the cremated animal bone are contemporaneous. This is consistent with the discovery of the pyre site in Trench 3.

The radiometric dates taken from charcoal recovered from the interior of the cave relate to the Graveyard (No. 12), Area W (No. 16) and Area V (No. 17). The date from the Graveyard was taken from a large lump of charcoal recovered from a rock cleft in the chamber.

Similar lumps of charcoal, clearly representing burnt sticks, were recovered in a number of areas in the cave and appear to be the remains of torches, probably used for lighting. This fragment returned a date of 1240±50 BP (Beta-137055), calibrated to AD 675–900.

The sample from Area W was recovered from redeposited sediment in the base of the shallow grave-cut that contained the articulated burial of a male. The sample returned a date of 1150±60 BP (Beta-150536), calibrated to AD 760–1010. The sample from Area V was recovered from the fill of the pit and returned a date of 1140±60 BP (Beta-150537), calibrated to AD 770–1010. Again, both of these dates are broadly similar to one another and date activity in these two discrete areas to the same general period as the activity in the enclosure and the deposition of the cremated animal bone.

A sample was also taken from human bone found in Area W (No. 18); however, the sample was inadvertently taken from bone recovered in the soil covering the articulated burial rather than from the articulated burial itself. Analysis of the sample confirmed the presence in the soil around and over the burial of bone that was not from the articulated burial. A date of 1180±40 BP (Beta-150538), calibrated to AD 680–890 was returned. This is slightly earlier than that from the charcoal sample.

The remaining twelve samples were all taken from unburnt human remains recovered from a number of areas within the cave and produced both the earliest date (No. 9) and the latest date (No. 19). The earliest date was from the tibia of a sub-adult in the Graveyard: 1550±50 BP (Beta-137052), calibrated to AD 430–645. The latest date was from an adult femur from Area T: 1020±40 BP (Beta-150539), calibrated to AD 890–1020.

A single sample (No. 6) was taken from a sub-adult ulna recovered from the soil at the base of the entrance shaft: 1190±40 BP (Beta-137048), calibrated to AD 680–885, a date similar to that from the adult femur recovered from Area W.

The remaining samples were taken from human bone recovered from the Graveyard and the Two-Star Temple. The samples from the Two-Star Temple (Nos 7 and 8) were from a sub-adult femur and an adult femur and returned dates of 1260±50 BP (Beta-13709) and 1220±40 BP (Beta-137051) respectively, calibrated to AD 645–795 and AD 665–815. These dates are earlier than those obtained from the surface and from areas within the Graveyard and the Entrance Gallery.

The remaining six samples, all from the Graveyard, were taken from both adult and sub-adult bone material. Five were from

Quadrants A and B, and the remaining one was from Quadrant C/D. Of the samples from Quadrants A and B (Nos 2, 3, 5, 10 and 14), three (Nos 2, 10 and 14) returned dates that were among the earliest from the site: 1270±40 BP (Beta-137044), 1330±50 BP (Beta-137053) and 1360±40 BP (Beta-137057) respectively, calibrated to AD 655–785, AD 635–780 and AD 645–770.

The two remaining samples from Quadrants A and B (Nos 3 and 5) gave dates of 1190±50 BP (Beta-137045) and 1210±40 BP (Beta-137047), calibrated to AD 670–895 and AD 675–880. Interestingly, these bones were recovered resting on and within soil overlying the circular stone setting containing the cremated animal bone, which gave a substantially later date. This clearly indicates the disturbed nature of the stratigraphy but also the mixing of bones of earlier and later date within the soil brought into the cave, probably during the final phase of burial.

The final sample from the Graveyard was taken from an adult thoracic vertebra recovered from a stone cleft on the western side of the chamber. It returned a date of 1140±40 BP (Beta-137046), calibrated to AD 705–910. The remaining sample from the cave interior was from an adult femur in Area X and returned a date of 1150±40 BP (Beta-132903), calibrated to AD 780–990. The date from the western side of the Graveyard is important, given that the analysis of the human bones suggests that there are more complete skeletal remains of two adults in Quadrants C/D, which is discussed above as evidence of a differing burial rite relating to the later burials in the cave.

In general the radiocarbon dates confirm the interpretation of a two-phase use of the cave as a place of burial. The earlier phase centres on the eighth century and is represented by dated samples from both the Two-Star Temple and the Graveyard. The later phase centres on the late ninth and the early tenth century and is represented by dated samples from the surface trenches, the deposit of cremated bone, Areas V, T, W and X, and Quadrants C/D on the western side of the Graveyard.

However, it is important to note that, although the sample confirmed an earlier and a later grouping of dates, only thirteen pieces of human bone were dated. This is a relatively small sample from an assemblage of over 3500 bones, and, given the disarticulated nature of most of the remains, there is no way of knowing whether some of the dated bones are from the same individual.

The artefacts from the cave represent a wide range of raw materials—silver, iron, copper alloy, bone, amber, glass, antler, ivory, and stone—and artefact types, from small glass beads to iron weapons. Many of the artefact types represented in the assemblage, such as iron shears and pig fibula pins, have a long currency in the archaeological record. However, the more closely datable objects from the cave, such as the silver hoard, the bone combs and the ringed pins, fit comfortably in the period AD 850–950.

The Irish sites providing parallels for the artefact assemblage from the cave range in date from AD 650–750/800 in the case of Garryduff, Co. Cork (O'Kelly 1963, 119), to the seventh–tenth centuries in the case of Lagore, Co. Meath (Hencken 1950, 1). Cahercommaun, Co. Clare, is dated to the ninth century, mainly on the basis of the decorated metalwork (Hencken 1938, 27–35). The site providing most parallels is Carraig Aille, Co. Limerick, where the occupation is dated to the eighth–tenth centuries (Ó Ríordáin 1949, 108). Interestingly, ringed pins and a small silver hoard, described as being of 'Viking type', are among the main indicators of a tenth-century date, similar to Cloghermore.

Most of the artefacts paralleled at early sites such as Garryduff are examples of types with a long survival, such as iron shears, and it is clear that the bulk of the identifiable material from the cave, whether based on Irish or on Scandinavian parallels, can be dated to a late ninth- to early tenth-century context. However, the evidence of burial ritual from Cloghermore, including horse burial and the cremation of animals and possibly of human remains, as well as cultic practices and the lack of evidence of such practice at other Scandinavian or Hiberno-Scandinavian burial sites in Ireland, may also be indicative of date. One is tempted on the basis of this evidence to conclude that the burials of Scandinavian character from Cloghermore are of late ninth- rather than early tenth-century date and that they represent a Scandinavian rather than a Hiberno-Scandinavian group.

Sheehan suggests that the silver hoard could not have been deposited before c. AD 880 (Chapter 6), so one can assume that the burials cannot be any earlier than this date. Yet, the annalistic reference to the attack on the base at Dún Mainne dates to AD 867 and suggests a Scandinavian presence close to Cloghermore earlier than the suggested earliest date for the deposition of the silver hoard. However, the assumption that these two dates cannot be accommodated in the context of Cloghermore presumes that the site at Dún Mainne was completely destroyed and abandoned in AD 867, which is not certain. The base may have continued or been re-founded after the attack. It is also true that the suggested

settlements/farmsteads in the hinterland of the base, including the
Cloghermore area, may not have been abandoned after the attack
and may have persisted for some time afterwards. The later burials
could conceivably, therefore, date to the second half of the ninth
century, before the recorded attack on the base at Dún Mainne.
Indeed, only one of the later radiocarbon dates appears to be too late
to fall within this period, that from Area T (No. 19).

| Sample no. | Material | Location | Radiocarbon age BP | Calibrated date AD | Lab. no. |
|---|---|---|---|---|---|
| 1 | Mid-shaft of adult femur (unburnt) | Area X | 1150±40 | 780–990 | Beta-132903 |
| 2 | Adult left ulna (unburnt) | The Graveyard, Quadrant A | 1270±40 | 655–785 | Beta-137044 |
| 3 | Adult left talus (unburnt) | The Graveyard, Quadrant B | 1190±50 | 670–895 | Beta-137045 |
| 4 | Adult thoracic vertebra (unburnt) | The Graveyard, Quadrant C/D | 1140±40 | 705–910 | Beta-137046 |
| 5 | Sub-adult left humerus (unburnt) | The Graveyard, Quadrant B | 1210±40 | 675–880 | Beta-137047 |
| 6 | Sub-adult right ulna (unburnt) | Entrance shaft | 1190±40 | 680–885 | Beta-137048 |
| 7 | Sub-adult right distal femur (unburnt) | Two-Star Temple, Quadrant E | 1260±50 | 645–795 | Beta-137049 |
| 8 | Adult right femur (unburnt) | Two-Star Temple, Quadrant G | 1220±40 | 665–815 | Beta-137051 |
| 9 | Sub-adult mid-shaft tibia (unburnt) | The Graveyard, Quadrant B | 1550±50 | 430–645 | Beta-137052 |
| 10 | Adult left calcaneus | The Graveyard Quadrant B | 1330±50 | 635–780 | Beta-137053 |
| 11 | Charcoal | Trench 1, post-hole | 1130±60 | 785–1025 | Beta-137054 |

TABLE 2—*Cloghermore radiocarbon determinations. The calibrated
dates are 2 sigma, or 95% probability.*

| Sample no. | Material | Location | Radiocarbon age BP | Calibrated date AD | Lab. no. |
|---|---|---|---|---|---|
| 12 | Charcoal | The Graveyard, Quadrant A | 1240±50 | 675– 900 | Beta-137055 |
| 13 | Animal long-bone fragment (burnt) | Cremation deposit | 1170±60 | 765–1010 | Beta-137056 |
| 14 | Adult right humerus (unburnt) | The Graveyard, Quadrant A | 1360±40 | 645–770 | Beta-137057 |
| 15 | Charcoal | Trench 3, pyre site | 1160±60 | 710–1000 | Beta-150535 |
| 16 | Charcoal | Area W | 1150±60 | 760–1010 | Beta-150536 |
| 17 | Charcoal | Area V | 1140±60 | 770–1010 | Beta-150537 |
| 18 | Adult left femur (unburnt) | Area W | 1180±40 | 680–890 | Beta-150538 |
| 19 | Adult right femur (unburnt) | Area T | 1020±40 | 890–1020 | Beta-150539 |

TABLE 2 (CONTD)—*Cloghermore radiocarbon determinations. The calibrated dates are 2 sigma, or 95% probability.*

## 8.2 SYNTHESIS

It is clear that the cave at Cloghermore is a burial site and that the excavated features on the surface—the D-shaped enclosure and the post- and slot-trench structures—relate to this use of the cave. The minimal stratigraphy within the cave, involving the bringing of the brown clay soil into the Graveyard and the Entrance Gallery but not into the Two-Star Temple, suggests two distinct phases of burial within the cave. The burial rite evidence indicates two differing rites: one involving the deposition of selected bones within the cave after the defleshing of the bones, and the other involving the interment of complete bodies within the cave, which were subsequently disturbed, probably as a deliberate act of desecration.

The analysis of the human bone from the cave supports this thesis, clearly showing that most of the individuals within the cave are represented by partial skeletal remains, the absence of smaller bones from the hands and feet being conspicuous and indicative of burial elsewhere before the deposition of disarticulated bones in the cave. It also shows the presence of more complete skeletal remains for a small number of individuals, and in many cases these bones have evidence of having been deliberately broken while they were still fresh and may still have had some flesh on them. The evidence of the removal of the skull from the articulated burial in Area W when the body was only partially decomposed suggests that this was indeed the case and that the complete burials were deliberately desecrated shortly after interment.

The animal bone from the cave is similarly scattered and disturbed, and analysis indicates that most of it originated from ritual activity rather than being indicative of the economy of the period. The minimal sample of animal bone from the Two-Star Temple, compared to the Graveyard and the Entrance Gallery, again suggests two different burial rites and by extension a temporal and cultural difference between the use of these areas for burial.

The radiocarbon dates from the site confirm an earlier and a later phase of burial. The earlier phase, represented by the deposition of defleshed, disarticulated skeletal remains without artefacts, centres on the eighth century. The later phase—characterised by the bringing in of the brown soil, the interment of complete bodies with artefacts, and burial rites involving the cremation of animals, the interment of parts of a horse etc.—centres on the late ninth and the early tenth century. The artefacts recovered from the cave were all found within the brown clay soil and seem to relate to the second phase of burial, represented by the interment of complete bodies. Indeed, the artefacts from the trenches excavated on the surface also appear to relate to this second phase of burial.

A number of the artefacts from the cave are of types that have a long currency in the archaeological record, although, in general, all of the artefacts would fit into a late ninth- early tenth-century context.

In effect, the cave seems to have been used as an ossuary during the first phase, and the dating of this activity suggests that the skeletal remains represent a pagan Irish population. The rite itself may be a continuation of a burial style from the pre-Christian Iron Age, preserved by a small local population that had not converted to Christianity. However, the rites associated with the later burials can only be compared, to a limited extent, in an Irish context, with antiquarian accounts of burials with a Scandinavian or Hiberno-

Scandinavian cultural context. The most accurate parallels for the burial rites associated with this second phase of burial occur outside of Ireland, in Scandinavia itself or in areas of Scandinavian settlement such as the Isle of Man and parts of Scotland. Indeed, the account of a Rus funeral on the Volga in AD 921 by Ibn Fadlan offers a convincing parallel for the rites represented at Cloghermore.

Many of the artefacts from the cave can be compared with material from Irish sites such as Lagore, Co. Meath, and Cahercommaun, Co. Clare. However, the Irish site with the broadest range of comparable material is Carraig Aille, near Lough Gur, Co. Limerick. It is significant that the Annals of Inisfallen record the establishment of a Viking base at Lough Gur in AD 926 (Ó Floinn 1998, 150).

Many of the artefacts can also be paralleled in the material from the Dublin excavations and other Scandinavian contexts in Ireland, but there are a small number of items that can be most closely paralleled within Scandinavia itself. These include the small iron anvil (170), the small spherical glass beads (80 and 81), the iron arrowhead (54) and the copper-alloy button (105). Parallels of any sort for the unusual bone handle (132) and the perforated ivory ball (91) are difficult to find. However, in the case of the ivory ball, either the walrus ivory or the finished object is an import, probably from Scandinavia.

All of the available evidence suggests that the second phase of burial is indicative of the use of the cave by a pagan Scandinavian or Hiberno-Scandinavian group. The complex nature of the pagan burial rites and the close similarity to aspects of the rites described by Ibn Fadlan suggest that the group had intimate knowledge of the rites as practised in Scandinavia and was not influenced by the Christian ethos prevailing in Ireland at the time.

Interestingly, the area of Scandinavia that provides the closest parallels for the burial rite and, indeed, for a number of the artefacts is southern Scandinavia (Fig. 57). There are specific comparanda for aspects of the horse burial—the inclusion of unburnt horse teeth in the cremation deposit and the burial of unburnt bones from the head and extremities of horses—in southern and eastern Sweden (Gräslund 1980, 60). This is contrary to the usual Scandinavian influences proposed for Ireland, where the initial raids are seen as the work of the Norse, with the Danes arriving in AD 851. The evidence suggests that in both Ireland and the Scottish islands the Norwegians were predominant, although there were in some instances violent clashes between the Norse and the Danes in Ireland (Sawyer 1982, 80).

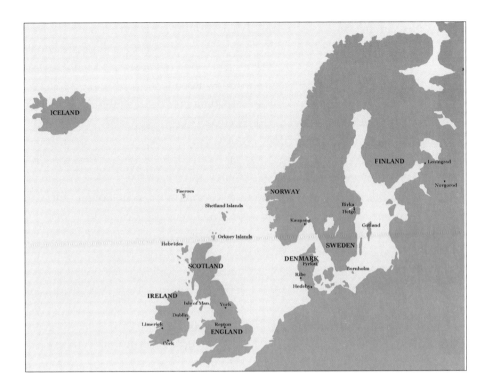

Indeed, the distribution within Scandinavia of artefacts of the type made or used in Ireland shows a clear concentration in the Norwegian area. This is often interpreted to mean that Norway was the main point of departure for the plundering raids on Ireland (Wamers 1985).

However, B. Ambrosiani (1998) feels that this evidence is biased owing to the differences in burial rite. Most of the finds from Norway, where the old custom of fully furnished burial was still practised, are from graves, while this style of burial had already been abandoned in Denmark. Yet, Sweden and southern Scandinavia have been seen as an important influence in the area of the importation and working of silver. Sheehan (2001b, 56), in analysing Irish Viking Age hoards, has stated that the recognisable imported objects in the hoards are derived, in the main, from southern Scandinavia and the Baltic region, a similar route to that of the Arabic coins from Ireland.

In looking in more detail at the Hiberno-Scandinavian silver-working tradition, both Graham-Campbell (Brooks and Graham-Campbell 1986, 96–8) and Sheehan (1998a, 194–8) state that the origins of the broad-band arm-ring type, as developed in Ireland, lie in ninth-century Denmark. In this light it is important to remember that parts of southern and eastern Sweden, including Skåne and Halland, were ruled by Denmark (Roesdahl 1987, 77).

FIG. 56
*Map showing major sites in Scandinavia, Britain and Ireland exhibiting parallels with material recovered from Cloghermore.*

Sheehan, in his analysis of the Cloghermore hoard, notes that both it and the Carraig Aille II hoard contain hack-silver arm-rings decorated using a punch with a serrated edge (Chapter 6). He suggests that this decorative technique, originating in southern Scandinavia, may be indicative of imported prototype rings or copies of them. Sheehan (2001a, 58) sees this southern Scandinavian influence as linked to the importance of this area and of the Baltic region as a source of the silver used to supply the Hiberno-Scandinavian silver-working tradition. Clearly, the importance of southern Scandinavia, including parts of Sweden, with respect to the importation and working of silver, discussed by Sheehan in more detail in Chapter 6, is not in question. However, this area has not previously been seen as an important influence on other aspects of Scandinavian and Hiberno-Scandinavian culture in Ireland.

There is obviously a case for reassessing the source of Scandinavian influences in Ireland, and the site at Cloghermore raises the possibility that southern Scandinavia may have had an influence beyond that already accepted for the silver-working tradition in Ireland.

## Who used Cloghermore?

As discussed in some detail above, the cave was used first by a probable non-Christian, local group and then by a Scandinavian or Hiberno-Scandinavian group. However, some comment on the size of these groups and the extent of the non-Christian element within the population of the area is necessary.

The analysis of the human remains from the cave suggests that there are a small number of burials that can be ascribed to the second phase of use, the minimum number being three adults and three children. When these are removed from the total minimum number of individuals, it leaves a minimum of twelve adults and twelve sub-adults.

The radiocarbon dates that relate to the early phase of use span the period from 1550±50 BP (Beta-137052) to 1190±40 BP (Beta-137048). Yet the earliest date is very much outside the range of the other dates from the cave, the next-earliest date being some 190 radiocarbon years later. The earliest date may truly reflect a very early usage of the cave, but it stands alone and is well outside the clustering of dates obtained from other bone samples from diverse areas of the cave. If this date is discounted, the radiocarbon dates relating to the earlier phase of use of the cave span a period of 170 radiocarbon years, approximately three or four generations.

On this basis the number of bones placed in the cave during this first phase of use is quite small and could not represent a large group. Indeed, the evidence suggests that the cave was used by a small family group, as a vault or ossuary, during the eighth century, the defleshed bones being placed in the cave according to a non-Christian rite.

As noted above, it is suggested that the second phase of use involved the burial of three adults—two male and one female—and three sub-adults, including the torso of a child in the pit in Area V. To this group should also be added the suggested cremation of a female that had been placed within the stone setting in the Graveyard but for which no skeletal evidence now remains.

The radiocarbon dates relating to this second phase of use range from 1170±60 BP (Beta-137056) to 1020±40 BP (Beta-150539); however, as with the earliest date from the cave, the latest date is well outside the range of the other dates. If this late date, from Area T, is discounted, the usage of the cave during this second phase spans only 40 radiocarbon years, at most a single generation and probably much less. Indeed, all of these burials could have been placed in the cave over a very short period of time. Again, this group of bones suggests a small family group, possibly an extended family, as one would expect to find in an isolated rural farmstead of the period, either in Ireland or in Scandinavia.

A small group, as outlined above, is also suggested by the artefact assemblage from the cave, when the numbers of artefacts of types known from Scandinavian graves of the period are assessed. The cave produced evidence of four ringed pins, four definite iron shears and six separate bone or antler combs. One of the combs, however, was recovered from the surface, in Trench 3, and another comb and one of the iron shears were recovered from the pit in Area V, clearly associated with the ritualistic treatment of a child burial. This leaves four separate combs and ringed pins from within the burial area of the cave, which are both items known from Scandinavian graves. This suggests the burial of at least four adults in the cave, the same number as suggested for this second phase of burial at the site. The artefacts also suggest that at least one burial of a male was accompanied by weaponry, including an axe, an arrowhead, a spearhead and a possible sword, and a shield boss is directly associated with the articulated burial in Area W.

Clearly, a burial was also associated with the interment of parts of horses and a horse harness. The presence of tools such as the iron saw, augur pit and anvil, as well as barrel padlocks, crucibles, nails, bolts and staples, may indicate that a toolbox or chest was placed in the cave, possibly as part of the burial of a craftsman.

The female grave-goods include the thirteen beads of bone, glass and amber, the items associated with weaving—the three spindle-whorls and the antler pin-beater—and possibly the decorated bone handle and the iron shears, given their possible association with weaving. Clearly, the artefact assemblage and the bone analysis suggest a small number of later burials, and the volume of artefacts from the cave shows that these burials were richly furnished with items ranging from weaponry and a horse harness to whetstones. The presence of women and children among the later burials, as well as domestic items of everyday use such as potboilers and tools, suggests a settled group rather than a raiding party.

The annalistic reference to a Scandinavian *dún*, or settlement, on the River Maine (Ó Corráin 1996) is the nearest recorded settlement site to Cloghermore. The use of the word *dún* may, as discussed above, indicate that this was a permanent settlement, also indicated by the annalistic reference to the taking of women prisoners at the site. If this settlement was permanent and functioned as a 'way-station' on the sea route between Cork and Limerick, as suggested by Sheehan *et al.* (2001), it probably also had a military garrison and controlled the hinterland of the settlement, both in terms of security and as a source of food and raw materials. Indeed, a military presence and influence within the hinterland of the settlement is suggested by the fact that the Ciarraige Luachra, the Eóganacht Locha Léin and the Uí Fidgeinte felt it necessary to launch a combined attack on the site. Perhaps small, family-sized groups from this permanent base moved out into the country to settle and farm nearby land to supply Dún Mainne with the food and raw materials such a settlement would have required.

Cloghermore lies only 16.5km from the suggested site of Dún Mainne (Ó Corráin 1996), and, as already noted, the nearest watercourse to Cloghermore is a tributary of the River Maine known as the Little River Maine. Perhaps the settlement at Dún Mainne was even closer to Cloghermore than the current village of Castlemaine. Indeed, a brief study of available aerial photography and first-edition maps of the area between the Maine estuary and the townland of Springmount to the east has suggested a number of possible previously unrecorded sites.

These include a levelled D-shaped enclosure, measuring *c.* 135m north-west/south-east by 120m north-east/south-west, in the townland of Ardcanaght. The site lies between the River Maine and one of its tributaries, *c.* 225m from the river at its nearest point (Pl. 42). A second, partially destroyed site in the townland of Rathmore is also D-shaped, with the straight side onto the River Maine. It measures *c.* 250m by 170m, with extant defences consisting of a double bank with an intervening ditch. The banks are up to 6.8m wide and 2.4m high, and the ditch is 3.7m wide. This site is only 8.5km south-south-west of Cloghermore. Unfortunately, this massive site has been disturbed over the years, both by land clearance and by drainage works on the River Maine; however, it is very probably the large fort (Rath Mór) referred to in the townland name. A third, smaller cropmark enclosure, close to the confluence of the River Maine and one of its tributaries in the townland of Castledrum, is also situated at the water's edge and measures *c.* 90m by 125m. The townland of Lonart, which clearly preserves the term *longphort*, is situated on the shores of Castlemaine Harbour and may also be the location of the Dún Mainne of the annals. Whatever the exact location of the site referred to in the annals, Cloghermore suggests that a small, family-sized group of Scandinavian or Hiberno-Scandinavian origin was settled in the hinterland of the cave.

In the context of a settlement in the environs of Cloghermore, it should be remembered that only a small portion of the surface of the reef was excavated. All of the excavated trenches are effectively within the D-shaped enclosure, which is clearly too small to contain

PL. 42
*Aerial view of the D-shaped enclosure at Rathmore on the River Maine.*

houses. Other structures and mounds have been noted higher up on the reef, but only further excavation would confirm whether these are coeval with the second phase of use of the cave.

Recent fieldwork has recorded more than 50 previously unrecorded earthworks and mounds within 4–5km of Cloghermore (Connolly 1999, fig. 20). Most of these sites may well be of prehistoric date, but only excavation can confirm this, and the possibility exists that one of these sites is the location of the suggested Scandinavian settlement in the area.

It is clear that this small group adopted the final burial place of a local, pagan group as their own and, after a number of alterations to the cave entrance and the construction of a number of structures on the surface, began burying their dead. The evidence suggests that this second phase of use of the cave, and consequently the suggested settlement, was short-lived, lasting at most a single generation and probably much less. With the abandonment of the suggested settlement, the cave entrance shaft was closed and sealed. However, it appears that this did not prevent the site from being desecrated shortly after its abandonment.

## 8.3 CONCLUSION

Cloghermore Cave is one of the most important sites excavated in Ireland in recent times. The evidence from the site suggests that pagan burial practices lingered on among small family groups well into the eighth century and that Christianity had not yet fully penetrated all levels of Irish society. It has previously been suggested that the conversion of Ireland was far from instantaneous and that pagan religious practice may have persisted for a time. The idea of defleshed and disarticulated human remains being placed in a cave in the eighth century will undoubtedly cause controversy in some circles. Yet, this conclusion is inescapable based on the findings from the cave and our limited knowledge of secular burial practice of the period.

As if this were not enough, the cave also contained the first Scandinavian or Hiberno-Scandinavian burials excavated in Ireland since the discovery of the burial at Eyrephort, Co. Galway, in 1940. Since the site was excavated in 1999–2000, further 'Viking' burials have been excavated in and around Dublin. In 2003, during excavations at South Great George's Street in Dublin, the remains of two male burials were uncovered. The first was placed in a shallow grave-cut, close to the edge of the 'Black Pool', oriented east–west (head to the west). The grave contained an iron shield boss of probable ninth-century date and an iron dagger. The second burial was placed on a hearth, though not burnt, and had been disturbed in antiquity. Fragments of iron were noted on the chest (Simpson 2003, 5). A similar burial had been excavated in 2002 at Great Ship Street, a short distance to the west. Here the torso and skull of a male were uncovered in a shallow grave-cut. The grave contained fragments of a sword, a silver finger-ring, and a decorative silver ring, an iron object and a bead, all three of which appear to have been worn around the neck. A sample from the burial returned a calibrated radiocarbon date of AD 665–865 (*ibid.*).

More recently, in 2004, the extended skeleton of a female aged 25–35 years, accompanied by an oval brooch at her right shoulder and fragments of a second in the chest area, was uncovered near the medieval church in Finglas (Wallace 2004, 7). The brooch is described as being from the Danish side of the Baltic and of ninth-century type. This burial is interpreted as that of a ninth-century 'Viking' lady of relatively high status (*ibid.*).

The excavations at Cloghermore seem to have precipitated a 'boom' in the discovery and excavation of 'Viking' burials that have a number of similarities with the articulated burial in Area W. The orientation of the male burials from Dublin and their location in shallow grave-cuts, as well as the presence in one of a dagger and a shield boss, can be paralleled by aspects of the articulated burial in Area W at Cloghermore. Indeed, the date suggested for these Dublin burials is the same as has been suggested here for those at Cloghermore. However, the range of evidence for horse burial, cultic practice, animal sacrifice and cremation at Cloghermore is beyond anything previously recorded in Ireland.

It has been suggested here that this range of evidence on burial ritual may indicate a date in the second half of the ninth century for these burials, placing them in the same date range as the burials from the cemeteries at Islandbridge and Kilmainham in Dublin. There is also the distinct possibility that the Cloghermore burials are of members of a Scandinavian rather than a Hiberno-Scandinavian population.

The location of the site in a rural setting in south-west Ireland is also important as it offers yet another indication that not all Scandinavian settlement was urban. Indeed, Cloghermore clearly suggests that the rural farmsteads seen in other areas settled by Scandinavians may well have been a regular feature of the settlement in Ireland also.

It is unfortunate that the site at Cloghermore had suffered disturbance over a long period of time, from shortly after the insertion of the last burials to the present day. Clearly, this has led to extensive scattering and damage to the human and animal bone assemblages from the site. However, it also appears, from information received and the nocturnal digging of holes within the cave during the period of the excavation, that the cave has been a target of treasure-hunters and metal-detectorists. Therefore, it is highly likely that artefacts have been removed from the cave and that much of the evident moving of rocks and soil, particularly in the Graveyard, is a result of this activity.

The townland of Cloghermore probably takes its name from the limestone reef under which the cave system is situated, and it is entirely appropriate that this location was the final resting place of probably the last non-Christian Irish people in the area and the first pagan Scandinavians. Cloghermore Cave: a pagan underworld in an increasingly Christian overworld.

# BIBLIOGRAPHY

Ambrosiani, B. 1998 Ireland and Scandinavia in the early Viking Age: an archaeological response. In H.B. Clarke, M. Ní Mhaonaigh and R. Ó Floinn (eds), *Ireland and Scandinavia in the early Viking Age*, 405–20. Dublin.

Ambrosiani, K. 1981 *Viking Age combs, comb making and comb makers in the light of recent finds from Birka and Ribe*. Stockholm Studies in Archaeology 2. Stockholm.

Andersen, A. 1968 *Mittelalterliche kämme aus Ribe*. Archaeologica Lundensia 3, Res Mediaevales. Lund.

Arbman, H. 1937 *Schweden und das Karolingische reich*. Stockholm.

Arbman, H. 1940 *Birka I: die gräber* (2 vols), vol. 1 [figures]. Stockholm.

Arbman, H. 1943 *Birka I:die gräber* (2 vols), vol. 2 [text]. Stockholm.

Armstrong, E.C.R. 1921 Some Irish antiquities of unknown use. *Antiquaries Journal* **2**, 6–12.

Arwidsson, G. and Berg, G. 1983 *The Mästermyr find: a Viking Age tool chest from Gotland*. Stockholm.

Batey, C. 1987 *Freswick Links, Caithness: a re-appraisal of the Late Norse site in its context*. British Archaeological Reports, British Series 179. Oxford.

Batey, C. 1993 Viking and Late Norse graves of Caithness and Sutherland. In C. Batey, J. Jesch and C. Morris (eds), *The Viking Age in Caithness, Orkney and the North Atlantic*, 187–203. Edinburgh.

Batey, C. and Sheehan, J. 2000 Viking expansion and cultural blending in Britain and Ireland. In W.F. Fitzhugh and E.I. Ward (eds), *Vikings: the North Atlantic saga*, 127–41. Washington.

Bassett, S., Dyer, C. and Holt, R. 1992 Introduction. In S. Bassett (ed.), *Death in towns: urban responses to the dying and the dead, 100–1600*, 1–7. Leicester.

Bersu, G. and Wilson, D.M. 1966 *Three Viking graves in the Isle of Man*. Society for Medieval Archaeology Monograph Series 1. London.

Biddle, M. 1990 Dress and hair pins. In M. Biddle (ed.), *Object and economy in medieval Winchester* (2 vols), vol. 2, 552–60. Oxford.

Biddle, M. and Kjølbye-Biddle, B. 1992 Repton and the Vikings. *Antiquity* **66**, 36–51.

Bieler, L. 1979 *The Patrician texts in the Book of Armagh*. Dublin.

Blackburn, M.A.S. and Pagan, H. 1986 A revised check-list of coin-hoards from the British Isles, *c*. 500–1100. In M.A.S. Blackburn (ed.), *Anglo-Saxon monetary history: essays in memory of Michael Dolley*, 291–313. Leicester.

Blindheim, C. 1981 Slemmedal-skatten: en liten orientering om et stort funn. *Viking* **45**, 5–31.

Blindheim, C., Heyerdahl-Larsen, B. and Tollnes, R.-L. 1981 *Kaupang—funnene*, vol. 1. Oslo.

Bøe, J. 1940 Norse antiquities in Ireland. In H. Shetelig (ed.), *Viking antiquities in Great Britain and Ireland* (6 vols), vol. 3. Oslo.

Boon, G.C. 1986 *Welsh hoards 1979–1981*. Cardiff.

Braathen, H. 1989 De norske vikingeskibsgraves alder: et vellykket norsk–dansk forskningsprojekt. In *Nationalmuseets Arbejdsmark*, 128–48. Copenhagen.

Bradley, J. 1988 The interpretation of Scandinavian settlement in Ireland. In J. Bradley (ed.), *Settlement and society in medieval Ireland*, 49–78. Kilkenny.

Bradley, J. 1995 Scandinavian rural settlement in Ireland. *Archaeology Ireland* **9** (3), 10–12.

Bradley, J. 1998 The monastic town of Clonmacnoise. In H. King (ed.), *Clonmacnoise studies. Volume 1: seminar papers 1994*, 42–56. Dublin.

Briggs, C.S. and Graham-Campbell, J.A. 1986 A lost hoard of Viking-Age silver from Magheralagan, Co. Down. *Ulster Journal of Archaeology* **39**, 20–3.

Brøndsted, J. 1936 Danish inhumation graves of the Viking Age. *Acta Archaeologica* **7**, 81–228.

Brooks, N.P. and Graham-Campbell, J. 1986 Reflections on the Viking-Age silver hoard from Croydon, Surrey. In M.A.S. Blackburn (ed.), *Anglo-Saxon monetary history: essays in memory of Michael Dolley*, 91–110. Leicester.

Buckley, L. 2000 Dunmore Cave: a Viking massacre site. *Paleopathology Association, Irish Section News* **3**, 5.

Burov, G.M. 1997 Human use of caves in the mountains of Crimea. In C. Bonsall and C. Tolan-Smith (eds), *The human use of caves*, 127–35. British Archaeological Reports, International Series 667. Oxford.

Callmer, J. 1977 *Trade beads and bead trade in Scandinavia c. 800–1000 AD*. Malmö.

Coleman, J.C. 1942 Cave excavation at Midleton, Co. Cork. *Journal of the Cork Historical and Archaeological Society* **47**, 63–76.

Collins, T. and Coyne, F. (forthcoming) Shape shifting: enclosures in the archaeological landscape.

Condell, L. 1985 Cloghermore Cave. *Irish Speleology* 3 (2), 52–3.

Connolly, M. 1996 The passage tomb of Tralee. *Archaeology Ireland* 10 (4), 15–17.

Connolly, M. 1997 Excavations at Ballycarty, Co. Kerry. In I. Bennett (ed.), *Excavations 1996*, 46–7. Bray.

Connolly, M. 1998 Copper axes and ringbarrows: ritual deposition or coincidence? *Archaeology Ireland* 12 (2), 8–10.

Connolly, M. 1999 *Discovering the Neolithic in County Kerry: a passage tomb at Ballycarty*. Bray.

Connolly, M. 2000 The underworld of the Lee Valley. *Archaeology Ireland* 14 (2), 8–12.

Connolly, M. and Coyne, F. 1996 A pilot survey of the Lee Valley, Tralee, Co. Kerry. Unpublished survey results, Kerry County Museum.

Connolly, M. and Coyne, F. 2000 Cloghermore Cave: the Lee Valhalla. *Archaeology Ireland* 14 (4), 16–19.

Cooney, G. 2000 *Landscapes of Neolithic Ireland*. London.

Cowie, T.G., Bruce, M. and Kerr, N.W. 1993 The discovery of a child burial of probable Viking-Age date on Kneep Headland, Uig, Lewis, 1991: interim report. In C. Batey, J. Jesch and C. Morris (eds), *The Viking Age in Caithness, Orkney and the North Atlantic*, 165–72. Edinburgh.

Coyne, F. 2004 Report on excavation at Clogher, Lixnaw, Co. Kerry. Unpublished, Department of the Environment, Heritage and Local Government.

Curle, C. 1982 *Pictish and Norse finds from the Brough of Birsay, 1934–74*. Society of Antiquaries of Scotland Monograph Series 1. Edinburgh.

Cusack, M.F. 1871 *A history of the kingdom of Kerry*. Dublin.

Dekówna, M. 1990 Unterschungen an Glasfunden aus Haithabu. In *Das archäologische Fundmaterial V*, 9–63. Berichte über die Ausgrabungen in Haithabu 27. Neumünster.

de Paor, L. 1976 The Viking towns of Ireland. In B. Almqvist and D. Greene (eds), *Proceedings of the Seventh Viking Congress*, 29–37. Dublin.

Doherty, C. 1998 The Vikings in Ireland: a review. In H.B. Clarke, M. Ní Mhaonaigh and R. Ó Floinn (eds), *Ireland and Scandinavia in the early Viking Age*, 288–330. Dublin.

Dolley, R.H.M. 1975 The 1973 Viking-Age coin find from Dunmore Cave. *Old Kilkenny Review* 1 (2), 70–9.

Dowd, M. 1997 The human use of caves in the south of Ireland. Unpublished MA thesis, University College Cork.

Drew, D.P. and Huddart, D. 1980 Dunmore Cave, County Kilkenny: a reassessment. *Proceedings of the Royal Irish Academy* **80**C, 341–422.

Dunlevy, M. 1988 A classification of early Irish combs. *Proceedings of the Royal Irish Academy* **88**C, 341–422.

Düwel, K. and Tempel, W.-D. 1970 Knochenkämme mit Runeninschriften aus Friesland. *Palaeohistoria* **14**, 353–91.

Dyer, J. 1972 Earthworks of the Danelaw frontier. In P.J. Fowler (ed.), *Archaeology and the landscape: essays for L.V. Grinsell*, 222–36. London.

Edwards, N. 1990 *The archaeology of early medieval Ireland.* London.

Eldjárn, K. 1956 *Kuml og haugfé úr heiðnum sið á Íslandi.* Akureyri. Reykjavík.

Ellis Davidson, H.R. 1964 *Gods and myths of northern Europe.* London.

Ellis Davidson, H.R. 1995 *The lost beliefs of northern Europe.* London.

Ellis Davidson, H.R. 1998 *Roles of the Northern goddess.* London.

Eogan, G. 1974 Report of the excavation of some passage graves, unprotected inhumation burials and a settlement site at Knowth, Co. Meath. *Proceedings of the Royal Irish Academy* **74**C, 11–112.

Fanning, T. 1970 Viking grave goods from near Larne, Co. Antrim. *Journal of the Royal Society of Antiquaries of Ireland* **100**, 71–8.

Fanning, T. 1981 Excavation of an early medieval cemetery and settlement at Reask, Co. Kerry. *Proceedings of the Royal Irish Academy* **81**C, 3–172.

Fanning, T. 1983 Some aspects of the bronze ringed pin in Scotland. In A. O'Connor and D.V. Clarke (eds), *From the Stone Age to the 'Forty Five: studies presented to R.B.K. Stevenson*, 324–42. Edinburgh.

Fanning, T. 1991 A Viking fashion in dress pins. In H. Bekker-Nielsen (ed.), *Tiende Tvaerfaglige Vikingesymposium*, 53–6. Odense.

Fanning, T. 1994 *Viking Age ringed pins from Dublin.* Medieval Dublin Excavations 1962–81, Series B, vol. 4. Dublin.

Freke, D.J. 1986 *Peel Castle excavations, interim report, 1986.* Peel.

Frazer, W. 1879 Description of a great sepulchral mound. *Proceedings of the Royal Irish Academy* **2**, 29–55.

Goodall, I.H. 1990 Locks and keys. In M. Biddle (ed.), *Object and economy in medieval Winchester* (2 vols), vol. 2, 1001–36. Oxford.

Graham-Campbell, J.A. 1976 The Viking-Age silver hoards of Ireland. In B. Almqvist and D. Greene (eds), *Proceedings of the Seventh Viking Congress*, 31–74. Dublin.

Graham-Campbell, J.A. 1980 *Viking artefacts.* London.

Graham-Campbell, J.A. 1987 Some archaeological reflections on the Cuerdale hoard. In D.M. Metcalf (ed.), *Coinage in ninth-century*

*Northumbria: the Tenth Oxford Symposium on Coinage and Monetary History*. British Archaeological Reports, British Series 180, 320–44. Oxford.

Graham-Campbell, J.A. 1988 A Viking-Age silver hoard from near Raphoe, Co. Donegal. In P.F. Wallace and G. Mac Niocaill (eds), *Keimelia: studies in medieval archaeology and history in memory of Tom Delaney*, 102–11. Galway.

Graham-Campbell, J.A. 1989 The coinless hoard. In H. Clarke and E. Schia (eds), *Coins and archaeology*. British Archaeological Reports, International Series 556, 53–61. Oxford.

Graham-Campbell, J.[A.] and Batey, C. 1998 *Vikings in Scotland: an archaeological survey*. Edinburgh.

Graham-Campbell, J.A. and Sheehan, J. 1996 A hoard of Hiberno-Viking arm-rings, probably from Scotland. *Proceedings of the Society of Antiquaries of Scotland* **125**, 771–8.

Gräslund, A.-S. 1965 *Rapport över arkeologisk undrersökning av fornl. Nr. 245*, Ljusdal l och I Skepptuna sn, Uppland ATA.

Gräslund, A.-S. 1980 *Birka IV: the burial customs. A study of the graves on Bjorko*. Stockholm.

Gräslund, A.-S. 2000 Religion, art and runes. In W.W. Fitzhugh and E.I. Ward (eds), *Vikings: the North Atlantic saga*, 55–72. Washington.

Grieg, S. 1929 Vikingetidens skattefund. *Universitets Oldsaksamlings Skrifter* **2**, 77–311.

Grieg, S. 1933 *Middelalderske byfund fra Bergen og Oslo*. Oslo.

Grieg, S. 1940 Viking antiquities in Scotland. In H. Shetelig (ed.), *Viking antiquities in Great Britain and Ireland* (6 vols), vol. 2. Oslo.

Hall, R. 1973 A hoard of Viking silver bracelets from Cushalogurt, Co. Mayo. *Journal of the Royal Society of Antiquaries of Ireland* **103**, 78–85.

Hall, R. 1976 Keyhole archaeology: Bootham Bar and All Saints Pavement. *Interim* **4**, 17–19.

Hall, R. 1978 A Viking-Age grave at Donnybrook, Co. Dublin. *Medieval Archaeology* **22**, 64–83.

Hallinder, P. and Tomtlund, J.-E. 1978 Rod-shaped blanks from Helgö. In K. Lamm and A. Lundstrom (eds), *Excavations at Helgö V:1. Workshop, part II*. Stockholm.

Hamilton, J.R.C. 1956 *Excavations at Jarlshof, Shetland*. Edinburgh.

Hardman, E.T. 1875 On two new deposits of human and other bones discovered in the cave of Dunmore, Co. Kilkenny. *Proceedings of the Royal Irish Academy* **12**, 168–76.

Harrison, S.H. 2001 Viking graves and grave goods in Ireland. In A.-C. Larsen (ed.), *The Vikings in Ireland*, 61–76, Roskilde.

Hayden, A. and Walsh, C. 1997 Small finds. In C. Walsh (ed.),

*Archaeological excavations at Patrick, Nicholas and Winetavern streets, Dublin,* 132–44. Dingle.

Hencken, H.O'N. 1936 Ballinderry crannog no. 1. *Proceedings of the Royal Irish Academy* 43C, 103–239.

Hencken, H.O'N. 1938 Cahercommaun: a stone fort in County Clare. *Journal of the Royal Society of Antiquaries of Ireland* 68, 1–82.

Hencken, H.O'N. 1942 Ballinderry crannog no. 2. *Proceedings of the Royal Irish Academy* 47C, 1–76.

Hencken, H.O'N. 1950 Lagore crannog: an Irish royal residence of the 7th to 10th centuries AD. *Proceedings of the Royal Irish Academy* 53C, 1–247.

Holmqvist, W. and Arrhenius, B. 1964 *Excavations at Helgö II. Report for 1957–1959.* Stockholm.

Hornig, C. 1993 *Das spätsächische Gräberfeld von Rullstorf Ldkr. Lüneberg.* Internationale Archäologie 14. Buch am Erlbach.

Hudson, R.G.S., Clarke, M.J. and Brennand, P.T. 1966 The Lower Carboniferous (Dinantian) stratigraphy of the Castleisland area, Co. Kerry. *Scientific Proceedings of the Royal Dublin Society,* Series A, 297–317.

Hughes, K. 1966 *The Church in early Irish society.* London.

Hurley, M.F. 1997 Stone artefacts. In M.F. Hurley and R.M. Cleary (eds), *Excavations at the North Gate, Cork, 1994,* 106–14. Cork.

Ingstad, A.S. 1995 The interpretation of the Oseberg Find. In O. Crumlin-Pedersen and B. Munche (eds), *The ship as a symbol in prehistoric and medieval Scandinavia,* 139–47. Copenhagen.

Ingstad, A.S. 1997 *The discovery of a Norse settlement in America,* vol. 1. Oslo.

Ingstad, A.S., Christensen, A.E. and Myrhe, B. (eds) 1992 *Osebergdronningens grav: vår arkeologiske nasjonalskatt i nytt lys.* Oslo.

Iregren, E. 1983 Förhistorika kremationer i Västmanland. In *Västmanlands fornminnesförening och Västmanlands Läns Museum Årsskrift,* 23–39. Theses and Papers in North-European Archaeology 2. Uppsala.

Johnson, R. 1999 Ballinderry crannóg no. 1: a reassessment. *Proceedings of the Royal Irish Academy* 99C, 23–71.

Jones, G. 1968 *A history of the Vikings.* London.

Kavanagh, R.M. 1988 The horse in Viking Ireland. In J. Bradley (ed.), *Settlement and society in medieval Ireland,* 89–121. Kilkenny.

Keeley Gibbons, E. and Kelly, E.P. 2003 A Viking Age farmstead in Connemara. *Archaeology Ireland* 17 (1), 28–32.

Kelly, E.P. 1986 Ringed pins of County Louth. *County Louth Archaeological and Historical Journal* 21, 179–99.

Kelly, E.P. and O'Donovan, E. 1998 A Viking *longphort* near

Athlunkard, Co. Clare. *Archaeology Ireland* **12** (4), 13–16.

Kelly, E.P. and Maas, J. 1999 The Vikings and the kingdom of Laois. In P. Lane and W. Nolan (eds), *Laois: history and society*, 123–59. Dublin.

Klindt-Jensen, O. 1957 *Bornholm i folkevandringstiden*. Copenhagen.

Klindt-Jensen, O. 1968 *Hoved og hove*. Kuml: Arbog for Jysk Arkaelogisk Selskab. Arhus.

Kruse, S.E. 1993 Silver storage and circulation in Viking-Age Scotland. In C. Batey, J. Jesch and C. Morris (eds), *The Viking Age in Caithness, Orkney and the North Atlantic*, 187–203. Edinburgh.

Lamm, K. 1970 Summary concerning Cemetery 150. In W. Holmqvist (ed.), *Excavations at Helgö III: report for 1960–1964*, 217–22. Stockholm.

Lees, A. and Miller, J. 1995 Waulsortian banks. In C.L.V. Monty, D.W.J. Bosence, P.H. Bridges and B.R. Pratt (eds), *Carbonate mud-mounds: their origin and evolution*, 191–271. International Association of Sedimentologists Special Publication 23. Oxford.

Leigh Fry, S. 1999 *Burial in medieval Ireland, 900–1500*. Dublin.

Lubin, V.P. 1997 Human use of caves in the Caucasus. In C. Bonsall and C. Tolan-Smith (eds), *The human use of caves*, 144–9. British Archaeological Reports, International Series 667. Oxford.

Lundström, A. 1981 Survey of the glass from Helgö. In A. Lundström and H. Clarke (eds), *Excavations at Helgö VII. Glass, iron, clay*, 1–38. Stockholm.

Mac Airt, S. (ed.) 1951 *The annals of Inisfallen*. Dublin.

Mainman, A.J. and Rogers, N.S.H. 2000 *Craft industry and everyday life: finds from Anglo-Scandinavian York*. The Archaeology of York 17/14. York.

Manning, C. 1987 Excavations at Moyne graveyard, Shrule, Co. Mayo. *Proceedings of the Royal Irish Academy* **87**C, 3–70.

Marshall, J.W. and Walsh, C. 1998 Illaunloughan, Co. Kerry: an island hermitage. In M.A. Monk and J. Sheehan (eds), *Early medieval Munster: archaeology, history and society*, 102–11. Cork.

Marshall, J.W. and Walsh, C. 2005 *Illaunloughan Island: an early medieval monastery in County Kerry*. Bray.

Märtensson, A.W. 1976 *Uppgravt förflutet för PK-banken i Lund*. Lund.

Monks, W. 1946–7 The Cave of Dunmore. *Old Kilkenny Review* **1**, 55–60.

Movius, H.L. 1935 Kilgreany Cave, Co. Waterford. *Journal of the Royal Society of Antiquaries of Ireland* **65**, 254–96.

Munksgaard, E. 1970 To skattefund fra ældre vikingetid: Duesminde og Kærbyholm, *Aarboger for Nordisk Oldkyndighed og Historie*, 52–62.

O'Brien, E. 1992a Pagan and Christian burial in Ireland during the first millennium AD: continuity and change. In N. Edwards and A. Land (eds), *The early Church in Wales and the West*, 130–7. Oxbow Monograph 16. Oxford.

O'Brien, E. 1992b A re-assessment of the 'great sepulchral mound' containing a Viking burial at Donnybrook, Dublin. *Medieval Archaeology* **36**, 170–3.

O'Brien, E. 1998a Viking burials at Kilmainham and Islandbridge. In H.B. Clarke, M. Ní Mhaonaigh and R. Ó Floinn (eds), *Ireland and Scandinavia in the early Viking Age*, 203–21. Dublin.

O'Brien, E. 1998b Viking burials at Kilmainham/Islandbridge. In C. Manning (ed.), *Dublin and beyond the Pale: studies in honour of Paddy Healy*, 35–44. Bray.

O'Brien, E. 2003 Burial practices in Ireland: first to seventh centuries AD. In J. Downes and A. Ritchie (eds), *Sea change: Orkney and northern Europe in the later Iron Age, 300–800*, 62–72. Angus.

Ó Corráin, D. 1996 Vikings III: Dún Mainne. *Peritia* **10**, 273.

Ó Corráin, D. 2001 The Vikings in Ireland. In A.-C. Larsen (ed.), *The Vikings in Ireland*, 17–28. Roskilde.

Ó Cróinín, D. 1995 *Early medieval Ireland, 400–1200*. London.

O'Donovan, J. 1848–51 *Annals of the kingdom of Ireland by the Four Masters*. Dublin.

Ó Floinn, R. 1998 The archaeology of the early Viking Age in Ireland. In H.B. Clarke, M. Ní Mhaonaigh and R. Ó Floinn (eds), *Ireland and Scandinavia in the early Viking Age*, 131–65. Dublin.

Oftedal, M. 1976 Scandinavian place-names in Ireland. In B. Almqvist and D. Greene (eds), *Proceedings of the Seventh Viking Congress*, 125–34. Dublin.

O'Kelly, M.J. 1956 An island settlement at Beginish, Co. Kerry. *Proceedings of the Royal Irish Academy* **56**C, 159–94.

O'Kelly, M.J. 1963 Two ring-forts at Garryduff, Co. Cork. *Proceedings of the Royal Irish Academy* **63**C, 17–125.

Ó Ríordáin, S.P. 1940 Excavations at Cush, Co. Limerick. *Proceedings of the Royal Irish Academy* **45**, 83–181.

Ó Ríordáin, S.P. 1942 The excavation of a large earthen ringfort at Garranes, Co. Cork. *Proceedings of the Royal Irish Academy* **47**C, 77–150.

Ó Ríordáin, S.P. 1949 Lough Gur excavations, Carraig Aille and the 'spectacles'. *Proceedings of the Royal Irish Academy* **52**C, 39–111.

Ó Ríordáin, S.P. and Hartnett, P.J. 1943 The excavation of Ballycatteen Fort, Co. Cork. *Proceedings of the Royal Irish Academy* **49**C, 1–43.

Ottaway, P. 1992 *Anglo-Scandinavian ironwork from Coppergate*. The Archaeology of York 17/6. London.

Petersen, J. 1928 *Vikingetidens smykker*. Stavanger.

Petersen, J. 1940 *Viking antiquities in Great Britain and Ireland* (5 vols), vol. 5. Oslo.

Petersen, J. 1951 *Vikingetidens redskaper*. Stavanger.

Philpott, F.A. 1990 *A silver saga: Viking treasure from the North-West*. Liverpool.

Raftery, B. 1994 *Pagan Celtic Ireland: the enigma of the Irish Iron Age*. London.

Ramskou, T. 1976 *Lindholm Høje gravpladsen*. Copenhagen.

Ryan, M., Ó Floinn, R., Lowick, N., Kenny, M. and Cazalet, P. 1984 Six silver finds of the Viking period from the vicinity of Lough Ennell, Co. Westmeath. *Peritia* **3**, 334–81.

Randsborg, K. 1980 *The Viking Age in Denmark: the formation of a state*. London.

Roes, A. 1963 *Bone and antler objects from the Frisian Terpmounds*. Haarlem.

Roesdahl, E. 1976 Otte Vikingetidsgrave i Sdr, Onsild. *Aarboger for Nordisk Oldkyndighed og Historie*, 22–51.

Roesdahl, E. 1977 *Fyrkat, en jysk Vikingeborg, 2. Oldsagerne og gravpladsen*. Copenhagen.

Roesdahl, E. 1982 *Viking Age Denmark*. London.

Roesdahl, E. 1987 *The Vikings*. London.

Roesdahl, E. 1995 *Hvalrostand, elfenben og i nordboerne Grønland*. Odense.

Rogers, P.W. 1999 Textile-making equipment. In A. MacGregor, A.J. Mainman and N.S. Rogers, *Bone, antler, ivory and horn from Anglo-Scandinavian and medieval York, 1964–1971*. The Archaeology of York 17/12. London.

Rygh, O. 1885 *Norske oldsager*. Christiana.

Salin, B. 1922 Fyndet från Broa i Halla, Gotland. *Fornvännen* **17**, 189–206.

Sander, B. 1997 *Excavations at Helgö XIII. Cemetery 116*. Stockholm.

Sawyer, P.H. 1982 *Kings and Vikings: Scandinavia and Europe, AD 700–1100*. London.

Scharff, R.F., Ussher, R.J., Cole, G.A.J., Newton, E.T., Dixon, A.F. and Westropp, T.J. 1906 The exploration of the caves of County Clare. *Transactions of the Royal Irish Academy* **33**B, 1–76.

Sevastopulo, G.D. 1982 The age and setting of Waulsortian limestones in Ireland. In K. Bolton, H.R. Lane and D.V. LeMone (eds), *Symposium on the environmental setting and distribution of Waulsortian facies*, 65–79. El Paso.

Sheehan, J. 1984 Viking Age silver arm-rings from Ireland. Unpublished MA thesis, University College Galway.

Sheehan, J. 1987 A reassessment of the Viking burial from Eyrephort, Co. Galway. *Journal of the Galway Archaeological and Historical Society* **41**, 60–72.

Sheehan, J. 1990 A Viking-Age silver arm-ring from Portumna, Co. Galway. *Journal of the Galway Archaeological and Historical Society* **42**, 125–30.

Sheehan, J. 1998a Early Viking-Age silver hoards from Ireland and their Scandinavian elements. In H.B. Clarke, M. Ní Mhaonaigh and R. Ó Floinn (eds), *Ireland and Scandinavia in the early Viking Age*, 166–202. Dublin.

Sheehan, J. 1998b Viking Age hoards from Munster: a regional tradition? In M.A. Monk and J. Sheehan (eds), *Early medieval Munster: archaeology, history and society*, 147–63. Cork.

Sheehan, J. 2000 Viking Age silver and gold from County Clare. In C. Ó Murchadha (ed.), *County Clare studies*, 30–41. Ennis.

Sheehan, J. 2001a Ireland's Viking-Age hoards: sources and contacts. In A.-C. Larsen (ed.), *The Vikings in Ireland*, 51–9. Roskilde.

Sheehan, J. 2001b Ireland's early Viking-age silver hoards: components, structure and classification. *Acta Archaeologica* **71**, 49–63.

Sheehan, J., Stummann Hansen, S. and Ó Corráin, D. 2001 A Viking Age maritime haven: a reassessment of the island settlement at Beginish, Co. Kerry. *Journal of Irish Archaeology* **10**, 93–119.

Shetelig, H. 1912 *Vestlandske Graver Fra Jernalderen*. Bergens Museums Skrifter. Ny. række Bd 11, No. 1. Bergen.

Sikora, M. 2000 Pagan horse burial and its implications: translations of Scandinavian culture to the Viking West. Unpublished MA thesis, University College Cork.

Simpson, L. 2003 Ninth-century Viking burials in Dublin. *Archaeology Ireland* **17** (3), 5.

Skre, D., Pilø, L. and Pedersen, U. 2001 *The Kaupang Excavation Project: annual report 2001*. Oslo.

Stenberger, M. 1961 Das gräberfeld bei Ihre im Kirchspiel Hellvi auf Gotland. *Acta Archaeologica* **32**, 1–134.

Straus, L.G. 1997 Convenient cavities: some human uses of caves and rockshelters. In C. Bonsall and C. Tolan-Smith (eds), *The human use of caves*, 127–35. British Archaeological Reports, International Series 667. Oxford.

Svanberg, F. 2003 *Death rituals in south-east Scandinavia AD 800–1000*. Stockholm.

Tempel, W.D. 1970 *Die Kämme aus Haithabu (Ausgrabungen 1963–1964)*. Berichte über die Ausgrabungen in Haithabu 4. Neumünster.

Thomas, C. 1981 *Christianity in Roman Britain to AD 500*. London.

Thornton, M.S. 1966 The Lower Carboniferous limestones of the Tralee Bay area, Co. Kerry, Ireland. Unpublished PhD thesis, Cambridge University.

Thunmark-Nylén, L. 1995 *Die Wikingerzeit Gotlands I: abbildungen der grabfunde.* Stockholm.

Turville-Petré  1975  *Myths and religion of the North: the religion of ancient Scandinavia.* London.

Ussher, R.J.  1885–6  Finds from the kitchen midden at Carrigmurrish, Whitechurch, Co. Waterford. *Journal of the Royal Society of Antiquaries of Ireland* **18**, 362–8.

Wallace, P.F.  1987  The economy and commerce of Viking Age Dublin. In K. Düwel, H. Jankuhn, H. Siems and D. Timpe (eds), *Untersuchungen zu Handel und Verkehr der vor- und frühgeschichtlichen Zeit in Mittel- und Nordeuropa, 4. Der Handel der Karolinger- und Wikingerzeit,* 200–45. Gottingen.

Wallace, P.F.  1992  *The Viking Age buildings of Dublin.* Medieval Dublin Excavations 1962–81, Series A, vol. 1, part 1. Dublin.

Wallace, P.F.  1998  The use of iron in Viking Dublin. In M. Ryan (ed.), *Irish antiquities: essays in memory of Joseph Raftery,* 201–22. Dublin.

Wallace, P.F.  2004  A woman of importance in ninth-century Finglas. *Archaeology Ireland* **18** (3), 7.

Wallace, P.F. and Ó Floinn, R.  1988  *Dublin 1000: discovery and excavation in Dublin 1842–1981.* Dublin.

Wamers, E.  1985  *Insularer Metallschmuck in wikingerzeitlichen Gräbern Nordeuropas. Untersuchungen zur skandinavischen Westexpansion.* ÖffaBücher 56. Neumünster.

Wamers, E.  1995  The symbolic significance of the ship-graves at Haiðaby and Ladby. In O. Crumlin-Pedersen and B. Munche (eds), *The ship as a symbol in prehistoric and medieval Scandinavia,* 149–59. Copenhagen.

Waterman, D.M.  1959  Late Saxon, Viking and early medieval finds from York. *Archaeologia* **97**, 59–105.

Welander, R.D.E., Batey, C. and Cowie, T.G.  1987  A Viking burial from Kneep, Uig, Isle of Lewis. *Proceedings of the Society of Antiquaries of Scotland* **117**, 149–74.

Wilde, W.  1861  *Catalogue of the animal materials and bronze in the museum of the Royal Irish Academy.* Dublin.

Wynne Foot, A.  1870–1  An account of a visit to the cave of Dunmore, Co. Kilkenny, with some remarks on human remains found therein. *Journal of the Historical and Archaeological Association of Ireland* **1**, 65–94.

Wyse-Jackson, P.N.  1999  The geology and palaeontology of the passage tomb, with comments on the significance of the fossils and geological finds. In M. Connolly, *Discovering the Neolithic in County Kerry: a passage tomb at Ballycarty,* 86–91. Bray.

# ARTEFACT CATALOGUE

## WORKED BONE, ANTLER AND IVORY

*Bone pin, 99E0431:2*

This pin was found in the soil layer that sealed the capstones covering the shaft leading to the cave system. It is 53mm long, 5mm wide at the head and 3mm thick.

The head of the pin is flattened, with a rectangular profile, and was perforated. However, the pin has broken across the middle of the 2mm-diameter perforation, and the broken portion of the head was not recovered. The pin shaft is round sectioned and has a distinct polish. In general this example is in good condition.

*Bone pin, 99E0431:3*

This pin is broken into two pieces: the upper portion is 66mm long, 7mm wide at the head and 3.5mm thick, and the lower portion is 28mm long (total length of pin: 94mm). The head of the pin is flattened, with a rectangular profile, and is bored 7mm from the top. The perforation was bored from both sides and has a diameter of 2.4mm. The shaft of the pin has a subcircular to oval profile with traces of polish, probably from use. In general the pin shows evidence of heavy wear and use. It was found in the same context as 99E0431:2 above.

*Antler pin-beater, 99E0431:14*

Fashioned from the central portion of an antler (the remains of soft tissue can be seen on one side of the point), this item is 183mm long, 18mm wide at the top, 2mm wide at the point and 10mm in average thickness. A number of faint cut-marks are clearly visible in the piece and may be the result of the manufacture of the point. The upper, wider end is irregularly shaped and may be broken (or unfinished). The point is highly polished and varies in colour from cream to yellow/brown. There are no visible indications of wear, and the tip is undamaged. This item was found in the brown clay inside the cave entrance.

*Bone gaming-piece, 99E0431:84*
The bead is dome shaped and made from the top of an animal bone. The flat base of the bead is unworked and clearly shows a cut-mark indicative of its having been cut from the top of a larger bone. The domed upper portion of the bead has a distinct patina. The bead is 13mm high, 15.5mm in diameter at the base and 7mm in diameter at the top. A perforation, 6mm in diameter, has been bored through the bead from the flat end.

*Decorated walrus ivory, 99E0431:91*
This spherical, circular-sectioned walrus ivory (A. MacGregor, pers. comm.) object is decorated on its outer surface by a series of incised concentric circles running around its circumference and has a central perforation. The perforation widens from the top (16mm in diameter) to the bottom (21mm in diameter). Two concentric circles are carved around the perforation at the top, 2mm apart; a further two, again 2mm apart, are carved around the middle of the object; and a single circle is carved around the perforation at the bottom. The object measures 25mm from top to bottom and 35mm from side to side.

*Bone plaque, 99E0431:99*
This triangular bone plaque is most likely the end from a belt or strap. It is 43mm long, 31mm wide at its base and 3mm thick. At a distance of 1.5mm from the base there is a rectangular perforation, 18mm long and 3.5–4mm wide. Directly above this are two circular perforations, 5mm apart, with diameters of 4mm and 3.5mm.

*Worked bone, 99E0431:106*
This oval-sectioned bone has a flattened, spatulate head at one end and tapers from this head toward a now missing point. It displays clear evidence of working and polishing and is probably an unfinished bone pin of a type common in the cave. It measures 85mm in overall length and is 5mm wide and 3mm thick. The flattened head measures 11mm by 10mm.

*Antler spindle-whorl, 99E0431:120*
This object is very degraded on one face and one side. The

better-preserved, upper face has been lightly polished. The total diameter of the spindle-whorl is 36mm, and it is 11mm thick. Eccentrically placed is a 13mm-diameter perforation.

*Bone point, 99E0431:125*
This eroded piece of bone is pointed at one end and flattened at the other end. It is very probably an unfinished bone pin. It measures 78mm in overall length, and the flattened upper end measures 15mm by 10mm.

*Bone pin, 99E0431:126*
This broken bone pin was found beside 99E0431:125 above. The pin has broken across the perforation through its flattened head. The pin measures 77mm in overall length; the remaining portion of the head measures 7mm by 6mm, and the surviving arc of the circular perforation shows that it was 2mm in diameter.

*Bone handle, 99E0431:132*
This handle was originally recovered in two pieces—one piece had been broken off from the butt end—which were refitted during conservation. The handle is curved and seven sided in section, tapering in size from the butt to the tip. The surface of the handle, at the butt end, is edged by two parallel, incised lines on the upper four of its seven faces/facets. The upper two faces are decorated with a series of four diamond motifs, running the length of the handle. The diamonds are formed by two parallel lines that zigzag down each face, meeting at the apex of the two faces of the handle. The two side faces of the handle are decorated at the narrower end, with a single zigzag/chevron motif again composed of two parallel lines. A slot, 13mm long and 5mm wide, has been cut through the narrow end of the handle, and part of a bone blade is still held inside the slot by a bone peg. The peg goes through the handle from one side to the other, and the handle and blade have broken across this peg. The total length of the handle is 111mm; the width and height at the butt are 20mm and 23mm.

*Bone pin head, 99E0431:134*
This piece of discoloured bone is clearly the flattened, perforated head of a pin similar to 99E0431:126 above. The surviving portion is 20mm long, 7mm wide and 1–2mm thick. The perforation is subcircular and measures 3mm by 2mm.

*Bone gaming-piece, 99E0431:135*
This piece is in a very eroded state and smaller than 99E0431:151 below, though of a similar type. It is composed of two separate pieces: a barrel-like, circular-sectioned and perforated piece of decorated bone and a short, pointed bone peg that fits into the central perforation. The barrel-like piece is 16mm high and is decorated with two incised lines running around its upper end and a similar pair of incised lines at the lower end. The lines are partially eroded; 2mm separate each pair, with the upper pair 6mm from the lower. The central perforation is 6mm in diameter at the top and 7mm at the bottom, and the total diameter of top and bottom is 12mm and 15mm. The circular-sectioned short peg is 30mm long and tapers from a diameter of 5.5mm at the top to 1.5mm at the point.

*Bone point, 99E0431:140*
This small, circular-sectioned bone point is slightly curved. It is 32mm long and tapers from a diameter of 11m at its flatter end to 2mm at the point.

*Bone gaming-piece, 99E0431:151*
This barrel-like piece of decorated bone is 19.5mm high and has a central perforation. The piece widens slightly from top to bottom and is circular sectioned. The upper edge of the piece is formed by a 4mm-wide raised area, which is decorated with a single incised line running around the body of the piece. There is a pair of similar incised lines running around the body of the piece midway along its height. The lines are 1mm apart, and there are traces of a failed/aborted third line below the second line. The base of the piece has a raised area, 3.5mm wide, similar to that at the top and also decorated with a single incised line. The central perforation is 9mm in diameter, and the diameter of the piece is 18mm at the top and 21mm at the base.

*Worked bone, 99E0431:154*
This irregularly shaped fragment of bone is unworked on its inner and outer surfaces except for the presence of one side of a broken perforation near one end. The bone is 45mm long, 9mm wide and 4mm thick. The remaining arc of the perforation is 4mm in diameter.

*Bone pin, 99E0431:156*
This bone pin is broken at its upper end along the base of the

perforation, and the point at the other end is also missing. The shaft of the pin is oval in section and originally had a flattened, perforated head. The pin measures 74mm in overall length and is 5mm wide and 3mm thick. The remains of the perforation are insufficient for its original diameter to be calculated.

### Decorated spindle-whorl fragment (burnt), 99E0431:175

This small bone fragment was cremated and probably shattered during this process. The piece was clearly from a perforated object with a flat, decorated upper face and a rougher, slightly domed lower face. The fragment measures 13mm by 12mm by 11mm. The remaining decoration consists of two concentric arcs carved around the remaining arc of the central perforation. The concentric arcs are 4mm from the central perforation and 1.55mm apart.

### Bone point, 99E0431:176

This curved piece of bone shows clear evidence of having been worked to a blunt point at one end, and the other end displays evidence of a break. It is circular sectioned and 84mm long, tapering from a diameter of 12mm at the broken end to 1.5mm at the point.

### Bone pin, 99E0431:187

This pin is shorter than many of the other examples but is, again, broken across the perforation through the flattened head. The pin is unpolished and measures 69mm in overall length. It is subcircular in section, 4mm wide and 3mm thick. The perforation of the flattened head was subcircular and 3.5mm in diameter.

### Decorated bone fragment, 99E0431:202

This small fragment is decorated on both faces, and the unbroken end is very carefully rounded and polished. The piece is flat and measures 29mm by 11mm by 2mm. One surface is decorated with three complete ring-and-dot motifs and half of a fourth, and the other face bears two complete motifs of similar type. In all cases the central dot is 1mm in diameter, and the surrounding ring varies from 4mm to 5mm in diameter.

## BEADS: AMBER, BONE, STONE AND GLASS

### Amber bead, 99E0431:41

This bead was retrieved from sieving the grey ash layer that overlay cremations in the Graveyard, this bead was very brittle and broke into four pieces shortly after retrieval. It is a disc-type bead, 10mm in diameter and 5.1mm thick, with a central perforation 2.4mm in diameter. The outer surface is a dark yellow/orange, but the interior is a much darker red, which may indicate exposure to heat and explain the brittle nature of the bead.

*Amber bead, 99E0431:44*
This bead was retrieved from sieving of the charcoal-rich layer that underlay the grey ash layer containing beads 41 and 48. This bead is intact but is probably quite brittle. It measures 10mm in diameter, is 5mm thick and has a central perforation 3.4mm in diameter. Coloration externally is the same dark yellow/orange as bead 41.

*Amber bead, 99E0431:48*
This bead was retrieved from sieving the grey ash layer that overlay the cremations in the Graveyard. Like bead 41, it was very brittle, and it broke into five pieces during retrieval. It is a disc-type bead, like amber beads 41 and 44; it measures 10mm in diameter, is 5mm thick and has a central perforation 4mm in diameter. Coloration internally and externally is the same as 41, again indicating exposure to heat, which would be consistent with the fact that all three were recovered from an ash layer containing cremated bone.

*Amber bead, 99E0431:64*
This bead is in the same style as the other amber beads described above. The disc bead is 11mm in diameter and 4.0–4.5mm thick. Eccentrically placed is a 4mm-diameter perforation.

*Bone spacer/bead, 99E0431:68*
This circular bone spacer/bead is in very good condition; it measures 7.5mm in diameter, is 2.5–3.0mm thick and has a central perforation 2.5mm in diameter.

*Amber bead, 99E0431:69*
This bead is broken, and the two remaining fragments account for approximately three-quarters of the total bead. It is similar in shape and form to the other amber beads recovered from the cave, although its height increases dramatically toward one side. The larger fragment measures 9mm across and 6mm in maximum height (3.5mm in minimum height) and is 2mm thick. The central perforation was originally 3.5mm in diameter. The smaller fragment measures 7mm across and 7mm in height and is 2.5mm thick.

*Bone spacer, 99E0431:79*
This bone spacer/bead has many small scratches on both faces. It measures 8mm in diameter and has a central perforation 2.5mm in diameter.

*Glass bead, 99E0431:80*
This small spherical glass bead measures 4.3mm in diameter, with a central perforation 1mm in diameter.

*Glass bead, 99E0431:81*
This is almost identical to 99E0431:80 above, though slightly larger, 5.2mm in diameter; the perforation is again 1mm in diameter.

*Stone spacer/bead, 99E0431:104*
This small stone disc is made from limestone with flecks of rock crystal. It measures 5.5mm in diameter and is 1mm thick. The central perforation is 2mm in diameter.

*Amber bead, 99E0431:110*
The bead is badly discoloured and has a major flaw/crack running through to the central perforation. It measures 11mm in diameter and is 3.9mm thick. The central perforation measures 3.8mm in diameter.

*Glass bead, 99E0431:143*
This cylindrical blue glass bead is decorated with yellow enamel around the centre of its body and at both ends. The bead measures 9mm in height and 9mm across and is 2mm thick. The upper and lower edges of the bead have had a thin, C-sectioned band of enamel applied. The upper band measures 2mm in maximum width, and the lower is 1.5mm. Around the body of the bead five hemispherical bosses of similar enamel have been applied. Four are intact, and the fifth is broken. They measure on average 2.5mm across and are 1.8mm high. The central perforation is 5mm in diameter.

*Bone spacer/bead, 99E0431:186*
This small bone disc-type bead is 4.5mm in diameter and 1mm thick. The central perforation is irregularly shaped (almost star shaped) and measures 1mm across.

## WORKED STONE

*Flint scraper, 99E0431:6*

This is a small possible scraper struck from a split flint pebble of cream to orange colour. It is 34mm long, 17mm wide and 7mm thick and was recovered from the dark brown clay with charcoal and bone inclusions that sealed the capstones covering the entrance to the shaft.

*Chert scraper, 99E0431:12*

This small piece of chert is triangular with a concave or hollow base at its wider end, which is quite sharp. It is 25mm long, 20mm wide and 9mm thick and was also found in dark brown clay that sealed the capstones covering the entrance to the shaft.

*Possible anvil stone, 99E0431:17*

This is a large block of red sandstone, again showing clear evidence of having been exposed to fire (blackened surface). This piece may be part of a larger anvil stone, as there are iron accretions on its surface. The outer surface is smooth and bears traces of pecking. The stone measures 147mm by 145mm by 128mm and was found in the soil that had fallen into the cave from the base of the shaft.

*Chert nodule, 99E0431:21*

This is a generally heart-shaped chert nodule that has had two flakes—one large and one small—struck from it. The larger bulb measures 45mm by 30mm and is situated on one side; the smaller measures 21mm by 14mm and is situated at the narrow end of the nodule. The whole stone measures 55mm by 53mm by 20mm and was found in the base of the shaft.

*Possible hammerstone, 99E0431:22*

This badly burnt fragment of a red sandstone cobble or possible hammerstone is irregularly shaped but bears clear evidence of wear at one end. It is 90mm long, 84mm wide and 64mm thick.

*Quernstone fragment, 99E0431:25*

This piece consists of one half of the upper stone of a rotary quern. It is made from red sandstone, and the break occurred across the central perforation. The stone was originally 360mm in diameter and 55mm thick; the central perforation was 80mm in diameter. The hole for the wooden turning handle is extant and measures 50mm by 25mm; however, a second hole has been bored from the side of the stone to intersect with the hole for the handle. This hole measures 47mm by 22mm and may have been fashioned to allow the fragment to be suspended. The stone was found in the material that had slipped into the cave from the base of the shaft, just inside the cave entrance, and has clearly been subjected to fire.

### Stone disc, 99E0431:34

This subcircular piece of greenstone has one rough convex surface and a concave depression on the other face, from which a piece has obviously been struck. The stone is oval in section and measures 70mm by 65mm by 10mm. It was found within the make-up of the large, inner bank of the D-shaped enclosure.

### Rock crystal microlith, 99E0431:37

This is a very small blade of clear rock crystal ('Kerry Diamond') with clear evidence of work around its edge. It is 8mm long, 6mm wide and 1mm thick and was found in the fill of a post-hole situated directly outside the outer bank of the D-shaped enclosure.

### Possible hammerstone, 99E0431:47

This rounded red sandstone cobble has been exposed to heat and has clear traces of wear and abrasion at one end; it measures 67mm by 56mm.

### Spindle-whorl, 99E0431:52

Made of green sandstone, this object has a flat base with rounded sides and a domed upper surface. There is considerable damage to the edge of the piece. It has a central perforation that widens from a diameter of 11mm on the domed upper surface to 35mm at the base. This item was recovered from the thin layer of soil on the stalagmite floor of the Two-Star Temple.

### Rock crystal, 99E0431:65

This small, triangular piece of rock crystal shows evidence of working on its broader end; it is 12mm long, 9mm wide and 5mm thick.

### Stone disc, 99E0431:71

This circular stone disc is flat on one face and domed on the other. It shows clear evidence of working around its edge and polishing on its domed surface and is chipped at a number of points around its edge. It measures 39mm in diameter and is 7mm thick.

*Stone crucible, 99E0431:100*
The vessel is made from light green stone, which has been identified as an iron-rich nodule, probably derived from boulder clays around the area. The total dimensions of the stone are 44mm by 42mm by 24mm. It has a broad U-shape in section and seems to be completely unworked externally. A hemispherical depression has been carved into the largest face of the stone, measuring 29mm by 27mm by 18mm deep.

*Red jasper fragment, 99E0431:107*
This is a small fragment of very fine, smooth red stone with a convex, polished outer surface. The stone has been identified as jasper (as have 204 and 222 below), a cryptocrystalline form of quartz with a distinctive red colour. Jasper occurs in Old Red Sandstone conglomerates on the Dingle Peninsula and is frequently found eroded from these rocks, as pebbles in streambeds. The stone measures 16mm by 14mm by 7mm.

*Perforated straw stalactite, 99E0431:112*
This unusual find has been broken at its narrower, unperforated end. It is circular sectioned and 61mm long. It tapers from a diameter of 4mm at the perforated end to 2mm at the broken end. The small circular perforation is 2mm in diameter.

*Stone spindle-whorl, 99E0431:138*
This whorl is made from slate/shale and bears clear evidence of wear around the central perforation, on both the upper and the lower surface. The lower surface has a large chip missing, extending from the perforation to the edge. The upper surface is slightly convex, and the lower is slightly concave. The whorl is 45mm in diameter and 6mm thick. The perforation is eccentrically placed and hourglass shaped in section. It is 9mm in diameter at both ends.

*Stone disc, 99E0431:142*
This stone disc is made from red sandstone and is badly chipped at one point on its edge. It is an elongated oval in section, measuring 62mm by 57mm, and is 9mm thick. It exhibits clear evidence of working around its edge.

*Flint, 99E0431:144*
This is an irregularly shaped piece of black/grey flint with much of

the white cortex remaining on its outer surface. It is struck but bears no traces of further working. It measures 32mm by 30mm by 7mm and was possibly for use with a fire steel or strike-a-light.

*Upper stone of rotary quern, 99E0431:177*
This fragment represents one quadrant of the upper stone of a rotary quern. It is made from green sandstone; the lower face is relatively flat but undressed, and the upper face rises from the edge of the stone toward the break at the centre. The original edge of the stone has been roughly rounded. The break has occurred around the location of the central perforation but is jagged and rough, leaving no indication of the original dimensions or shape of the perforation. The ragged nature of the break at this point and the generally unfinished nature of the stone may indicate that the break occurred during the manufacturing process. The stone measures 270mm in maximum length, 182mm in maximum width and 64mm in maximum thickness.

*Stone axehead, 99E0431:179*
This is the possible blade end of a small stone axehead made from silt/mudstone. The butt end is missing, the break having occurred 51mm from the cutting edge. The cutting edge shows clear evidence of having been worked, and a large flake, measuring 20mm by 17mm, has broken off from one face where it slopes downward to form the cutting edge. The piece was obviously unfinished, as only the sides and edges are smoothed, the central area of each face being rough and unfinished. The axehead is 51mm long, 51mm wide and 20mm thick at the broken end.

*Saddle quern/grinding stone fragment, 99E0431:198*
This roughly square fragment of red sandstone is broken on two sides. The remaining portion has a relatively flat base on one side, which curves toward the original edge of the stone. The original edge of the stone is rounded. The upper surface is gently curved and very smooth. It is 146mm long and 134mm wide and measures 65mm in maximum thickness.

*Stone rubber, 99E0431:199*
This oval-sectioned fragment of red sandstone was found in association with 99E0431:198 above. It is broken at its wider end and tapers slightly to a blunt point, where there is some chipping. The stone is

very smooth, and one face is slightly more rounded than the other, although both show clear evidence of pecking to roughen the centre of each face. The stone is 156mm long, 88mm wide and 60mm thick.

*Worked stone, 99E0431:208*
This irregularly shaped piece of limestone has been smoothed and polished, possibly by use. It has a very clearly defined, 4mm-wide groove around its body, which shows evidence of wear. The stone measures 41mm by 24mm by 20mm.

*Chert, 99E0431:211*
This irregularly shaped lump of chert has been struck at a number of points; it measures 51mm by 45mm by 17mm.

*Stone disc fragment, 99E0431:214*
This fragment of green sandstone is flat with a finely bevelled outer edge. It bears clear evidence of pecking on both flat surfaces and around the edge. It measures 79mm by 42mm by 12mm.

*Worked stone, 99E0431:215*
This piece is a broad U-shape in section and has clear evidence of chiselling internally. It is made of similar stone to the stone crucible, 99E0431:100, and may be the remains of a failed attempt to make a slightly larger example. It measures 60mm by 51mm and is 10mm thick.

*Worked stone, 99E0431:218*
This is a small triangular fragment of worked stone measuring 33mm by 9mm by 6mm. It has a bevelled edge and is charred from exposure to fire.

*Potboiler, 99E0431:219*
This red sandstone ball, though partly water rolled, shows evidence of pecking on its surface. It measures 75mm by 47mm.

*Water-rolled jasper, 99E0431:222*
This ovoid stone is red and has a distinct polish from use. It has been identified as jasper, similar to 99E0431:204 and 107 above. It measures 30mm by 21mm by 8mm.

*Stone disc, 99E0431:223*
This subcircular sandstone disc is blackened from exposure to fire

and shows evidence of pecking around its bevelled edge. It measures 35mm by 34mm by 8mm.

## WHETSTONES/SHARPENING STONES

### Whetstone, 99E0431:7

This flat rectangular piece of green sandstone has rounded ends and slight scorings on one smooth face; it is 71mm long, 49mm wide and 8mm thick. The stone was found in the layer of dark brown clay with charcoal and bone inclusions that overlay the capstones sealing the shaft entrance.

### Sharpening stone, 99E0431:18

This large block of red sandstone is broken at one end, with some damage to the extant rounded end. The stone is square sectioned, and the outer surfaces are smooth. One face has a distinct polish and bears very fine scorings. The stone is 210mm long, 145mm wide and 50mm thick and was found in the same context as 99E0431:7 above.

### Broken whetstone/cobble, 99E0431:19

This irregularly shaped piece of red sandstone bears clear evidence of pecking on its outer surface and of having been exposed to fire; it appears to have shattered off a larger, smooth, red sandstone cobble or whetstone. The stone was also found in the clay that had tumbled into the cave from the base of the shaft.

### Whetstone, 99E0431:30

This is a very finely polished rectangular piece of micaceous siltstone with rounded ends. Clear traces of wear and very fine scorings are visible on both faces. The stone is 159mm long, 42mm wide and 19mm thick and was found in the clay that had fallen into the cave from the base of the shaft.

### Whetstone, 99E0431:32

This square-sectioned, rectangular piece of green sandstone is very finely worked and has a distinct polish, with fine scorings visible on one face and one side. It is 126mm long, 29mm wide and 27mm thick and was found in the yellow clay at the base of the shaft, immediately outside the cave entrance.

### Sharpening stone, 99E0431:36

This triangular piece of red sandstone is broken at its narrower end.

The stone has a single, deep groove, up to 8mm deep, running over each face and around the surviving end. The stone is 70mm long, 55mm wide at the wider end, 29mm wide at the narrower end and 26mm thick. It was found at the base of the bank that forms the D-shaped enclosure around the entrance shaft.

*Whetstone, 99E0431:50*
This very finely made square-sectioned piece of green sandstone has a distinct polish on three sides. It is 254mm long, 30mm wide and 29mm thick. There are iron accretions on one side and one face. The stone was found in the upper layer of trampled clay/mud in the Graveyard

*Boat-shaped whetstone, 99E0431:116*
This beautifully crafted whetstone is made from a red/brown micaceous siltstone and measures 82mm in overall length. The stone tapers from a maximum width of 24mm near the middle to 8.5mm and 12.5mm at either end. The stone is 12mm in maximum thickness, but this also tapers toward both ends. The surface of the stone is perfectly smooth and bears no markings.

*Perforated whetstone, 99E0431:141*
This small pendant whetstone is made from a similar material to the small boat-shaped whetstone. It is broken, and only the upper portion was recovered. The stone is very smooth and has become waisted in shape from wear. The surface of one face bears six small scratches close together. The stone is 58mm long and narrows from 17mm near the top to 11mm in the middle, where it is heavily worn. The stone is 11mm thick, and the circular perforation near the upper end is 5.5mm in diameter.

*Whetstone, 99E0431:155*
This subrectangular piece of red sandstone is chipped at the slightly wider end. It is 125mm long, 37mm wide and 26mm thick. It is made from a very coarse-grained sandstone and displays clear evidence of its manufacture and use.

*Whetstone, 99E0431:197*
This is a very smooth, subcircular-sectioned and rounded piece of limestone with several small scratches on one surface and fire blackening on the other. It is 82mm long, 22mm wide and 19mm thick.

## MISCELLANEOUS STONE

The finds 99E0431:8, 10, 11, 13, 20, 31, 35, 49 and 217 were all stones/pebbles of no archaeological significance and have not been described.

*Water-rolled quartz pebbles, 99E0431:4:1–2*

These two water-rolled white quartz pebbles were recovered from the soil filling the entrance shaft and bear clear evidence of having been exposed to fire. 99E0431:4:1 is oval sectioned and measures 37mm by 22mm by 14mm. 99E0431:4:2 is badly cracked from heat, has a subcircular section and measures 45mm by 28mm by 17mm.

*Water-rolled green sandstone pebble, 99E0431:5*

This is a water-rolled green sandstone pebble with an oval section. It measures 20mm in diameter and is 7mm thick. It was recovered from the same context as 99E0431:4 above.

*Quartz fragment, 99E0431:15*

This square-sectioned piece of white quartz is 53mm long, 33mm wide and 28mm thick. It was recovered from the soil filling the entrance shaft.

*Green sandstone fragment, 99E0431:27*

This fragment of a rounded, smooth, green sandstone cobble bears clear evidence of having been exposed to intense heat, which probably resulted in the shattering of the cobble. The stone measures 78mm by 48mm and was found in the clay that had fallen into the cave from the base of the shaft.

*Quartz crystal, 99E0431:33*

This tiny clear quartz crystal was recovered from the fill of a post-hole outside the outer bank of the D-shaped enclosure. It measures 5mm by 4mm by 3mm.

*Red sandstone block, 99E0431:38*

This is a square-sectioned fragment of a badly burnt block of red sandstone. The outer surfaces are smooth but uneven, and one face has a slightly concave surface. The stone has stalagmite accretions from the cave and measures 155mm by 155mm by 66mm. It was found in the upper layer of trampled clay/mud in the Graveyard and may be part of the possible anvil stone, 99E0431:17 above.

*Two fragments of burnt and broken red sandstone, 99E0431:43*
The smaller of the two pieces is irregularly shaped with two smooth outer surfaces bearing clear evidence of burning. The evidence of breaking on all but two planes suggests that it was shattered by heat. This stone is 70mm long, 34mm wide and 30mm thick. The larger fragment is a block of red sandstone that has been broken at two points, again probably owing to exposure to heat. All of the remaining outer surfaces are smooth, and one face has a slightly concave surface. This stone is 137mm long, 120mm wide and 56mm thick. Both stones were found in the grey ash layer that overlay the cremation deposits in the Graveyard.

*Quartz crystal, 99E0431:54*
This faceted crystal of clear quartz was recovered from the thin layer of soil on the stalagmite floor of the Two-Star Temple. It is 25mm long, 13mm wide and 6mm thick.

*Two angular quartz fragments, 99E0431:56:1–2*
These two fragments originally probably formed one large piece. Both show clear evidence of having been exposed to intense heat, the outer surface being completely reddened. 99E0431:56:1 measures 90mm by 66mm by 45mm; and 99E0431:56:2 measures 80mm by 50mm by 35mm. These fragments were found in the clay that had fallen into the cave from the base of the shaft.

*Water-rolled quartz pebble, 99E0431:57*
This water-rolled quartz pebble has a subrectangular section with rounded sides and ends. It has three deep scorings on one face, 25–35mm long. The pebble is 70mm long, 60mm wide and 25mm thick.

*Water-rolled quartz pebble, 99E0431:58*
This pebble, similar to 99E0431:57, has a subrectangular profile with rounded sides and ends. There are a number of pits on the surface of the stone but no traces of working. The stone shows evidence of having been exposed to fire. It was found in the upper layer of trampled clay/mud in the Graveyard.

*Chert, 99E0431:59*
This is a triangular-sectioned piece of chert with a flat base and irregular sides. It is 34mm long, 24mm wide and 11mm thick. It was

recovered from underneath the topsoil in the trench that exposed the entrance shaft to the cave.

### Potboiler, 99E0431:92

This large green sandstone is clearly water rolled and displays no obvious signs of working. It measures 62mm by 45mm.

### Potboiler, 99E0431:121

This is a sub-spherical potboiler of red sandstone. It displays some slight chipping and possible evidence of pecking and also shows evidence of having been exposed to fire (blackened/charred). It measures 75mm by 70mm by 40mm.

### Rock crystal, 99E0431:149

This piece of finely faceted rock crystal has traces of wear. The crystal has a very fine front face and a rougher rear face, with traces of metal attached to it. It measures 21mm by 15mm by 11mm.

### Flint flake, 99E0431:192

This small cream/white flint flake bears no definite evidence of having been struck but has clear marks from wear along its edges. It measures 38mm by 25mm by 9mm. It may be for use with a fire steel or strike-a-light.

### Fragment of jasper, 99E0431:204

This is a small, irregularly shaped piece of fine, smooth red stone. It measures 22mm by 16mm by 13mm and seems to have been chipped from a larger piece.

### Quartz pebble, 99E0431:206

This small quartz pebble has been rounded, probably by water action, and has been highly polished. It is cream coloured and oval in section and measures 22mm by 20mm by 8mm.

### Stone with iron accretions, 99E0431:210

This flat, oval piece of black limestone has a large number of iron accretions on one surface. It measures 57mm by 36mm by 14mm.

### Chert, 99E0431:212

This small, irregularly shaped chert fragment measures 23mm by 17mm by 11mm.

*Chert with iron accretions, 99E0431:213*
This is an irregularly shaped piece of chert with iron staining and accretions. It measures 47mm by 38mm by 15mm.

*Water-rolled stone, 99E0431:216*
This rounded stone is white and oval in section. It measures 50mm by 34mm by 14mm.

### POTTERY/CLAY

*Post-medieval pottery fragment, 99E0431:28*
This small fragment of coarse redware has a black glaze on one face and measures 34mm by 19mm by 9mm. It was recovered from the upper layer of soil over the capstones of the entrance shaft.

*Crucible sherd, 99E0431:97*
This fragment is from the body and rim of a clay crucible made from a grey clay with quartz grit temper. The sherd is cracked from heat, and the inner surface exhibits the red colour characteristic of oxidisation. The sherd is irregularly shaped, measuring 25mm by 22mm by 9mm thick, tapering toward the rim.

*Clay spool, 99E0431:205*
This subcircular-sectioned item is made of clay and has clear traces of iron and threading around its exterior, as if it had been screwed into something as a stopper or had thread or wire wound around it. The piece is 21mm long and measures 12mm by 10mm across the end.

### IRON

*Axehead, 99E0431:1*
The axehead is of iron, and all surfaces were badly corroded and covered in mud and dirt. The axe weighs 590g and obviously still contains a high proportion of metal. The axe has a very obvious break at the butt, where the back of the axe appears to have been curved around to form a socket for hafting. The axe measures 127mm in maximum length, 94mm in maximum width at the blade and 39mm in width at the butt (where the curvature for the socket begins). The maximum thickness of the axe is 14mm, and it is 6.5mm thick at the blade. The thickness decreases gradually toward the curved portion at the back, which is 6.5mm thick. This was probably to enable this portion of the axe to be hammered back to form the

socket. The darker rust discoloration at the centre of the breaking point indicates that the break occurred when the axe was already rusty, rather than in antiquity. The axe was not recovered during the excavations in the cave but by cavers; its exact context is therefore not known, but it was reported as having been found in the Graveyard.

*Nail, 99E0431:24*
This badly corroded iron nail has a 16mm-long, slightly bent, round-sectioned shaft, tapering to a blunt point, and a domed, circular head, 7mm in diameter.

*Bar, 99E0431:29*
This badly corroded, round-sectioned iron bar is slightly bent at one end, with evidence of an old break at the other. It is 127mm long and 6mm in diameter and was recovered from the clay that had fallen inside the cave entrance from the base of the shaft.

*Fragment, 99E0431:39*
This is a generally rectangular, badly corroded and heavily accreted iron fragment, 39mm long, 13mm wide and 8mm thick. There are clear traces of wood adhering to the iron.

*Ferrule and portion of blade (fused to ferrule), 99E0431:45–6*
This badly corroded item was recovered from the trampled mud that formed the upper soil layer in the Graveyard. The ferrule is 107mm long and consists of a 44mm-long shaft leading down to a hollow socket, which widens toward its base. A triangular fragment has been broken from one side of the socket, and there is a small hole through the face directly opposite the break. The socket is 63mm long and widens from 17mm where it meets the shaft to 33mm at base. The socket is 35mm deep and measures 24mm by 14mm at base. The small hole is 2.5mm in diameter. Fused to the socket, close to the broken area, is a small portion of an iron blade, which measures 54mm by 34mm and is 2.5–3mm thick.

*Barrel padlock mechanism, 99E0431:51*
This unusual iron object is formed by a flattened iron band that has been folded over on itself at least four times. One end of the band terminates in a ring, formed by folding the band into a tubular form and then bending it back on itself. The ring feature is subcircular, measuring 14mm by 12mm, with a 6mm-diameter hole through the

centre. There are two smaller fixed rings on one side of the piece, on separate folds of the band. The rings are 7mm in overall diameter. Attached to the last fold of the band, midway along its length, is a semicircular plate/mount, measuring 21mm across its base and 19mm in height. Corroded to the top of the remaining folds of the bands is a large circular ring, 24mm in overall diameter, with a 15mm-diameter perforation. The iron band that forms the main body of the piece is 18–14mm wide and 1.5–2mm thick.

### Arrowhead, 99E0431:53

This item is very badly corroded and was recovered from the thin layer of soil that overlay the stalagmite floor in the Two-Star Temple. The arrowhead consists of a 68mm-long shaft topped by a relatively flat, triangular blade. The shaft appears to have originally been hollow for part of its length. There is a small break at the base of the shaft/socket. The shaft widens from 7mm where it meets the blade to 12.5mm at base. The blade is an elongated oval in section and appears to have a rounded tip. It is 29mm long, 3mm wide at the tip, 11mm wide at the base and 4mm in maximum thickness.

### Fragments, 99E0431:55:1–3

These are three very small, corroded iron fragments. Fragment 1 is a slightly bent/curved, generally circular-sectioned iron rod, 33mm long and 3.5mm in diameter; it widens and flattens slightly at one end to 5mm in width. Fragment 2 is an irregularly shaped, hollow iron fragment, 14mm long, 8mm wide and 5mm thick, with a clear break at one end. Fragment 3 is a short, badly corroded, hollow, circular-sectioned iron rod, 13mm long and 5mm in diameter, which clearly fits to the broken end of Fragment 2.

### Staple and strap, 99E0431:62:1–2

The U-shaped staple is formed from a roughly circular-sectioned iron bar that has been flattened at one end, the other end clearly being broken. The piece is 30mm long, and the two sides of the U are 8mm apart. The flattened side is 23mm long, 8mm wide and 3mm thick. The strap is a flat, subrectangular-sectioned iron strip, 34mm long, 7.7mm wide and 3mm thick.

### Staple, 99E0431:63

This rectangular iron staple is badly corroded. It is made from a rectangular-sectioned piece of iron that has been bent over to form the staple. It tapers slightly toward the ends of both arms and measures 22mm by 10mm by 7mm.

*Augur fragment, 99E0431:70*
This corroded fragment narrows from the broken end to the rounded tip and is a shallow C-shape in section. It is 45mm long, 17mm wide at the broken end, 4mm wide at the tip and 3.5mm thick. This is possibly the tip from an augur or a spoon bit.

*Fragments, 99E0431:77:1–13*
All thirteen of these fragments are very badly corroded and have a heavy layer of accretions, including timber. Fragment 1 is 62mm long, 37mm wide and 22mm in maximum thickness. Fragment 2 is 65mm long, 29mm wide and 20mm in maximum thickness. Fragment 3 is 30mm long, 29mm wide and 28mm in maximum thickness. Fragment 4 is 37mm long, 25mm wide and 17mm in maximum thickness. Fragment 5 is 40mm long, 27mm wide and 19mm in maximum thickness. Fragment 6 is 25mm long, 21mm wide and 9mm in maximum thickness. Fragment 7 is 27mm long, 13mm wide and 2mm in maximum thickness. Fragment 8 is 22mm long, 11mm wide and 4mm in maximum thickness. Fragment 9 is 25mm long, 25mm wide and 6mm in maximum thickness. Fragment 10 is 24mm long, 14mm wide and 6mm in maximum thickness. Fragment 11 is 26mm long, 14mm wide and 6mm in maximum thickness. Fragment 12 is 14mm long, 10mm wide and 3mm in maximum thickness. Fragment 13 is 13mm long, 10mm wide and 6mm in maximum thickness.

*Fragments, 99E0431:78:1–2*
These two fragments fit together to comprise a roughly triangular piece of metal that is an elongated oval in section. Fragment 1 measures 30mm by 22mm by 5mm, and Fragment 2 measures 20mm by 16mm by 5mm. The whole piece is 43mm long and 22mm wide.

*Fragments, 99E0431:85:1–12*
All of these fragments are very badly corroded, with a heavy layer of accretions. Fragment 1 measures 65mm by 35mm and is 12mm thick. Fragment 2 measures 42mm by 23mm and is 12mm thick. Fragment 3 measures 46mm by 25mm and is 16mm thick. Fragment 4 measures 34mm by 17mm and is 13mm thick. Fragment 5 measures 32mm by 13mm and is 2mm thick. Fragment 6 measures 26mm by 13mm and is 2mm thick. Fragment 7 measures 26mm by 16mm and is 3.5mm thick.

Fragment 8 measures 26mm by 12mm and is 4mm thick. Fragment 9 measures 25mm by 20mm and is 9mm thick. Fragment 10 measures 24mm by 15mm and is 4mm thick. Fragment 11 measures 22mm by 17mm and is 4mm thick. Fragment 12 measures 19mm by 11mm and is 9mm thick.

*Staple, 99E0431:86*
This is a subcircular-sectioned iron bar that has been bent over to form a U-shape. It is very badly corroded, and one side of the U is slightly longer than the other: 52mm, as opposed to 48mm. The sides of the piece are 8.5mm apart, and the bar is 4.5mm wide and 3.5mm thick.

*Fragments, 99E0431:88:1–2*
Both of these fragments are badly corroded. Fragment 1 is a very rough, irregular piece, 55mm long, 32mm wide and 27mm thick. Fragment 2 is an oval-sectioned bar that appears to have been tubular; it is 42mm long, 7mm wide and 3.5mm thick.

*Fragments, 99E0431:89:1–3*
Fragment 1 is an iron nail/rivet with wood attached. It tapers from the wider head to its square-sectioned tip and is slightly curved. It is 23mm long, 7mm wide at the head and 1.5mm wide at the tip. Fragment 2 is an irregularly shaped fragment that measures 14mm by 12mm and is 4mm thick. Fragment 3, an iron bar, is circular in section, 22mm long and 7mm in diameter.

*Fragments, 99E0431:9:1–6*
These six very small, badly corroded fragments have wood fragments attached. Fragment 1 measures 23mm by 19mm and is 3mm thick. Fragment 2 measures 20mm by 14mm and is 2.5mm thick. Fragment 3 measures 16mm by 13mm and is 5mm thick. Fragment 4 measures 14mm by 10mm and is 5mm thick. Fragment 5 measures 13mm by 13mm and is 4mm thick. Fragment 6 measures 12mm by 8mm and is 3mm thick.

*Fragments, 99E0431:93:1–7*
Fragment 1 is a large, heavy piece of curved iron from a larger object; it measures 52mm by 42mm and is 10mm in maximum thickness. Fragment 2 is part of a blade, broken at its wider end and badly corroded. The blade is triangular sectioned with a straight upper edge and a gently curving cutting edge. It is 67mm long, 23mm in

maximum width and 6mm in maximum thickness and is part of a draw knife. Fragment 3 is a triangular fragment from the tip of a blade; it is triangular sectioned, 28mm long, 18mm in maximum width and 2mm thick. Fragment 4 is an irregular lump of iron that measures 24mm by 13.5mm and is 11mm thick. Fragment 5 is a curved fragment that has been folded/bent over on itself. It is made from a thin strap/bar of iron and is 2.5mm thick and 12mm wide. Fragment 6 is an irregular fragment that measures 15mm by 10mm and is 3mm thick. Fragment 7 is an irregular fragment that measures 16mm by 8mm and is 5mm thick.

### Knife, 99E0431:94
This small iron knife is very corroded. The blade is triangular sectioned and has a slightly curved back, the edged side being straight. The tang is an elongated oval in section and is set inside the line of the back of the blade. The blade is 54mm long, 10.5mm wide and 4mm thick. The tang is 29mm long, 6mm wide and 2.5mm thick.

### Horse harness, 99E0431:95
This is a small, P-shaped and badly corroded iron fragment, rounded at both ends. It is 23mm long; the shaft is 4mm in diameter, and the head is 8.7mm in diameter. It may be a link or toggle from a leather horse harness.

### Fragments, 99E0431:101:1–7
All seven fragments are badly corroded. Fragment 1 is a flat, roughly rectangular object broken at its wider end; the narrow end terminates in a curved hook-like feature. The object is 54mm long, 25mm wide and 2mm thick. The hook feature is 7mm long and 3mm in diameter. Fragment 2 measures 22mm by 17mm and is 2.8mm thick. Fragment 3 measures 19mm by 9mm and is 4mm thick. Fragment 4 measures 24mm by 9.5mm and is 3mm thick. Fragment 5 measures 12mm by 6mm and is 3mm thick. Fragment 6 measures 12mm by 8mm and is 4mm thick. Fragment 7 measures 9mm by 8mm and is 4.5mm thick.

### Fragments, 99E0431:102:1–13
These are thirteen irregularly shaped iron fragments. Fragment 1 is part of a triangular-sectioned iron blade, 24mm long, 19mm wide and 3mm thick. Fragment 2 measures 15mm by 12mm and is 2mm thick. Fragment 3 measures 23mm by 16mm and is 5.5mm thick. Fragment 4 measures 30mm by 18mm and is 5mm thick. Fragment 5 measures

19mm by 15mm and is 4mm thick. Fragment 6 measures 18mm by 11mm and is 6mm thick. Fragment 7 measures 12mm by 12mm and is 5mm thick. Fragment 8 measures 16mm by 14mm and is 6mm thick. Fragment 9 measures 14mm by 10mm and is 4mm thick. Fragment 10 measures 12mm by 8mm and is 9mm thick. Fragment 11 measures 15mm by 10mm and is 4mm thick. Fragment 12 measures 14mm by 10mm and is 2mm thick. Fragment 13 measures 14mm by 8mm and is 5mm thick.

*Fragments, 99E0431:103:1–2*
Fragment 1 is an iron nail with a rounded head 11mm in diameter and 7.5mm high. The square-sectioned shaft tapers from the head to the tip. It is 44mm long and 6mm wide. Fragment 2, a shears bow, is a C-shaped object made from a flattened iron bar and has been broken at both ends. It is 51mm long, 14mm in maximum width and 3.5–4.5mm thick. There is wood remaining inside the curve of the bar at one end.

*Fragments, 99E0431:109:1–14*
All fourteen fragments are badly corroded, with a heavy layer of accretions. Fragment 1 is the mid-portion of a blade, 40mm long, 25mm wide and 4mm thick. Fragment 2 is the mid-portion of a blade, 33mm long, 25mm wide and 4mm thick. Fragment 3 is 34mm long, 12mm wide and 2mm thick. Fragment 4 is U-sectioned, 40mm long and 6mm wide; the U is 3.5mm deep. Fragment 5 is a square-sectioned, curved bar; it is 43mm long across the curve, 4mm wide and 4mm thick. Fragment 6 is 20mm long, 9mm wide and 5mm thick. Fragment 7 is 19mm long, 18mm wide and 2mm thick. Fragment 8 is a domed nail head, 8mm in diameter and 5mm high. Fragment 9 is a nail head with part of a shaft. The shaft is 8mm long, tapering from the head; the head measures 9mm by 8mm and is 3mm high. Fragment 10 is 15mm long, 13mm wide and 2mm thick. Fragment 11 is 16mm long, 13mm wide and 2mm thick. Fragment 12 is 12mm long, 11mm wide and 2mm thick. Fragment 13 is 10mm long, 8mm wide and 2mm thick. Fragment 14 is 15mm long, 9mm wide and 6mm thick.

*Fragments, 99E0431:118:1–9*
Fragment 1 is 32mm long, 14mm wide and 5mm thick; Green patina in the centre of the fragment indicates that it is at least partially made from copper alloy. Fragment 2 is 24mm by 13mm and 7mm in maximum thickness. Fragment 3 is 25mm by 13mm and 2mm in maximum thickness. Fragment 4 is 20mm by 14mm and 2mm in maximum thick-

ness. Fragment 5 is 16mm by 12mm and 3mm in maximum thickness. Fragment 6 is 13mm by 11mm and 4mm in maximum thickness. Fragment 7 is 14mm by 10mm and 4mm in maximum thickness. Fragment 8 is 14mm by 12mm and 2mm in maximum thickness. Fragment 9 is 13mm by 10mm and 1.5mm in maximum thickness.

*Fragments, 99E0431:127:1–12*

All twelve fragments are badly corroded, with a heavy layer of accretions. Fragment 1 is a straight, circular-sectioned bar, 39mm long and 4mm in diameter. Fragment 2 is 35mm long, 21mm wide and 7mm thick. Fragment 3 is 29mm long, 29mm wide and 9mm thick. Fragment 4 is 25mm long, 21mm wide and 4mm thick. Fragment 5 is 25mm long, 14mm wide and 9mm thick. Fragment 6 is 20mm long, 17mm wide and 9mm thick. Fragment 7 is 17mm long, 11mm wide and 2.5mm thick. Fragment 8 is 16mm long, 14mm wide and 5mm thick. Fragment 9 is 25mm long, 14mm wide and 1.5mm thick. Fragment 10 is 17mm long, 16mm wide and 7mm thick. Fragment 11 is 19mm long, 14mm wide and 9mm thick. Fragment 12 is 17mm long, 12mm wide and 7mm thick.

*Fragments—iron shears, 99E0431:128:1–8*

Fragment 1 is curved and hook shaped, formed from a rectangular-sectioned, thin iron bar. The longer arm of the fragment is 60mm long, and the curved end is 23mm long; the bar is 14mm wide and 4mm thick. Fragment 2 is a rectangular- to square-sectioned bar, 50mm long, 10mm wide and 5mm thick, that fits to the longer end of Fragment 1. Fragment 3 is a rectangular-sectioned bar, 52mm long, 11mm wide and 7mm thick, that fits to the shorter end of Fragment 1. Fragment 4 is a short section of rectangular-sectioned bar, 24mm long, 11mm wide and 7mm thick, that fits to the other end of Fragment 3. Fragment 5, 37mm long, 11mm wide and 7mm thick, fits to the end of Fragment 4. Fragment 6 is a short section of bar that broadens at one end to form a triangular-sectioned probable blade. The blade is broken, and the remaining part is 23mm long, 24mm wide and 3.5mm thick. Fragments 1, 2, 3, 4, 5 and 6 together form a U-shaped object with 13.5mm between the two arms and the portion of blade set edge on to the opposing arm: an iron shears.

Fragment 7 is blade fragment, probably from the shears, but it does not fit to the above fragments; it is 25mm long, 24mm wide and 4–6mm thick. Fragment 8 is an irregular, flat piece of very thin iron measuring 75mm by 35mm and 2mm thick.

*Shears, 99E0431:129*

This is one side of a broken iron shears, originally recovered in three parts and refitted during conservation. The blade is triangular in section, with a straight cutting edge and a back that is straight for 54mm of its length before running sharply down to the tip. The blade is 104mm in total length and tapers from 24mm wide at the shoulder to 3mm at the tip. The handle/tang is round sectioned, 85mm long and 6mm in diameter. The total length of the piece is 189mm.

*Shears blade, 99E0431:130*

This blade was originally recovered in two pieces and was fitted together during conservation. The blade is triangular in section and broken at the tang; it has a straight back, with a slightly curved cutting edge. The blade is 85mm long and tapers from 20mm wide in the middle to 1.5mm at the tip. The tang is broken but was offset to the blade; the remaining portion of the tang is 10mm long, 7mm wide and 5.5mm thick. The total length of the blade is 95mm.

*Shears fragments, 99E0431:131:1–3*

Fragment 1 is part of an iron blade with a partial tang. The tang has a D-shaped section; it remains to a length of 20mm and is 8mm wide. The blade is triangular in section and tapers from the tang; it is 26mm long, 25mm in maximum width and 3mm thick. The total length of the object is 46mm. Fragment 2 is part of an iron blade. The fragment is triangular in section, with a straight upper edge and a slightly curved cutting edge, tapering sharply from its broken end to the point. It is 42mm long, 20mm in maximum width and 3mm thick. Fragment 3 is another triangular-sectioned blade fragment, 30mm long, 18.5mm in maximum width and 3mm thick.

*Bucket handle, 99E0431:137*

This small iron bucket handle was originally recovered in four pieces, which were fitted together during conservation. The handle is formed from a flattened iron bar, which widens from the back of the hooked ends toward the top of the handle. At the upper curve of the handle the bar is flattened at right angles to the rest of the handle to form a handhold area. The external width of the handle is 147mm, and the internal width is 118mm. The bar is 14mm wide at the handhold area and only 2.5mm wide at the hooked ends.

### Draw knife fragments, 99E0431:139:1–3

Fragment 1 is a badly corroded iron fragment perforated at its intact end. It is curved and has partially separated at its broken end, indicating that it was tubular/hollow. The piece is 55mm long, 23mm wide at the broken end, 14mm wide at the perforated end and 4.5mm thick. The perforation is 4.6mm in diameter. Fragment 2 is an unidentifiable iron fragment measuring 14mm by 10m by 5mm. Fragment 3 is an iron fragment measuring 12mm by 7mm by 4mm. Fragments 2 and 3 are possibly from the draw knife represented by Fragment 1.

### Shield boss fragments, 99E0431:145:1–3

These three irregularly shaped, concave fragments may be from an iron shield boss or umbo. Numerous fragments of wood were accreted to the surface of the fragments. Fragment 1 measures 66mm by 49mm and is 3mm thick. Fragment 2 measures 61mm by 40mm and is also 3mm thick. Fragment 3 measures 46mm by 33mm and is 2.7mm thick. Fragments 1 and 2 fit together to form a domed piece, and Fragment 3 is undoubtedly from the same object.

### Fragment with rivet, 99E0431:146

This flat, rounded iron fragment measures 31mm by 16mm by 3mm and is a shallow V-shape in section. It is pierced near one end by a square-headed rivet, 7.5mm long. The rivet head measures 6mm square.

### Plate/strap, 99E0431:147

This flat, rectangular-sectioned iron plate/strap is 67mm long, 15mm wide and 1.5mm thick.

### Fragments, 99E0431:148:1–14

All of these fragment are badly corroded, with heavy accretions. Fragment 1 measures 34mm by 26mm and is 9.5mm thick. Fragment 2 measures 23mm by 11mm and is 2mm thick. Fragment 3 measures 18mm by 17mm and is 8mm thick. Fragment 4 measures 17mm by 17mm and is 2.5mm thick. Fragment 5 is a hook-like subcircular-sectioned bar. The shaft is 28mm long; the curved hook feature is 9mm long; and the bar is 4mm in diameter. It is possibly part of an item of horse harness. Fragment 6 is a Y-shaped circular-sectioned bar. The stem is 10mm long; the arms are 9mm and 15mm long; and the bar is 3.5mm in diameter. Fragment 7 measures 18mm by 9mm and is 2mm thick. Fragment 8 measures 16mm by 13mm and is 1.5mm thick. Fragment 9 measures 9mm by 9mm and is 2mm thick. Fragment 10 measures by 9mm and is 2mm thick. Fragment 11 measures 13mm by 8.5mm and is 2mm thick. Fragment 12 measures 11mm by 8mm and is 2mm thick. Fragment 13 measures 15mm by 10mm and is 2mm thick. Fragment 14 measures 15mm by 11mm and is 2mm thick.

*Saw, 99E0431:150:1–5*
Fragment 1 is a roughly L-shaped piece of iron. The longer arm is formed by a flat iron plate, 35mm long, 14mm wide and 2mm thick, and the shorter arm is formed by a circular-sectioned bar set at an angle to the plate. The bar is 8mm long and 4mm in diameter. Fragment 2 is a broad V-shaped, circular-sectioned iron bar that fits to the similar bar of Fragment 1; each arm of the V is 9mm long. Fragment 3 is a second L-shaped fragment of the same form as Fragment 1, to which it fits. The flat plate of this fragment is 15mm long, and the circular-sectioned bar, set at right angles to the plate, is also 15mm long. Fragments 1, 2 and 3 fit together to form an object measuring 69mm in maximum length, with the circular-sectioned bars rising from the ends of the flat plate like the remains of a handle: the fragments probably represent a small saw. Fragment 4 is hollow and triangular sectioned, 19mm long, 15mm wide and 6mm in maximum thickness. Fragment 5 is part of the same object as Fragment 4; it is 16mm long, 14mm wide and 4mm thick. Fragments 4 and 5 are probably from the same object as the other fragments.

*Button/stud, 99E0431:153*
This circular iron button or stud is very corroded but bears clear textile impressions on its surface. The upper surface is flat, and the rear of the button stud is slightly convex, with the corroded remains of an attachment centrally placed. It measures 12mm in diameter and 5mm in maximum thickness. The central attachment at the rear measures 6mm by 5mm and is 1.2mm thick.

*Bar fragment, 99E0431:157*
The fragment is slightly curved and tapers in width toward both ends. The ends of the bar are square sectioned, but the central area is an elongated rectangle in section. The fragment is 100mm long, 7mm wide at the ends, 15mm wide in the centre and 4mm thick.

*Fragments, 99E0431:158:1–4*
Fragment 1 measures 11mm by 8.5mm and is 2mm thick. Fragment 2 measures 36mm by 19mm and is 2mm thick. Fragment 3 measures 18mm by 17.5mm and is 2mm thick. Fragment 4 measures 22mm by 16mm and is 8mm thick.

*Dibbler, 99E0431:159*
This is a hollow, circular-sectioned, iron ferrule-like object that tapers to a blunt point and still has part of a wooden handle in the hollow socket at its wider end. It is 54mm long; the socket at the wider end is 11mm in diameter; and the dull point is 2.5mm in diameter.

*Fragments, 99E0431:160:1–3*
Fragment 1 is a lightly curved, oval-sectioned iron fragment that tapers from one end to the other; both ends are broken. It is 50mm long, 2–10mm wide and 4mm thick. Fragment 2 is an irregularly shaped iron fragment measuring 25mm by 17mm and 4.5mm thick. Fragment 3 is an iron knife, formed, in the main, from a rectangular-sectioned bar. One end of the object is triangular and is offset to the rectangular handle-like bar, which extends from its wider end. The fragment is 57mm long, and the triangular end is 20mm long and 10mm wide. The handle-like feature is 7.5mm wide and 3mm thick.

*Shears, 99E0431:163:1–2*
This piece was recovered in two parts and consists of a long stem, broken midway along its length. The stem is circular sectioned, 5mm in diameter and 110mm long. The blade is triangular, 33mm long, 11mm wide and 2mm thick. The total length of the piece is 143mm, and it appears to represent one side of an iron shears.

*Bar fragment, 99E0431:164*
This is a fragment of a curved, subcircular-sectioned iron bar, 40mm long and 8mm in diameter.

*Fragments, 99E0431:165:1–4*
Fragment 1 is part of an iron blade. The triangular-sectioned blade has a straight upper edge and a slightly curved cutting edge. It is 49mm long and measures 19.5mm in maximum width and 3.5mm in maximum thickness. Fragment 2, also part of an iron blade, fits to one end of Fragment 1. It is triangular sectioned with a rounded tip

and has a number of wood fragments adhering to the blade. It is 30mm long, 20mm wide and 3.3mm thick. Fragments 1 and 2 together give a blade that is 79mm long. Fragment 3 is an iron fragment measuring 17mm by 16mm and 4mm thick. Fragment 4 is a tubular iron fragment 21mm long and 4mm in diameter.

*Fragment, 99E0431:166*
This irregularly shaped lump of iron measures 21mm by 16mm by 13mm.

*Fragments, 99E0431:167:1–4*
All four fragments are very badly corroded, with a heavy layer of accretions, including wood. Fragment 1 measures 31mm by 13mm and is 9.5mm in maximum thickness. Fragment 2 measures 27mm by 18mm and is 14mm in maximum thickness. Fragment 3 measures 19mm by 11mm and is 5mm in maximum thickness. Fragment 4 measures 18mm by 16mm and is 9mm in maximum thickness.

*Staple, 99E0431:168*
The staple is U-shaped, with charcoal fragments attached to its surface. One side of the object is straight, and the other is slightly curved; the straight side is D-shaped in section, and the curved side is oval in section. The object is 20mm long and 21mm in maximum width.

*Fragments, 99E0431:169:1–2*
These are two small, thin iron fragments. Fragment 1 measures 27mm by 8mm and is 1mm thick. Fragment 2 measures 20mm by 18mm and is 4mm thick.

*Anvil, 99E0431:170*
This large, heavy, corroded fragment is T-shaped in section, the cross arm of the T being formed by a very thick, slightly curved and square-sectioned plate, 35mm long, 20mm wide and 7mm thick. The rest of the fragment is composed of a subrectangular iron plate measuring 35mm by 34mm by 5mm.

*Fragments, 99E0431:171:1–2*
Fragment 1 is heavy, irregularly shaped and slightly concave. Probably from a large vessel, it measures 73mm by 65mm and is 4.5mm thick. Fragment 2 is a badly corroded iron ring that measures 26mm by 25mm and is 8mm thick.

*Fragments, 99E0431:173:1–2*

Fragment 1 is an iron nail with a square-sectioned shaft tapering from top to tip. The shaft is 40mm long, 4.5mm wide at the top and 1.5mm wide at the tip. The head is badly corroded but appears to have been round and slightly domed; it is 9mm in diameter and 3.5mm high. Fragment 2 is very badly corroded but appears to be an iron staple with the arms clenched together. It is 49mm long and 17mm wide at the rounded top, and the circular-sectioned bar from which it is formed measures 4mm in diameter.

*Fragments, 99E0431:174:1–5*

These are five irregularly shaped iron fragments. Fragment 1 measures 21mm by 15mm and is 6mm thick. Fragment 2 measures 16mm by 12mm and is 6mm thick. Fragment 3 measures 16mm by 10mm and is 7mm thick. Fragment 4 measures 12mm by 7mm and is 5mm thick. Fragment 5 measures 10mm by 9mm and is 4mm thick.

*Fragments, 99E0431:178:1–2*

Fragment 1, from an iron bar, is circular in section for 35mm of its length and rectangular in section for the remaining 41mm. It tapers in width from the circular-sectioned end to the narrower, rectangular end, where it is bent to form an L-shape. The longer arm is 76mm long, and the bent section is 12mm long. The maximum width of the object is 10mm, and its minimum width, at the tip of the curved/bent section, is 4mm. Fragment 2, from a dibbler, is conical, hollow and circular in section and tapers sharply from the wider, socket end to its blunt tip. Part of the wall of the socket is missing. The fragment is 38mm long; the hollow socket measures 10.5mm in diameter and is *c.* 15mm deep.

*Clench-bolt, 99E0431:180*

This badly corroded item consists of a circular-sectioned shaft, which tapers from top to bottom, surmounted by a flat, rectangular head. The shaft is 52mm long and measures 4–10mm in diameter. The head measures 23mm by 17.5mm and is 7mm thick.

*Fragment, 99E0431:182*

This heavy, irregularly shaped lump of iron measures 55mm by 34mm and is 17mm thick.

*Blade fragment, 99E0431:184*

This is a badly corroded, slightly curved iron fragment that tapers toward both ends. Both ends exhibit evidence of breaks. It is subrectangular in section, 81mm long, 15mm wide and 3.5–4mm thick.

*Fragment, 99E0431:185*

This large, heavy, L-shaped piece of iron is rectangular in section. Around its outer edge, it is 68mm long on one side and 64mm on the other. The ends are 24mm and 30mm wide, and it is 2.5–3mm thick. It appears to have a D-sectioned rim at its wider end and may be from a large vessel.

*Fragment, 99E0431:188*

This irregular lump of iron measures 29mm by 22mm by 17mm.

*Fragments, 99E0431:189:1–2*

These are two very small, irregularly shaped fragments. Fragment 1 measures 16mm by 10mm and is 8mm thick. Fragment 2 measures 8mm by 6mm and fits to Fragment 1.

*Nail, 99E0431:190*

This is a small, corroded piece of the circular-sectioned shaft of a nail; it is 29mm long and 5mm in diameter.

*Fragment, 99E0431:191*

This is a very corroded and irregularly shaped lump of iron. It has a rounded head, 17mm in diameter, attached to a 7mm-diameter bar, which flattens out for most of its length. The entire piece is 74mm long, 20mm wide and 15mm thick.

*Barrel padlock (iron and tin), 99E0431:194*

This item was badly corroded when recovered, and unfortunately most of the iron is now converted to oxide. It was impossible during conservation to remove any further accretions to reveal the reinforcement plates or the twisted spiral rods (as seen in the X-ray), placed on each side of the reinforcement bar. However, the removal of accretions, where possible, revealed that the lock was made from two tinned plates, reinforced by two outer plates and a circular band. The two circular plates measure 35mm in diameter and are fitted to either side of a cylindrical iron core, with a now broken iron reinforcement bar rising from its outer surface. The remains of this bar are 11m high and 9mm in diameter. The iron core is 16mm wide and *c.* 31mm in diameter.

*Ring, 99E0431:195*
This badly corroded iron ring has an internal diameter of 45mm. The ring is rounded to rectangular in section; the inner and outer faces are flattened, and the sides are slightly rounded. The ring is 7mm wide and measures 6mm in maximum thickness, although its dimensions and general shape have been greatly affected by corrosion.

*Staple, 99E0431:196*
This badly corroded iron staple is formed from a curved iron bar, 5mm wide and 2.5mm thick. The two arms of the staple touch, and the end of the longer arm bends outward at right angles to the body of the staple. The staple is 25mm in maximum length and 20.5mm in maximum width.

*Ring, 99E0431:200*
This iron ring is 44.3mm in internal diameter and in much better condition than 99E0431:195 above. It is generally square in section; the inner face and both sides are flat, although the outer face is slightly rounded. The ring is 6.5mm wide and 6.5mm thick. On one side of the ring are the corroded remains of a smaller ring or moulding through which the larger is attached. The remains suggest that the central element of this feature was originally circular, 9mm in internal diameter, 4.5mm wide and 4.5mm thick. This ring/moulding is enclosed in corrosion, although there is evidence of a break on its outer side, suggesting that it was originally part of a larger feature, possibly a horse-bit link. This ring and 99E0431:195 were recovered within 15cm of each other and are probably the remains of a horse-bit.

*Loop-headed pin, 99E0431:201*
This iron fragment is badly corroded but appears to have had a hollow, rounded head, formed by curving over the flattened end of the D-sectioned shaft, now broken. The extant portion of the shaft is 19mm long and 3.5mm wide; the head measures 8mm in diameter.

*Horse-bit link, 99E0431:207*
This circular-sectioned rod has been curved into a hook at one end and is beginning to curve into a second hook at its broken end. It is

60mm long and 20mm wide at the hooked end, and the bar measures 4mm in diameter.

## Handle/hook fragment, 99E0431:220

This corroded fragment is made from a circular-sectioned iron bar that has been curved at one end, giving it a J-shape. The piece is 66mm long; the bar measures 5mm in diameter and may have been tubular.

## Handle, 99E0431:221

This badly corroded iron handle retains part of the iron vessel from which it has broken. The wall of the vessel is 4mm thick. The handle is circular sectioned, 11mm in diameter and 7-shaped. The upper, straight arm of the handle is 23mm long, and the sloping arm is 54mm long.

## Nail, 99E0431:224

This corroded fragment is probably the remains of a nail. It consists of a circular shaft crowned by a domed head. The shaft is 54mm long and 6mm in diameter. The head is 11mm in diameter, at the base, and 6mm high.

## Fragment, 99E0431:225

This large, heavy iron fragment is rectangular sectioned and has been broken at both ends. It is badly corroded, 50mm long, 34mm wide and 3.5mm thick.

## Rivet fragment, 99E0431:226

This corroded iron fragment is D-shaped in section and displays evidence of having broken from a larger piece. It has a domed head and may be a rivet. It measures 11mm across and is 4mm high.

## Fragment, 99E0431:227

This fragment is quite thin and is curved, giving it a C-shaped section. It measures 19mm by 18mm by 1mm.

## Fragment, 99E0431:228

This irregularly shaped fragment is badly corroded; it appears to have two small domed features on its exterior surface and is slightly curved. It measures 18mm by 13mm by 3.5mm; the domed features are 4mm in diameter.

*Fragment, 99E0431:229*
This is a small, thin-walled, curved fragment, very similar to 99E0431:227 above, and probably from the same artefact. It measures 18mm by 8mm by 1mm.

### COPPER/BRONZE

*Copper-alloy fragment, 99E0431:9*
This very small fragment was recovered from the fill of the shaft that led into the cave system. It measures 6.37mm by 5.24mm and is 3.10mm thick.

*Copper-alloy fragment, 99E0431:26*
This small copper-alloy fragment was recovered on the surface in Quadrant D of the Graveyard. It is 16.2mm long, 12mm wide and 2.7mm thick. X-ray photography revealed a perforation close to the edge of the fragment.

*Possible copper-alloy rim fragment, 99E0431:40*
This piece was recovered from the ash overlying the cremated remains in the Graveyard. It is 17.7mm long, 6.52mm wide and 3mm thick. The piece has a distinct curvature and may be part of the rim of a larger object.

*Copper-alloy pinhead, 99E0431:42*
This small, rounded copper alloy-fragment was also recovered from the ash overlying the cremated remains in the Graveyard. It has a maximum diameter of 5.6mm and weighs only 3.9g. X-ray photography of the item revealed that it has a hollow interior and possible decoration lines on its surface.

*Copper-alloy ringed pin, 99E0431:82*
This plain-ringed, loop-headed ringed pin is undecorated. The ring is D-shaped in section, the upper and the lower face being flattened. The ring measures 18.7mm in external diameter and 13.2mm in internal diameter and is 2.7mm thick. The ring narrows sharply as it nears the loop head of the pin and is held tightly within the loop, possibly in a pivot. The upper surface of the ring is badly pitted. The loop head of the pin is damaged: a piece at the base of the loop, nearest the shank, is missing. The loop is 4mm wide and measures 2.5mm in internal diameter. The shank of the pin is rounded to rectangular in section; the front and back surfaces of the shank are

flattened, and the side surfaces are rounded. The shank is 87.2mm long and is a constant 2.5mm wide and 1.7mm thick, to a point 15mm from the tip of the pin, where it narrows sharply to a point. The total length of the ringed pin is 115.2mm.

*Copper-alloy fragments, 99E90431:87:1–4*
These three small fragments were retrieved by sieving. Fragment 1, the largest, is very thin and curved, measuring 8mm by 6.5mm by 0.7mm. Fragment 2 is similarly thin and measures 6mm by 3.5mm. Fragment 3 is a thin fragment measuring 5mm by 4mm. Fragment 4 is very small piece of metal that is difficult to identify as being part of a larger item; it is very thin and irregularly shaped, measuring 18mm by 4mm.

*Copper pin, 99E0431:96*
This copper pin is curved/bent at a point approximately one-third of the way down the shaft. The shaft is circular sectioned and capped by a hemispherical head decorated with a single lightly engraved line running around its body. The pin measures *c.* 37mm in overall length and 0.5mm in diameter. The head measures 2mm in diameter and is 1mm high.

*Copper-alloy button, 99E0431:105*
This small copper-alloy button has a domed head and a large, perforated tang/shank. The domed head is 7.1mm in diameter and 4.2mm high. The shank/tang is 6mm wide, 5mm long and 1mm thick, and the perforation is 2.8mm in diameter.

*Copper-alloy fragments, 99E0431:108:1–2*
Fragment 1 measures 6mm by 2.5mm. Fragment 2 measures 9mm by 6.5mm and is 3.5mm thick.

*Copper-alloy fragments, 99E0431:114:1–4*
These are four very small, unidentifiable fragments. Fragment 1 measures 5mm by 3mm and is 1mm thick. Fragment 2 measures 6mm by 4mm and is 1.5mm thick. Fragment 3 measures 6mm by 6mm and is 1mm thick. Fragment 4 measures 5mm by 4mm and is 1.2mm thick.

*Copper-alloy ringed pin, 99E0431:115*
This loop-headed ringed pin has an unusual, broken ring and was

found with the articulated burial in Area W. The pin shaft is badly pitted and corroded and tapers gently from its looped head to a blunt point. The shaft is slightly bent at a point 25mm from the base of the looped head and is subcircular in section. The pin is 92mm long, 3.8mm wide at the base of the looped head, 0.6mm wide at the point and 2.6mm in average thickness/diameter. The looped head is formed by flattening the pin shaft and curving it over on itself to form an aperture 3.6mm in internal diameter. The flattened loop is 5mm wide and 1mm thick.

The ring is damaged, and the lower portion is missing, but it is clearly not of the types described by Fanning (1994). The remaining portions of either side of the ring are D-shaped in section, the rear of the ring being flat and the front slightly rounded. Both sides of the ring flare out as they approach the looped head of the pin and have flattened, circular terminals/flanges that rest against the sides of the pinhead, preventing any movement of the ring through the pinhead. A circular-sectioned iron bar extends through the pinhead from the terminals, allowing movement of the ring up and down. Although the lower part of the ring is missing, on one side there is a 2.2mm-long portion of a straight bar, which ran across the ring, and a recessed rear plate. This suggests that the lower part consisted of a D-shaped setting or plate, which had been decorated with red enamel, some of which still adheres to the remains of the recessed setting. However, there is no evidence to suggest whether the ring was annular. The remains of the ring have an internal diameter of 13mm, and the ring is 3mm wide and 1mm thick at the lower end and 4mm wide and 2mm thick at the terminals on either side of the looped pin-head.

*Copper-alloy buckle tang, 99E0431:119:1–2*
These two pieces fit neatly together and originally formed one piece. Fragment 1 appears to be the square-sectioned shaft of a buckle tang with some iron accretions. It is 38mm long and 2.5mm in diameter. Fragment 2, which also has some iron accretions, consists of a flattened, subrectangular-sectioned piece of metal that has been folded over to form a loop. It measures 12mm by 6mm by 4mm.

*Copper pin, 99E0431:122*
This is a straight copper-alloy pin with a flattened head. The pin is 27mm long and tapers to a point. It is circular in section and 1mm in diameter, and the flattened head is 2mm in diameter.

*Copper-alloy fragment, 99E0431:133*
This very small, thin copper-alloy fragment measures 5mm by 4mm.

*Copper-alloy pin shaft, 99E0431:152*
The pin shaft is circular sectioned, tapering to a point with evidence of a break at one end. It is 37mm long and 1.2mm in diameter.

## BONE COMBS AND FRAGMENTS

*Bone comb fragments, 99E0431:60:1–4*
Fragment 1 is a small triangular piece decorated with a single incised line running down its side and a pair of incised lines running around one end. The upper surface is decorated with cross-hatching. The fragment is 10mm long, 9mm wide and 3.5mm thick. Fragment 2 is decorated with a pair of parallel incised lines down its remaining length. Outside these lines, running to the edge of the fragment, are seven incised lines, and the area inside them is decorated with cross-hatching. The fragment is 19.5mm long, 10.5mm wide and 3mm thick. Fragment 3 has similar decoration to Fragment 1: a pair of parallel lines running down the side of the fragment and around one end. The upper surface is decorated with cross-hatching. The fragment is broken across a peg/rivet-hole, 3mm in diameter, and is 18mm long, 10mm wide and 2.5mm thick. Fragment 4 is part of a single-sided teeth-plate and has three intact teeth, 16.5–18mm long, and four broken teeth; the top of the plate is also broken.

*Bone comb fragment, 99E0431:67*
This fragment is from the upper portion of a teeth-plate. The top of the plate has a gabled form and a perforation, which was clearly bored from the outer, more polished side, where it is 5mm in diameter. Midway along the length of the plate each edge bears the remains of a perforation, one of which contains the remains of a bone peg. This perforation was 3mm in diameter, and the other, broken perforation was of similar size. The plate originally bore six teeth, now broken. The fragment measures 25mm by 15mm by 2mm.

*Bone comb fragments, 99E0431:75:1–4*
These four fragments were found close together in Area Z. Fragment 1 is curved and has broken from a larger side-plate. The inside of the curve is marked with sixteen incised lines caused by the cutting of the teeth, spread across its surface. The lines vary in length from 1.5mm to 5mm. The upper surface of the fragment is decorated with

cross-hatching and appears to have broken across four peg/rivet-holes, 3–4mm in diameter. The fragment is 57mm long, 10mm wide and 7mm thick. Fragment 2 is from a curved, trapezoidal-sectioned side-plate and is probably part of the same comb as Fragment 1. The inside of the curve is decorated with five incised lines, arranged into two pairs of parallel lines, with a single line close to the wider, broken end. The upper surface is, again, decorated with incised cross-hatching. The fragment is broken at both ends, across peg/rivet-holes 3mm in diameter, and there is a complete perforation, 3mm in diameter, near the narrower end. The fragment is 36mm long, 11–16mm wide and 5.2mm thick. Fragment 3 is small fragment and has an upper surface decorated with incised hatching; it is part of the same comb as Fragments 1 and 2 and is 26mm long, 12mm wide and 7mm thick. Fragment 4, also from the same comb, is slightly curved and is decorated with the same incised cross-hatching. It is broken at both ends, across two peg/rivet-holes, 4mm and 5mm in diameter. The fragment is 25mm long, 7mm wide and 5.5mm thick.

*Bone comb plate, 99E0431:76*

This 49mm-long fragment has six intact teeth, 21.5–23mm long. One side of the plate is more polished than the other, and the original break occurred along the line of a 3mm-diameter perforation positioned 7mm above the intact teeth. At a point 16mm above the teeth a second, larger perforation occurs. This was clearly bored from the more polished side and measures 5mm in maximum diameter. The top of the plate has been finished to a gabled form.

*Bone comb, 99E0431:83:1–5*

This partial comb was originally recovered in five pieces, which were fitted together during conservation. It is a heavy, roughly made comb with D-sectioned side-plates, held in place by three iron rivets and two bone pegs. The comb is very badly eroded, but one side-plate shows traces of a border formed by two parallel lines; small cuts from the teeth are also visible. Both side-plates are broken at the same end; they are 84mm and 81mm long and 20–23mm wide. One end of the teeth-plate is intact and shows it to have been of a gabled form. The extant plate originally had 35 teeth, of which seventeen are intact. The maximum length of the extant teeth is 23mm. The total length of the comb is 96mm, and the total width is 45mm.

*Bone comb, 99E0431:98:1–4*

Fragment 1 is 39mm long, 15mm wide and 3mm thick. It is undecorated and C-shaped in section but has been charred by fire. One end of the fragment is complete, and the other end has a relatively recent break. The break occurred around an iron rivet, part of which is extant. There is a second, intact iron rivet through the plate, 5.5mm from the complete end. On the rear of the plate, 24mm from the complete end, there is a 2.5mm-diameter perforation containing part of a bone peg.

Fragment 2 comprises two fragments of side-plate riveted and pegged to part of a double-sided teeth-plate, which has ten intact teeth, the length and nature of which indicate that the teeth of this comb were relatively short. Other teeth on the plate are represented by stubs. The comb broke around a corroded iron rivet, which is still intact, and a small bone peg, 3mm in diameter, is also still intact. The side-plates are similar to Fragment 1, which fits to one end, and are 39mm and 37mm long. The teeth-plate extends 13mm beyond the original end of one of the side-plates.

Fragment 3 is small fragment of teeth-plate that fits to one end of Fragment 2 and shows that the end of the comb was formed by the straight-sided teeth-plate. It has the remains of six teeth and is 29mm long and 12mm wide, narrowing in width toward the end of the comb.

Fragment 4 is a tiny fragment of teeth-plate that fits to the opposite end of the comb to Fragment 3. It measures 7mm by 6mm.

The completed comb measures 88.5mm in maximum length, 43mm in width at the intact end of the teeth-plate and 11mm in maximum width at the broken end. The maximum length of the remaining teeth is 9mm.

*Bone comb fragments, 99E0431:111:1–4*

These fragments consist of two decorated pieces (1 and 2), which fit together, and two pieces (3 and 4) that are the remains of teeth-plates, probably from this fragmentary comb.

Fragments 1 and 2 originally broke along the centre of a perforation and together form a narrow, thick, rectangular-sectioned comb side-plate. Fragment 1 is 16mm long, 9mm wide and 4mm thick. Fragment 2 is triangular and forms the end of the plate; it is 15mm long, 10mm wide and 4.5mm thick.

Fragment 3 is rectangular and undecorated but bears evidence of two broken perforations *c.* 3mm in diameter. It originally had four teeth, which are now broken, and it measures 2mm by 14mm by 1.5mm.

Fragment 4 is roughly rectangular and also originally bore four teeth, now broken. It has two extant perforations—the smaller is 3mm in diameter, and the larger 4mm—and the arcs of two further, broken perforations *c.* 3mm in diameter. It measures 25mm by 12mm by 2mm.

The whole side-plate is 27mm long across the base and 15mm long across the top. It is decorated with two pairs of parallel lines, 1.5mm apart, which run from the bottom to the top of the plate, forming a chevron motif. The upper edge of the plate is decorated with eight short cuts, which run over the front face of the piece. The perforation through the plate is 3mm in diameter.

*Decorated bone side-plate fragments, 99E0431:117:1–2*
Both fragments are probably from the decorated side-plate of a bone comb. Both have flat, undecorated rear surfaces and curved upper surfaces, indicating that the side-plate was originally C-shaped in section. Fragment 1 is roughly triangular, 19mm long, 9mm wide and 2mm thick. The decoration consists of two parallel lines, 1.5mm apart, which run the length of the fragment close to its original edge; a third line runs at an angle to these for a length of 10mm. Fragment 2 is irregularly shaped and has been badly charred by fire; it is 19mm long, 10mm wide and 2mm thick. Its decoration also consists of a pair of parallel lines 1.5mm apart, running for a length of 10mm along its original edge. A second pair of lines running at an angle to these occurs for a length of 7mm across the middle of the fragment.

*Bone comb fragment, 99E0431:123*
This is a fragment of a double-sided teeth-plate with nine intact and three broken teeth on one side and ten intact and two broken teeth on the other. The teeth are a maximum of 12mm long. The plate is clearly broken at both ends, at one end across a subcircular peg/rivet-hole 3.5–4mm in diameter. The plate is 20mm long and measures 39.5mm in maximum width.

*Bone comb fragment, 99E0431:124*
This undecorated fragment comes from a double-sided teeth-plate. The bases of seven teeth can be discerned on one side, but only two can be identified on the other. The fragment measures 23mm by 13mm by 2mm.

*Bone comb, 99E0431:136*
This was originally recovered in six pieces, which were fitted together

during conservation. The small, particularly finely made comb has two decorated side-plates, each of which is outlined/edged by a pair of parallel lines 1mm apart. One plate has a series of dots placed inside the inner line. Both ends of each plate are decorated. On the dot-ornamented plate, one end has a series of three concentric arcs extending from the corners of the border, the area between each arc being decorated with random dots. The other end has two less symmetrical arcs; the space between the two arcs is decorated with dots, and that between the inner arc and the border has two lightly incised lines and dots. Both sets of arcs are finished with a lightly incised motif at the inner extent of the arcs. The other plate has similar decoration at the ends. At one end there are two arcs; the space between them is decorated with dots, and the space between the inner arc and the border is decorated with incised parallel lines running from the border to the inner arc. The other end is the same except for the addition of a poorly drawn third arc with no decoration inside it. The by motif again finishes the decoration. The two plates are 55mm long, 16mm wide, rectangular in section and held in place by three iron rivets.

The teeth-plate is broken across one of these rivets, and the remaining plate had 48 teeth on one side and 49 on the other, of which 23 and 34 are intact. Light saw-marks from the cutting of the teeth are visible on the edges of the side-plates. One end of the teeth plate is intact and indicates that each end was slightly curved toward the main body of the comb. The teeth are a maximum of 15mm long, and the intact end of the teeth-plate extends 4mm beyond the side-plate. The comb measures 59mm in total length and 45mm in total width.

*Bone comb, 99E0431:181*

This item was originally recovered in six pieces, which were fitted together during conservation. Both of the decorated, D-sectioned side-plates are formed of two fragments and are almost complete.

On one plate the decorated surface is divided into three panels by single incised lines running down the sides of the plate and parallel pairs of incised lines running across the width of the plate. Each of the end panels is decorated with incised cross-hatching, and the central panel is decorated with a saltire motif, each arm of the cross composed of two parallel lines. The left panel has two intact pegs in 2.5mm- and 3mm-diameter perforations, and the middle panel has one empty perforation, 2.5mm in diameter. The right panel has two perforations, 4mm and 3mm in diameter. All of the panels are 16mm wide and 16mm high, and (from left to right) they are 20mm, 23mm and 23mm long. The plate is 79mm long, 23mm wide and 3mm thick.

The other plate is divided into four panels by a pair of incised parallel lines running down each side of the plate and five groups of three parallel lines running the width of the plate. The panels are 11mm high and 11mm wide, and (from left to right) they are 12mm, 11mm, 13mm and 20mm long. The leftmost panel is badly damaged, and the second from left has an intact bone peg through a 3.5mm-diameter perforation. The rightmost panel has an intact peg, which has been decorated as part of the three parallel lines edging the panel; it also contains an empty 2.5mm-diameter perforation. The plate is 79mm long, 23mm wide and 4mm thick, and its edge is decorated with a series of short incised lines.

A single double-sided teeth-plate was recovered and replaced during conservation. None of the teeth are intact, but the plate originally had thirteen teeth on each side.

*Decorated bone fragment, 99E0431:183*
This irregularly shaped, rough piece of bone is charred on its lower (inner) surface; the upper surface bears a C-sectioned line running across it, 18mm long and 1.5mm wide. The fragment measures 25mm by 16mm by 2.5mm.

*Bone comb side-plate fragment, 99E0431:193*
This is a small undecorated fragment from the corner of a bone comb side-plate; it measures 10mm by 5mm by 3mm.

*Decorated bone fragment, 99E0431:203*
This subtriangular bone fragment is decorated on both sides with a pair of parallel incised lines running the length of the fragment. The lines are 1.5mm apart on one face and 0.9mm apart on the other face. The fragment, which is clearly broken at its wider end, measures 9mm by 6mm and is 2mm thick.

CLAY PIPES

*Clay-pipe stem, 99E0431:172*
The stem is undecorated and increases in diameter from top to bottom; it is 42mm long and measures 5.5–8mm in diameter.

# HUMAN SKELETAL REMAINS

*Linda G. Lynch*

## INTRODUCTION

This section reports on the osteoarchaeological analysis of the human skeletal remains recovered from Cloghermore Cave. As detailed above, the remains were recovered over the course of two seasons: 1999 and 2000. The bones recovered during the first season were analysed by A. Chamberlain and A. Witkin of the University of Sheffield (Chamberlain and Witkin 2000). During the second season the present author was on-site and subsequently analysed the skeletal remains recovered during that period. In order to minimise disparity in the results of the analyses of essentially a disarticulated assemblage by three individual osteoarchaeologists, it was decided to re-analyse the remains from the first year. Therefore the skeletal remains examined in this section were analysed entirely by the present author to reduce inaccuracies in the results.

The methods used to excavate the cave have been described in detail above. There are three main divisions within the cave system from which human bone was recovered: the Two-Star Temple, the Graveyard and the Entrance Gallery. The Two-Star Temple—the innermost area from the entrance shaft—is linked to the Graveyard by a passage (Area Y), from which no human remains were recovered. It is therefore unlikely that there is any post-depositional mixing of bones from the Two-Star Temple with remains from the rest of the cave. The bones in the Two-Star Temple and possibly some bones from the Graveyard date to the earliest phase of burial activity at this site, *c.* eighth century.

The Graveyard and the Entrance Gallery are situated to the south of the Two-Star Temple and represent the second phase of burial, dated to the tenth century. Both the Graveyard and the Entrance

Gallery present a number of problems in the analysis of the human bone sample. On plan the two areas are relatively distinct, but in reality the gradient drops quite sharply from the Entrance Gallery to the Graveyard. There is considerable evidence of human intervention in the cave in recent times (even before scientific excavation).

When this evidence is combined with a variety of taphonomic factors over the centuries, such as water action, and with the apparent burial and/or depositional procedures (see below) initially used in antiquity, it is probable that there is at least some mixing of the skeletal deposits between the main areas of the Entrance Gallery and the Graveyard. These issues will be elaborated on below, particularly in the examination of the possible number of individuals deposited in the cave.

In addition to the main areas noted above, a number of relatively distinct areas of deposition were recorded in both the Graveyard and the Entrance Gallery, and these will be particularly examined in relation to the demographic profile of the skeletal remains. A small side chamber, Area Z, was present to the north of the Graveyard and contained human remains. In the Entrance Gallery the main deposit of human bone came from Area X, and human bone was also recovered from Areas U and W, which were elongated chambers running east at the eastern side of the Entrance Gallery. Just inside the entrance to the cave a small pit (Area V) was excavated and was found to contain a quantity of both human animal and non-human animal bone (from here on referred to as human and animal bone respectively). In addition, human remains were recovered from a shelf of rock (Area T) and from the backfill of the entrance shaft itself. All of these areas (Z, in the Graveyard, and X, U, W, V, T and the entrance shaft, in the Entrance Gallery) will be referred to again below in detail. All areas of the three primary divisions of the cave were fully excavated, thus ensuring full recovery of the skeletal remains.

## Materials

It is important at this point to clarify the terms used in relation to the human remains recovered from Cloghermore Cave. Disarticulation is defined as the 'complete reduction of the soft tissues that hold bone together within a joint in a living organism' (Roksandic 2002, 101). Technically, therefore, a completely skeletonised individual with all of the bones in the correct anatomical position is considered disarticulated (*ibid.*). However, osteoarchaeological literature systematically refers to the state of such an individual as articulated, while both isolated individual bones and commingled bones are referred to as disarticulated (see, for example, Mays 1998; Ubelaker 1989). In this study any human bones that were recovered in the correct anatomical position, regarding two bones or more, are considered articulated, while commingled and scattered bones are considered disarticulated.

A considerable volume of human skeletal remains was recovered during the two seasons of excavation at Cloghermore Cave. Virtually all were uncovered in a disarticulated state, jumbled and churned throughout the earthen deposits of the cave. The exceptions were the articulated spine of a child in Area U and the articulated but truncated remains of an adult male recovered from Area W inside the entrance. The condition of the skeletal remains is examined in more detail below; however, most were fragmentary. Only seventeen complete adult long bones were recovered, seven of which were from the single articulated skeleton, and the fragments were considerably mixed together. Some fragments displayed peri-mortem breaks (with sharp edges indicative of breakages of fresh bone); other bones were broken sometime after disposal in antiquity; and other fragments exhibited fresh breaks that probably occurred during and after the excavation despite careful handling.

All of the areas of the Two-Star Temple, the Graveyard and the Entrance Gallery were completely excavated, thus maximising the recovery of human bone fragments. Owing to the context of recovery—a cramped underground location in artificial light—and the primarily disarticulated nature of the human remains, all of the excavated soil was brought to the surface, labelled by its area of recovery. The earth was then sieved on-site. This allowed for the recovery of some minute finds, as well as small bones, including animal and human foetal remains and some of the smaller bones of more mature humans. The bones of animals and humans were then separated, bagged, labelled and removed for specialist analysis. No discernible stratigraphy was recorded in the cave, and therefore bones were labelled by the area (or segment of the main area) of recovery. All discernibly articulated material was excavated *in situ*. All of the bones were examined for any pathological conditions.

Finally, Table 1 details the human bones that were sent for dating. Although these bones no longer exist, they have been included in certain elements of the analysis, particularly in the examination of the minimum number of individuals and demographic profiles. Unfortunately, owing to an oversight, the bones were not weighed, nor were the lengths of the complete long bones recorded, before they were sent for analysis, and these bones are therefore excluded from certain aspects of the analysis. More detail is provided in the relevant sections.

| Age | Area | Bone | Sample no. |
|---|---|---|---|
| Adult | Area X | Mid-shaft of femur | 1 |
| Adult | Graveyard, Quadrant A | Left ulna | 2 |
| Adult | Graveyard, Quadrant B | Left talus | 3 |
| Adult | Graveyard, Quadrant C/D | Thoracic vertebra | 4 |
| Adult | Two-Star Temple, Quadrant G | Right femur | 8 |
| Adult | Graveyard, Quadrant B | Left calcaneus | 10 |
| Adult | Graveyard, Quadrant A | Right humerus | 14 |
| Adult | Area W | Left femur | 18 |
| Adult | Area T | Right femur | 19 |
| Sub-adult | Graveyard, Quadrant B | Left humerus | 5 |
| Sub-adult | Entrance shaft | Right ulna | 6 |
| Sub-adult | Two-Star Temple, Quadrant E | Right distal femur | 7 |
| Sub-adult | Graveyard, Quadrant B | Mid-shaft tibia | 9 |

TABLE 1—*Human bones sent for radiocarbon dating.*

## Scope of the study

The analysis of the human remains recovered from Cloghermore Cave was undertaken with the aim of examining a number of factors. The primary aim was to complete a detailed database on all of the fragments recovered. This database facilitated the further analysis of the assemblage, particularly with regard to determining the minimum number of individuals represented in the sample, establishing demographic profiles, examining the living stature of the adult individuals, analysing dental remains and considering the pathological lesions evident in the remains. All of these analyses were hampered somewhat by the disarticulated nature of the assemblage.

Further extensive analysis was carried out to examine the nature of the bone within the cave, in order to evaluate the procedures that were involved in the deposition of the remains within the cave and whether any distinctive processes were apparent in this original deposition/s. Post-depositional alterations to the assemblage were also considered. This involved an examination of the condition and state of preservation of the individual bones and an assessment of the weights of bones recovered. In addition, the more substantial bone deposits were examined with a view to establishing the frequency of representation of the various bone types.

## Methodology

A disarticulated assemblage presents a unique challenge to the osteo-archaeologist. When the skeletal remains of a number of individuals are commingled, the problem of establishing the number of individuals represented in the sample becomes apparent. The most practical and widely used method is to count the numbers present of each bone type (for example, how many left proximal humeri are present) using a database and to suggest that the greatest number of any single bone present represents the minimum number of individuals (MNI) present in the sample. Once these figures are correlated with the age and sex profile of the sample, a more conclusive MNI may be reached (see Ubelaker 2002). Other methods of analysing the demography of commingled remains exist (*ibid.*), but the method described above was the most expedient with regard to this site.

This MNI is 'minimum' for a number of reasons. There are inherent biases within any excavated skeletal assemblage (see Haglund and Sorg 1997; 2002). There is an exceptionally wide variety of taphonomic factors to which human remains may be subject (see Fig. 1). This means that the final osteological sample may not represent the host population, either in terms of demographic profiles, health and disease or in terms of the processes involved in the ritual of deposition (Fig. 1).

The sex of adult individuals in this population was assessed by examining morphological traits: firstly, from the bones of the pelvis, and, secondly, from the skull (after Buiskstra and Ubelaker 1994, 16–20). In addition, metrical data were used (after Bass 1995). In certain instances (see below) consideration was also given to overall robustness of skeletal elements.

There is considerable debate regarding the reliability of sexing of sub-adult bones (see Scheuer and Black 2000). However, studies by Schutkowski (1993) indicate that certain traits, in sub-adult pelvic bones in particular, may be used in the determination of sex. Schutkowski's (*ibid.*) methods for determining the sex of sub-adult individuals were used in the present study in order to gain insight into the sex profile of sub-adults deposited in this cave, although it is acknowledged that these methods have yet to be fully tested.

The assessment of the age at death of adult individuals in Cloghermore Cave was based primarily on the degeneration of various skeletal elements, as well as on rates of epiphysial fusion (after Scheuer and Black 2000). These include morphological changes in the pubic symphysis (after Brooks and Suchey 1990) and changes in the auricular surface of the ilium (after Lovejoy *et al.* 1985). Rates of dental attrition were used where possible (after Brothwell 1981, 71–2), but the disarticulated nature of the assemblage militated against its extensive use. Adult ages at death were assigned to three categories: 'young adult', (17–<25 years), 'middle adult' (25–<45 years) and 'old adult' (45+ years).

The ages at death of the sub-adult population were determined on the analysis of dental remains, including calcification and eruption of teeth (after Moorrees *et al.* 1963a; 1963b; Ubelaker 1989, 64), and on assessment of the growth and fusion of bones (after Scheuer and Black 2000; Scheuer *et al.* 1980; Schwartz 1995). The ages at death of sub-adults can generally be more accurately determined

FIG. I
*Factors that can affect an archaeological skeletal assemblage (adapted from Waldron 1987, 56, fig. 6, and Mays 1998, 14, fig. 2.1 (after Meadow 1980)).*

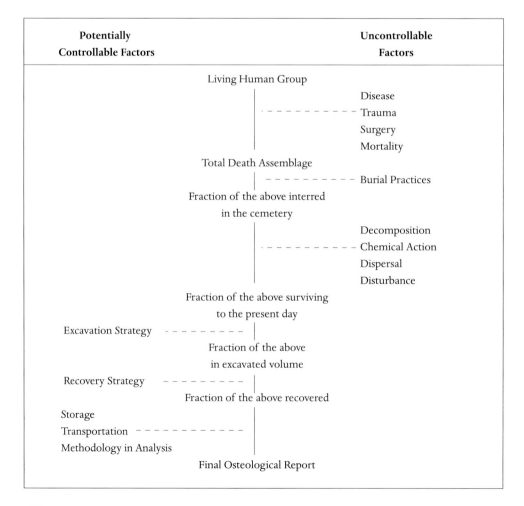

| Potentially Controllable Factors | | Uncontrollable Factors |
|---|---|---|
| | Living Human Group | |
| | | Disease |
| | — — — — — — — — | Trauma |
| | | Surgery |
| | | Mortality |
| | Total Death Assemblage | |
| | — — — — — — — — | Burial Practices |
| | Fraction of the above interred in the cemetery | |
| | | Decomposition |
| | — — — — — — — — | Chemical Action |
| | | Dispersal |
| | | Disturbance |
| | Fraction of the above surviving to the present day | |
| Excavation Strategy | — — — — — — — | |
| | Fraction of the above in excavated volume | |
| Recovery Strategy | — — — — — — — | |
| | Fraction of the above recovered | |
| Storage | | |
| Transportation | — — — — — — — — | |
| Methodology in Analysis | | |
| | Final Osteological Report | |

than adults, and these more specific data have been provided in the text where relevant. However, in some instances in the analysis the sub-adults have been grouped into broader age categories as follows: <1 year; 1–<6 years; 6–<12 years; 12–<17 years.

Finally, all complete long bones were measured in order to provide information on stature. The equations of Trotter (1970) were used in this regard. In addition, all teeth were recorded individually, and any dental diseases were noted, as well as any skeletal pathological lesions. All percentages in the analysis have been rounded to one decimal place.

The analysis of the well-preserved articulated adult male skeleton recovered from Area W was also undertaken using the methods outlined above.

A detailed discussion of the osteoarchaeological analysis is provided in this appendix, but the results are examined in their wider context in the main report in this volume.

## OSTEOLOGICAL ANALYSIS

### Demographic profiles

The MNI as established exclusively on bone counts for each of the main areas of the cave is provided in Table 2. This table also provides a total figure for the MNI of both adults and sub-adults from the entire combined cave, which includes excavated areas and bone recovered by potholers (location of recovery 'unknown').

There is an immediate disparity between the totals derived from the three primary divisions of the cave and the totals for the entire cave. This is due to the methods used to calculate the initial total MNI. It is based exclusively on bone counts with no consideration of the age at death or the sex of the individuals, or of the contexts of origin. In addition different bone elements gave the MNI from each of the three primary areas. Detailed analysis of the minimum

| Location | Adult | Sub-adult |
|---|---|---|
| Two-Star Chamber | 3 | 3 |
| Graveyard | 7 | 7 |
| Entrance Gallery | 5 | 6 |
| Total* | 13 | 12 |

* Total based on the combined results of bone counts.

TABLE 2—*Minimum number of individuals for each primary division and for the total assemblage, based exclusively on bone counts.*

number of individuals recovered in the various areas of the cave is provided below and is subdivided into adult and sub-adult individuals: as will be seen, the MNI totals vary quite dramatically.

### Adult demographic profiles

Table 3 shows the numbers of specific adult bones, and therefore the minimum number of adult individuals, recovered from the Two-Star Temple.

| Bone | Left | Right | Central/ unsided |
|------|------|-------|---------|
| **Long bones** | | | |
| Humerus, proximal | — | 1 | |
| Humerus, distal | 2 | 3 | |
| Ulna, proximal | 3 | 2 | |
| Ulna, distal | — | 1 | |
| Radius, proximal | 1 | — | |
| Radius, distal | — | — | |
| Femur, proximal | — | 1 | |
| Femur, distal | — | 1 | |
| Tibia, proximal | — | 1 | |
| Tibia, distal | 2 | — | |
| Fibula, proximal | — | 1 | |
| Fibula, distal | 1 | 1 | |
| **Irregular bones** | | | |
| Temporal | 1 | — | |
| Maxilla | — | — | |
| Mandible | — | 1 | |
| Clavicle, medial | 2 | 2 | |
| Clavicle, lateral | 3 | 2 | |
| Scapula | 2 | 1 | |
| Manubrium | | | — |
| Ilium | 1 | 1 | |
| Pubis | — | — | |
| Ischium | 1 | — | |
| Patella | — | — | |
| **Vertebrae** | | | |
| C1 | | | 1 |
| C2 | | | — |

TABLE 3—*Numbers of individuals as represented by adult bones recovered from the Two-Star Temple, all areas and contexts. Numbers in parentheses indicate actual numbers of bones recovered (adapted from Ubelaker 1974).*

| Bone | Left | Right | Central/ unsided |
|---|---|---|---|
| **Vertebrae** | | | |
| C3–C7 | | | 1 (5) |
| T1–T12 | | | 2 (17) |
| L1–L5 | | | 2 (7) |
| Sacrum | | | 1 |
| Coccyx | | | — |
| **Hand bones** | | | |
| Scaphoid | — | — | |
| Lunate | 1 | — | |
| Triquetral | — | 1 | |
| Pisiform | — | — | |
| Trapezium | — | — | |
| Trapezoid | — | — | |
| Capitate | — | 1 | |
| Hamate | — | — | |
| Metacarpal 1 | 1 | — | |
| Metacarpal 2 | — | — | |
| Metacarpal 3 | — | — | |
| Metacarpal 4 | — | — | |
| Metacarpal 5 | — | 1 | |
| Proximal phalanges 1–5 | | 1 (1) | |
| Intermediate phalanges 2–4 | | | — |
| Distal phalanges 1–5 | | | 1 (1) |
| **Foot bones** | | | |
| Calcaneus | 2 | 1 | |
| Talus | 1 | 1 | |
| Cuboid | — | 1 | |
| Navicular | — | 1 | |
| First cuneiform | 1 | — | |
| Second cuneiform | — | — | |
| Third cuneiform | — | — | |
| Metatarsal 1 | — | 1 | |
| Metatarsal 2 | — | 1 | |
| Metatarsal 4 | 1 | — | |
| Metatarsal 5 | — | — | |
| Proximal phalanges 1–5 | | | — |
| Intermediate phalanges 2–4 | | | — |
| Distal phalanges 1–5 | | | 1 (1) |

TABLE 3 (CONTD)—*Numbers of individuals as represented by adult bones recovered from the Two-Star Temple, all areas and contexts. Numbers in parentheses indicate actual numbers of bones recovered (adapted from Ubelaker 1974).*

The table above indicates that there were at least three adults in this area. It was possible to determine that at least one of these three individuals was female and another was male. It was not possible to confirm the sex of the third individual. The assessment of age at death for these individuals was hindered by the fragmentary and incomplete nature of the bones in the area. Although all preserved epiphyses were fully fused, indicating maturity, a single third upper molar indicated the presence of a young adult, but this evidence is inconclusive. Unfortunately, no other, more accurate indicators of age were available for analysis.

The numbers of adult bones recovered from the combined areas of the Graveyard and the Entrance Gallery (including the articulated skeleton) are given in Table 4. The greatest number recovered from

| Bone | Left | Right | Central/unsided |
|---|---|---|---|
| **Long bones** | | | |
| Humerus, proximal | 6 | 2 | |
| Humerus, distal | 3 | 7 | |
| Ulna, proximal | 8 | 9 | |
| Ulna, distal | 6 | 3 | |
| Radius, proximal | 7 | 5 | |
| Radius, distal | 8 | 5 | |
| Femur, proximal | 3 | 1 | |
| Femur, distal | 2 | 2 | |
| Tibia, proximal | 5 | 5 | |
| Tibia, distal | 6 | 3 | |
| Fibula, proximal | 2 | 1 | |
| Fibula, distal | 4 | 5 | |
| **Irregular bones** | | | |
| Temporal | 6 | 8 | |
| Maxilla | 2 | 2 | |
| Mandible | 6 | 4 | |
| Clavicle, medial | 6 | 3 | |
| Clavicle, lateral | 9 | 5 | |
| Scapula | 9 | 11 | |
| Manubrium | | | 5 |
| Ilium | 6 | 9 | |
| Pubis | 5 | 4 | |
| Ischium | 6 | 6 | |
| Patella | 4 | 5 | |

TABLE 4—*Numbers of individuals as represented by adult bones recovered from the Graveyard and the Entrance Gallery (including the articulated skeleton), all areas and contexts. Numbers in parentheses indicate actual number of bones recovered (adapted from Ubelaker 1974).*

| Bone | Left | Right | Central/unsided |
|---|---|---|---|
| **Vertebrae** | | | |
| C1 | | | 10 |
| C2 | | | 11 |
| C3–C7 | | | 4 (19) |
| T1–T12 | | | 6 (65) |
| L1–L5 | | | 7 (35) |
| Sacrum | | | 7 |
| Coccyx | | | 5 (5 first segments) |
| **Hand bones** | | | |
| Scaphoid | 1 | 2 | |
| Lunate | 3 | 2 | |
| Triquetral | — | 3 | |
| Pisiform | — | 1 | |
| Trapezium | 1 | 1 | |
| Trapezoid | 1 | 1 | |
| Capitate | 1 | 1 | |
| Hamate | 1 | 2 | |
| Metacarpal 1 | 2 | 3 | |
| Metacarpal 2 | 2 | 2 | |
| Metacarpal 3 | 4 | 1 | |
| Metacarpal 4 | 2 | 2 | |
| Metacarpal 5 | 3 | 4 | |
| Proximal phalanges 1–5 | | | 3 (30) |
| Intermediate phalanges 2–4 | | | 4 (25) |
| Distal phalanges 1–5 | | | 2 (20) |
| **Foot bones** | | | |
| Calcaneus | 7 | 7 | |
| Talus | 9 | 7 | |
| Cuboid | 5 | 4 | |
| Navicular | 3 | 6 | |
| First cuneiform | 5 | 4 | |
| Second cuneiform | 2 | 2 | |
| Third cuneiform | 3 | 4 | |
| Metatarsal 1 | 4 | 5 | |
| Metatarsal 2 | 7 | 3 | |
| Metatarsal 3 | 5 | 5 | |
| Metatarsal 4 | 7 | 3 | |
| Metatarsal 5 | 4 | 5 | |
| Proximal phalanges 1–5 | | | 3 (23) |
| Intermediate phalanges 2–4 | | | 1 (6) |
| Distal phalanges 1–5 | | | 1 (4) |

TABLE 4 (CONTD)—*Numbers of individuals as represented by adult bones recovered from the Graveyard and the Entrance Gallery (including the articulated skeleton), all areas and contexts. Numbers in parentheses indicate actual number of bones recovered (adapted from Ubelaker 1974).*

the combined areas is eleven right scapulae and eleven second cervical vertebrae, and therefore the minimum number of adults present is eleven. This broadly agrees with the MNI as established by the bone counts for the separate areas of the Graveyard and the Entrance Gallery in Table 2.

The age at death and sex of the adults from the Graveyard and Entrance Gallery were analysed to determine whether the MNI as provided by the bone count (Table 4) was an underestimation. However, owing to a variety of factors, the typical diagnostic assessors of age at death and sex were not available for examination. The information that was recorded on these basic demographic elements was therefore restricted.

In the area of the Graveyard there were at least three young adults, one of whom was female, one male and the other of undetermined sex. There were at least two middle adults in the Graveyard: one female and one male. Two teeth with severe attrition from the Graveyard suggest the presence of an old adult, but there is no other conclusive evidence. In addition to this demographic evidence, there are four each of the left and right temporals from female individuals, indicating that there are at least two more females of undetermined age at death.

Similar evidence is available from the area of the Entrance Gallery. There is a minimum of one young female adult, as well as at least one middle adult female and one middle adult male, in addition to the almost complete and articulated skeleton of a middle adult male. Also, a single fragment of hip bone, combined with dental evidence, indicates the presence of a single old adult of undetermined sex.

The correlation of the age at death and sex profiles with the bone counts indicates that there are two additional adults in the area of the Entrance Gallery and the Graveyard when the combined totals are considered (Table 5, compare with Table 2).

| Location | Age | | | | Total |
|---|---|---|---|---|---|
| | Young adult | Middle adult | Old adult | Adult of undetermined age | |
| Two-Star Temple | — | — | — | 3 (1F; 1M) | 3 |
| Graveyard | 3 (1F; 1M) | 2 (1F; 1M) | — | 2 (2F) | 7 |
| Entrance Gallery | 1 (F) | 3 (1F; 2M) | 1 | — | 5 |
| Total | 4 (2F; 1M) | 5 (2F; 3M) | 1 | 5 (3F; 1M) | 15 |

TABLE 5—*Final adult MNI (based on bone counts, age at death, and sex). Numbers identified by sex are in parentheses.*

*Sub-adult demographic profiles*

As noted earlier, much of the bone assemblage recovered from Cloghermore Cave was highly fragmented. All of the human bone recovered was separated into adult and sub-adult on the basis of the size and maturity of the skeletal element. However, it is possible that some adult bone has inadvertently been classed as sub-adult bone and vice versa. This is due to the differential fusion rates of a number of skeletal elements. For example, fusion of the medial end of the human clavicle may not be complete until 30 years, and the proximal fibula can fuse at any age between 12 years and 20 years (Scheuer and Black 2000, 251, 425). In general, however, it was clear from the size of the bone whether it was from an adult or a sub-adult individual. Therefore the figures provided in the descriptions below are presumed to be as accurate as is feasible with the sample in question. A similar process of examining the sub-adult bones is used here as with the adults.

The numbers of sub-adult individuals recovered from the Two-Star Temple as provided exclusively by bone counts are shown in Table 6.

| Bone | Left | Right | Central/unsided |
|---|---|---|---|
| **Long bones** | | | |
| Humerus, proximal | 1 | 1 | |
| Humerus, distal | 2 | 1 | |
| Ulna, proximal | 1 | — | |
| Ulna, distal | — | — | |
| Radius, proximal | — | 1 | |
| Radius, distal | — | — | |
| Femur, proximal | 3 | 3 | |
| Femur, distal | 3 | — | |
| Tibia, proximal | 1 | 1 | |
| Tibia, distal | 1 | — | |
| Fibula | | | 3 |
| **Irregular bones** | | | |
| Temporal | 2 | 2 | |
| Maxilla | — | 1 | |
| Mandible | 2 | 1 | |

TABLE 6—*Numbers of individuals as represented by sub-adult bones recovered from the Two-Star Temple, all areas and contexts. Numbers in parentheses indicate actual number of bones recovered (adapted from Ubelaker 1974).*

| Bone | Left | Right | Central/unsided |
|------|------|-------|-----------------|
| Clavicle, medial | I | 2 | |
| Clavicle, lateral | I | 2 | |
| Scapula | I | 2 | |
| Manubrium | | | — |
| Ilium | 2 | 2 | |
| Pubis | 2 | 2 | |
| Ischium | 2 | 3 | |
| Patella | I | — | |
| **Vertebrae** | | | |
| C1 | | | 2 |
| C2 | | | 2 |
| Cervical centra | | | 2 (9) |
| Cervical arches | 2 (7) | 2 (6) | |
| Thoracic centra | | | 2 (15) |
| Thoracic arches | 2 (14) | 2 (22) | |
| Lumbar centra | | | 2 (8) |
| Lumbar arches | 2 (6) | 2 (9) | |
| Sacral vertebrae | | | 2 (7) |
| Coccyx | | | — |
| **Hand bones** | | | |
| Carpals | | | I (I) |
| Metacarpals | | | I (I) |
| Phalanges | | | I (5) |
| **Foot bones** | | | |
| Calcaneus | I (I) | — | |
| Talus | I (I) | — | |
| Other tarsals | | | I (6) |
| Metatarsals | | | I (6) |
| Phalanges | | | I (2) |

TABLE 6 (CONTD)—*Numbers of individuals as represented by sub-adult bones recovered from the Two-Star Temple, all areas and contexts. Numbers in parentheses indicate actual number of bones recovered (adapted from Ubelaker 1974).*

The bone counts indicate that the minimum number of sub-adults in the Two-Star Temple is three (based on the femora and the ischia). However, further analysis of the sub-adult assemblage from this area indicates the presence of at least four individuals. This is determined from the age profile of the sample. A single femur represents a neonate, while dental remains clearly indicate the presence of three individuals whose ages at death were 4–6 years, 6–7 years and 9–10 years. Based on pelvic morphological traits, at least one of the latter two individuals was possibly a male child. It was not possible to determine the sex of any of the other sub-adults in the Two-Star Temple. The actual minimum number of sub-adults in the Two-Star Temple is therefore four individuals.

The minimum number of sub-adults as represented per diagnostic bone recovered from the Graveyard and Entrance Gallery combined is illustrated in Table 7. Again, these figures are based exclusively on bone counts.

| Bone | Left | Right | Central/unsided |
|---|---|---|---|
| **Long bones** | | | |
| Humerus, proximal | 4 | 5 | |
| Humerus, distal | 4 | 6 | |
| Ulna, proximal | 4 | 6 | |
| Ulna, distal | 2 | 5 | |
| Radius, proximal | 4 | 3 | |
| Radius, distal | 2 | 3 | |
| Femur, proximal | 5 | 6 | |
| Femur, distal | 3 | 4 | |
| Tibia, proximal | 6 | 5 | |
| Tibia, distal | 4 | 3 | |
| Fibula | | | 6 |
| **Irregular bones** | | | |
| Temporal | 5 | 3 | |
| Maxilla | 9 | 6 | |
| Mandible | 6 | 4 | |
| Clavicle, medial | 4 | 3 | |
| Clavicle, lateral | 5 | 6 | |
| Scapula | 5 | 5 | |
| Manubrium | | | 1 |
| Ilium | 8 | 6 | |
| Pubis | 2 | 3 | |
| Ischium | 6 | 6 | |
| Patella | | | 1 |
| **Vertebrae** | | | |
| C1 | | | 6 |
| C2 | | | 9 |

TABLE 7—*Numbers of individuals as represented by sub-adult bones recovered from the Graveyard and the Entrance Gallery, all areas and contexts. Numbers in parentheses indicate actual numbers of bones recovered (adapted from Ubelaker 1974).*

| Bone | Left | Right | Central/unsided |
|------|------|-------|-----------------|
| Cervical centra | | | 3 (15) |
| Cervical arches | 4 (17) | 3 (15) | |
| Thoracic centra | | | 4 (38) |
| Thoracic arches | 5 (54) | 5 (55) | |
| Lumbar centra | | | 4 (19) |
| Lumbar arches | 4 (18) | 4 (20) | |
| Sacral vertebrae | | | 3 (14) |
| Coccyx | | | — |
| **Hand bones** | | | |
| Carpals | | | — |
| Metacarpals | | | 1 (8) |
| Phalanges | | | 2 (16) |
| **Foot bones** | | | |
| Calcaneus | 4 | 6 | |
| Talus | 4 | 4 | |
| Other tarsals | | | 1 (2) |
| Metatarsals | | | 2 (17) |
| Phalanges | | | 1 (5) |

TABLE 7 (CONTD)—*Numbers of individuals as represented by sub-adult bones recovered from the Graveyard and the Entrance Gallery, all areas and contexts. Numbers in parentheses indicate actual numbers of bones recovered (adapted from Ubelaker 1974).*

The combined bone count from the Graveyard and Entrance Gallery indicates that there were at least nine sub-adults in this area, based on the left maxilla and the second cervical vertebra. Seven of the nine maxillae were retrieved from the Graveyard. The ages at death of these seven individuals are as follows: one infant (*c.* 6 months), one individual aged 1–3 years, two individuals aged 3–5 years, one individual aged 4–5 years, one individual aged 7–8 years, and one individual aged 8–9 years. The additional two maxillae from the area of the Entrance Gallery represent one child aged *c.* 2 years and one child aged 1–3 years at the time of death. However, in addition to this MNI of nine sub-adults, there is clear skeletal and dental evidence of a neonate individual in the Entrance Gallery. Furthermore, a single vertebral fragment of a foetal human was recovered from the Entrance Gallery. There is no substantial evidence of any other sub-adults in these areas. Therefore the actual minimum number of individuals from the combined areas of the Graveyard and the Entrance Gallery is eleven.

The ilia of the infants—the infant from the Graveyard and the neonate from the Entrance Gallery—are morphologically female. In addition, one right ilium from a young male child (1–6 years) was recovered from the Entrance Gallery, and a right and a left ilium from a young male child (1–6 years) were identified from the Graveyard.

The final MNI of the sub-adult individuals is given below in Table 8. If this is compared with Table 2, it is apparent that some numbers differ: primarily through the increase in individuals in the Two-Star Temple (because of the inclusion of another infant, not recognised through bone counts alone) and the decrease in individuals in the Entrance Gallery (see note, Table 8). However, the total number of sub-adult individuals of all areas increased from twelve to fifteen from the initial counts through detailed correlation of bone counts with age at death profiles in particular.

| Location | Age | | | | MNI |
|---|---|---|---|---|---|
| | <1 year | 1–<6 years | 6–<12 years | 12–<17 years | |
| Two-Star Temple | 1 | 1 | 2 (1M) | — | 4 |
| Graveyard | 1 (F) | 4 (1M) | 2 | — | 7 |
| Entrance Gallery | 2 (1F) | 2 (1M) | — | — | 4* |
| Total | 4 (2F) | 7 (2M) | 4 (1M) | — | 15 |

\* If the Graveyard and the Entrance Gallery are considered completely separately, the MNI for the Entrance Gallery rises to 7 on the basis of six distal right humeri and foetal remains. However, to ensure accuracy in the analysis of these two areas, which are inextricably linked, the same skeletal elements were used to calculate the MNI, excepting the clear evidence of foetal/infant remains as described in the text.

TABLE 8—*Final sub-adult MNI (based on bone counts, age at death, and sex). Numbers identified by sex are in parentheses.*

*Demographic profiles of specific areas*
The presence of isolated deposits of bone within the Graveyard and primarily the Entrance Gallery has already been noted. These include the Graveyard (excluding Area Z), Area Z in the Graveyard, and Areas X, U, W, V and T and the entrance shaft within the Entrance Gallery. These areas have been described in detail in the main report, particularly with regard to the finds retrieved from them. The physical separateness of all of these smaller areas within the confines of the larger chambers, combined with the information on the finds

recovered, warrants an examination of the demographic profile of the bone deposits within them. It is unlikely, given the interpreted and known history of the cave, that at the time of excavation these bone deposits were preserved precisely as deposited in antiquity. However, areas such as Area Z, the pit in Area V, Area T and Area W are more obviously isolated from the main bone deposits and appear to be clearly distinct areas. It is clear that in all cases, however, there has been sporadic intermixing, by whatever method, with the adjoining larger deposits of bone. In no instance was a complete skeleton recovered from any of these sub-areas (excepting the articulated male adult in Area W). It is highly probable that portions of the individuals contained within these areas have been intermingled, either via taphonomic factors or through human intervention, with the bones in the larger areas of the cave and vice versa.

THE GRAVEYARD (EXCLUDING AREA Z)
The isolated position of Area Z within the Graveyard dictated the necessity to assess the demographic profiles of both of these areas independently. The bone counts of the adult remains recovered from the Graveyard (excluding Area Z) is six adults. This is confirmed by analysis of the age and sex profile of the sample. There are at least three females (one young adult, one middle adult and one adult of undetermined age at death) and two males (one young adult and one middle adult). In addition, two teeth suggest the presence of an older adult, but this evidence is inconclusive as the wear pattern may have occurred as a result of unusual mastication habits. The total weight of adult bone recovered from the Graveyard (excluding Area Z) was 6307g. All of the body parts were relatively well represented, with cranial bones at 12.1 per cent, torso bones at 29.3 per cent and limb bones at 58.6 per cent by weight, and there is no evidence of selective deposition within this area.

The MNI of the sub-adult bone from the Graveyard (excluding Area Z) is seven individuals (seven left maxillae). As noted above (see demographic profiles), the ages at death of these seven individuals are estimated as one infant (c. 6 months), one individual aged 1–3 years, two individuals aged 3–5 years, one individual aged 4–5 years, one individual aged 7–8 years and one individual aged 8–9 years. There is no evidence of further sub-adults in this area. The total weight of bone recovered was 1965g. All of the skeletal elements were well represented, with cranial remains at 31.2 per cent, torso fragments at 26.7 per cent and limb bones at 42.1 per cent.

AREA Z

In Area Z of the Graveyard there were the remains of at least two adults, one aged 33–45 years and the other aged 17–25 years at the time of death. At least one of these individuals was female, but it was not possible to ascertain which. A total of 699g of adult bone was recovered from Area Z. Based on bone weight, the adult skeletons comprised 26.9 per cent cranial, 32.8 per cent torso and 40.3 per cent limb remains. These figures compare with the expected rates of recovery of 18.2 per cent cranial, 23.1 per cent torso and 58.7 per cent limb remains (McKinley 1989, 68). Although there does not appear to be any significant bias toward the inclusion or exclusion of any of the main body parts in Area Z, it is apparent that the 699g of adult bone recovered is not representative of the complete deposition of two adult skeletons (given that the weight of the incomplete articulated skeleton from Area W was 2106g). This suggests that there may have been some form of selected deposition within this area.

The bone count of the sub-adult remains indicates a minimum of two individuals. However, the dental remains clearly indicate the remains of at least three individuals. One individual was 2–3 years, one was 5–6 years, and the third was 9–10 years at the time of death. It was not possible to determine the sex of any of these individuals. The total weight of sub-adult bone recovered was 120g; 86.7 per cent comprised cranial remains, and the remainder consisted of vertebral and hip fragments, with hand phalanges represented by just 1g of bone. This suggests that there was a deliberate attempt to include primarily sub-adult cranial remains in this area, although none of the latter remains could be considered complete.

It is unlikely that there was significant mixing between this area and that of the main Graveyard, and the recovered deposits may be representative of the original pattern of deposition.

AREA X

In Area X of the Entrance Gallery the adult bone counts indicate the remains of a minimum of two individuals (two left mandibles): one a female aged 17–25 years, and the other a male aged 25–35 years at the time of death. The total weight of adult bone recovered from this area was 626g, comprising 13.9 per cent cranial, 60.3 per cent torso and 25.8 per cent limb remains. When these figures are compared with the expected rates of recovery (18.2 per cent, 23.1 per cent and 58.7 per cent respectively; McKinley 1989, 68), it is apparent that the torso in particular is dominant in the adult bone sample from this area and that the limbs are under-represented. As with Area Z, examined above, it is evident that 626g is not representative of two complete adult individuals. It is noted also that the position of Area X within the cave is on the direct line of access to the cave from the entrance shaft. In this regard it is probable that this area was used for a time as an access route to the lower chambers of the cave. It is difficult to determine whether the bones recovered from here are representative of deliberate deposition or piling of bones in one of the final uses of the cave with the deposition of the male adult burial in Area W. However, the sub-adult bones reveal some interesting information regarding the origin of the sample in Area X.

The sub-adult bone count from this area indicated the remains of at least two individuals. However, analysis of the age profile of the sub-adults revealed the presence of two individuals aged 1–3 years at the time of death (two left maxillae), one individual aged 8–10 years (right maxilla) and a neonate (the well-preserved remains of a female). Therefore the sub-adult remains in Area X represent at least four individuals. The total weight of sub-adult bone recovered from Area X was 336g. Cranial bones comprised 42.4 per cent of the total sub-adult bone recovered, which suggests that there may have been deliberate deposition of sub-adult cranial remains in this area. The inherent problems in the interpretation of this area have been mentioned above. However, the well-preserved remains of a neonate individual were recovered from Area X: none of these bones were damaged post-mortem, in comparison to virtually all of the other skeletal remains recovered from this area and indeed from the cave in general (with the exception of the articulated adult in Area W). Although it is difficult to interpret the nature or origin of deposition of the human bones within this area of access, the foetal remains may have been among the last to be deposited in the cave, given the excellent preservation of the bones.

AREA U

Bone counts indicated a minimum of two adults in this area. From the dental remains there was evidence of one individual aged 25–35 years and another individual aged 45+ years at the time of death. However, there was skeletal evidence of two female adults (two right distal humeri) and a male adult, giving a minimum number of three adults. The total weight of adult bone recovered from Area U was 1276g. Cranial remains comprised 4.5 per cent of the total adult bone from this area, the torso 46.2 per cent, and the limbs 49.3 per cent.

When compared with the expected rates of 18.2 per cent, 23.1 per cent and 58.7 per cent (McKinley 1989, 68), this suggests significant under-representation of cranial bones and over-representation of torso elements.

A small number of sub-adult bones were recovered from Area U. The bone count indicates a minimum of two individuals; this is not contradicted by analysis of the ages at death and the sex of the individuals. Dental remains indicate that these individuals were aged 1–3 years and 7–9 years at the time of death. It was not possible to determine the sex of these individuals. The total weight of sub-adult bone recovered was 333g; cranial remains comprised 9.9 per cent, and torso was represented by 55.3 per cent. This suggests that there may have been a bias toward the exclusion of sub-adult cranial remains from this area and the inclusion of torso elements. However, there are inherent problems in examining rates of representation by weight of sub-adult remains, which are examined in more detail below with regard to the analysis of bone weights. It was also apparent that most of the sub-adult remains recovered from this area were from the younger child, with all skeletal elements represented. In comparison, the older child was represented only by a small number of teeth, some torso remains and lower limb fragments. Again, a certain degree of selective deposition is apparent in this sub-adult sample, but it is possible that virtually the complete remains of the younger child were deposited here. Indeed, during the excavation the arm and part of the vertebral column of this individual were recovered in an articulated position, in contrast to most of the human bone fragments in the immediate area.

AREA W

In Area W the bone count indicates that, in addition to the remains of the articulated male adult, there was one other male adult. Two single teeth suggest that the ages at death of these individuals may be 17–25 years and 25–35 years, but this evidence is insufficient because the teeth may be from a single individual (including the articulated male adult) and the different wear patterns may be a result of factors such as mastication habits. A total of 2521g of adult bone was recovered from Area W (including the articulated skeleton). The articulated skeleton comprised 83.5 per cent (2106g) of the total adult bone. Cranial remains comprised just 0.1 per cent of the sample, the torso 43.4 per cent, and the limbs 56.5 per cent. Clearly, cranial remains are virtually absent while torso remains are over-represented. There is substantial evidence of the remains of another male in the area but certainly not in an articulated state. Given that the disarticulated bone in Area W comprises just 415g (16.5 per cent of the total), the remains of this additional adult are quite incomplete. The disarticulated remains also showed biases toward particular skeletal elements. Hand and foot bones comprised 21.9 per cent of the disarticulated bone; scapula, vertebrae and ribs comprised 40.5 per cent; and arm bones comprised 25.3 per cent. This indicates a clear bias in the disarticulated sample toward the deposition of the torso, arms, and hands and feet (negligible portions of these bones were absent from the articulated skeleton).

A tiny amount of sub-adult bone—just five fragments, weighing a total of 5g—was retrieved from Area W. The bone count indicated an MNI of one individual. However, the vertebral remains indicated an individual aged 1–3 years at the time of death while a single tooth represented an individual aged 6–7 years. It was not possible to determine the sex of either of these individuals. These sub-adult remains should be considered as intrusive elements within this area.

AREA V

In the pit in Area V a very small quantity of adult bone was recovered, indicating an MNI of one, an adult of undetermined sex and age at death. Six of the ten fragments  recovered were foot phalanges, which—on the basis of size and colour—appear to be from the same individual. The total weight of adult bone recovered from the pit was 12g. The small size of the sample may initially appear to indicate that it was intrusive; however, the pit was a sealed context, and the likelihood of the bones accidentally being included in the sample is small. The foot phalanges are from a single individual. In addition, one cranial fragment, fragments of at least one rib, and a single vertebral fragment were recovered (the last displayed evidence of the pathological condition spondylolysis). It is possible that the remains were deliberately deposited in the pit, where the primary bone deposits consisted of sub-adult remains.

The sub-adult bone count from the pit in Area V indicated an MNI of one. The bones were almost exclusively (87.8 per cent) from the torso of a young child. However, additional sub-adult remains were recovered through the examination of four metatarsals recovered from the pit. These bones indicated the presence of two young individuals (1–6 years) and one older sub-adult (7–12 years). Vertebral remains indicated that one of the younger individuals was aged 1–3 years at the time of death. It was not possible to determine the sex of any of these individuals. The total weight of sub-adult bone from the pit was 42g.

In summary, the human remains from Area V consisted almost exclusively of a child's torso (aged 1–3 years at the time of death); additional individuals—at least one adult, one child aged 1–6 years and one child aged 7–12 years—were represented almost exclusively by foot bones.

## AREA T

The remains of at least two adults (two right ilia) were recovered from Area T. At least one of these was aged 35–39 years at the time of death, and at least one was female. A total weight of 331g of adult bone was recovered from Area T. No cranial remains were recovered; the torso comprised 57.7 per cent of the bone, and the limbs 42.3 per cent. This indicates that cranial elements may have been deliberately excluded from this area. In addition, the total bone weight of 331g is clearly not representative of two complete adult skeletons.

The sub-adult bone count from Area T indicated an MNI of one. However, further examination revealed the remains of another sub-adult: a single left neural arch of a thoracic vertebra of a foetus was also recovered. Although it is not possible to determine accurately the age at death of this individual, the size of the bone indicates a mature but not full-term foetus. The majority of the sub-adult remains recovered from this shelf are those of an individual aged 6–8 years at the time of death. It was not possible to determine the sex of this individual. The total weight of bone recovered was 116g, comprising 23.3 per cent cranial, 37.9 per cent torso and 38.8 per cent limb remains.

## ENTRANCE SHAFT

The bone counts from the entrance shaft gave an MNI of two adults, which is confirmed by an examination of age and sex profile. Left hip fragments indicate the remains of at least one female aged 30–34 years at the time of death. Further left hip fragments, in addition to scapulae and a humerus fragment, indicate the remains of a male individual aged 22–35 years at the time of death. A total weight of 1266g of adult bone was recovered from the entrance shaft, comprising 0.9 per cent cranial, 43.5 per cent torso and 55.6 per cent limb remains. Cranial remains are under-represented while torso fragments are over-represented, suggesting deliberate selection. The total weight of bone is not representative of two complete adult skeletons.

Thirteen fragments of sub-adult bone were recovered from the entrance shaft, the bone count indicating an MNI of one. Examination of the age profile of the recovered bones indicated the remains of one individual (aged 6–12 years) represented by a variety of bones: cranial (8.1 per cent), torso (23 per cent) and limb (68.9 per cent). A single tooth represented the remains of a child aged 2–3 years. The minimum number of sub-adults recovered from within the entrance shaft is therefore two. It was not possible to determine the sex of either of these individuals. The total weight of sub-adult bone recovered from the entrance shaft was 122g. It seems probable that the remains of the younger child (2–3 years) were intrusive within this sample of sub-adult bones.

Given that the shaft had been deliberately backfilled, it is possible that the skeletal remains were deliberately selected and included in the fill as disarticulated remains. Excavation of the ground surface of the exterior of the entrance shaft revealed just four human bones: three adult fibulae fragments and an unsided distal half of a tibia from a possible neonate. This suggests that human remains were uncommon on the ground surface surrounding the entrance to the cave and that care was taken to deposit all bones within the cave.

A summary of the demographic profiles for each individual area within the cave system is given in Table 9.

*Summary of demographic profiles*
Fifteen adults and fifteen sub-adults were identified from the cave. Of the adults whose ages at death could be determined, 90 per cent were aged between 17 and 45 years. A clear concentration of individuals aged less than 6 years at the time of death was apparent, with 36.7 per cent of the total population aged in this category.

The sex profile of the population is more complex, and it was not always possible to correlate an individual whose age at death could be determined with their sex. It was possible to determine the sex of twelve of the fifteen adults (Table 10). It was possible to determine the sex of only four of the fifteen sub-adults. There were at least two female infants (including one neonate) and two young male children (1–<6 years).

**Stature**
Thirteen complete adult long bones were recovered from the entire cave, as well as five that were sent for radiocarbon dating. The lengths of the five long bones sent for dating (see Table 1) were not

| Location | Adult MNI | Adult bone weight (g) | Sub-adult MNI | Sub-adult bone weight (g) |
|---|---|---|---|---|
| Graveyard (excluding Area Z) | 6<br>3F (YA, MA, AA),<br>2M (YA, MA), other ? | 6307 | 7<br>infant (c. 6 months);<br>1–3 years; 3–5 years x 2;<br>4–5 years; 7–8 years;<br>8–9 years | 1965 |
| Area Z | 2<br>1F age?<br>1YA, 1MA | 699 | 3<br>(2–3 years; 5–6 years;<br>9–10 years) | 120 |
| Area X | 2<br>1F (YA), 1M (MA) | 626 | 4<br>(female neonate;<br>1–3 years x 2; 8–10 years) | 336 |
| Area U | 3<br>2F, 1M<br>(1MA, 1OA, other ?) | 1276 | 2<br>(1–3 years; 7–9 years) | 333 |
| Area W | 2<br>2M (MA (articulated); other?) | 2521 | 2<br>(1–3 years; 6–7 years) | 5 |
| Area V | 1<br>MA | 12 | 3<br>(1–3 years; 1–6 years;<br>7–12 years) | 42 |
| Area T | 2<br>1F, 1MA | 331 | 2<br>(foetus; 6–8 years) | 116 |
| Entrance shaft | 2<br>1F (MA), 1M (MA) | 1266 | 2<br>(2–3 years; 6–12 years) | 122 |

TABLE 9 —*Summary of demographic analysis of specific areas within the cave. YA = young adult; MA = middle adult; OA = old adult; AA = adult, age undetermined.*

| Sex | Age at death | | | |
|---|---|---|---|---|
| | Young adult | Middle adult | Old adult | Adult of undetermined age |
| Female | 2 | 2 | — | 3 |
| Male | 1 | 3 | — | 1 |

TABLE 10—*Sex profile of the adult population.*

recorded. Seven of the thirteen bones measured with regard to stature are from the single articulated burial recovered from Area W (Table 11). Table 11 also provides details of the estimated stature from each of the thirteen long bones. An estimated stature is provided for each of the complete long bones from the articulated skeleton, but the actual estimated stature of this individual—as used in the data below—is based on the tibia, as this bone is considered the most reliable indicator of stature (after Bass 1995).

| Area | Bone | Side | Sex | Length (mm) | Estimated stature (cm) |
|------|------|------|-----|-------------|------------------------|
| Two-Star Temple | Ulna | R | ? | 246 | 165.1–162.8 |
| Graveyard | Ulna | L | M | 254 | 168.0±4.32 |
| Graveyard | Radius | L | ? | 231 | 166.3–164.4 |
| Graveyard | Radius | L | F | 205 | 152.1±4.24 |
| Entrance Gallery | Humerus | L | M (artic.) | 308 | 165.3±4.05 |
| Entrance Gallery | Humerus | R | M (artic.) | 316 | 167.8±4.05 |
| Entrance Gallery | Ulna | R | M (artic.) | 266 | 172.5±4.32 |
| Entrance Gallery | Ulna | L | M | 251 | 166.9±4.32 |
| Entrance Gallery | Radius | L | M (artic.) | 240 | 169.7±4.32 |
| Entrance Gallery | Radius | R | M (artic.) | 248 | 172.8±4.32 |
| Entrance Gallery | Radius | L | M | 233 | 167.1±4.32 |
| Entrance Gallery | Tibia | L | M (artic.) | 353 | 167.6±3.37 |
| Entrance Gallery | Fibula | L | M (artic.) | 347 | 164.8±3.29 |

TABLE 11—*Intact adult long bones recovered by area, plus stature estimate (after Trotter 1970); artic. = from the articulated burial in Area W.*

It was possible to estimate the stature of a single adult female from the cave. The estimated height was 152.1cm (from the left radius). The average statures of females from the Early Christian sites of Solar, Co. Antrim, and Kilshane, Co. Dublin, were 157cm and 160cm (L. Buckley, pers. comm.), suggesting that the female from Cloghermore was considerably smaller than her contemporaries. However, it is important to note that the upper limb bones are not the most reliable indicators of living stature (after Bass 1995). In addition, there may be considerable variation in stature within any population, and a single individual may not necessarily be representative of a host population.

Male height estimates ranged from 166.9cm (left ulna from the Entrance Gallery) to 168.0cm (left ulna from the Graveyard) and averaged 167.4cm (when the left tibia was taken as representing the height of the articulated male). The average statures of males from the Early Christian sites of Solar, Co. Antrim, and Kilshane, Co. Dublin, were 171cm and 173cm (L. Buckley, pers. comm.), indicating that—as with the single female above—the males from this site were shorter than their contemporaries. However, similar problems to those encountered with the female stature estimate above should be taken into account here. Only disarticulated upper limb bones were available in the estimation of the statures of both the males and the female, which are not the most reliable indicators of either sex or stature.

## Dental remains

All of the teeth recovered from the cave were recorded individually, and pathologies were also noted. A total of 141 adult teeth and 194 sub-adult teeth were recovered. The former consist exclusively of fully matured permanent teeth, and the latter include both erupted and unerupted deciduous teeth and immature permanent teeth. The majority of the teeth were recovered loose, but some were still *in situ* in the mandible or maxilla. No dental remains were recovered in an articulated state within a distinct burial, which obviously hampers the dental analysis. However, all instances of the main dental diseases were recorded, and the information regarding the adult teeth is summarised below (Table 12).

| Disease | Teeth | |
|---|---|---|
| | n | % |
| Calculus | 96 | 68.1 |
| Caries | 10 | 7.1 |
| Enamel hypoplasia | 7 | 5.0 |

TABLE 12—*Dental disease in recorded adult teeth.*

The disarticulated nature of the assemblage militates against any attempt to analyse frequencies of dental diseases in the adult individuals. However, the results are given here as they may give some indications of the oral health of the host population.

Deposits of calculus were especially evident on the adult dental remains, with 68.1 per cent of teeth affected. Calculus, which is calcified or mineralised plaque, is a common finding on archaeological remains. The aetiology is multi-causal, but its formation is aided by alkaline in the mouth and a high-protein diet (Lieverse 1999). The high proportion of teeth with calculus in the sample suggests at least a diet high in protein. However, aspects such as poor oral hygiene should also be considered.

The prevalence of carious lesions (cavities in the enamel) in the adult population is relatively low, just 7.1 per cent (no dental caries were recorded on sub-adult teeth). The frequency of dental caries has increased over time, particularly with the increased consumption of refined sugars from the post-medieval period onward. Sugars are known to be cariogenic (Hillson 1986, 293; Woodward and Walker 1994). There is also some evidence to suggest that carbohydrates may be a contributory factor, although this is not certain (Hillson 1986, 293). In studies of the prevalence of dental caries (by tooth) in early medieval, medieval and post-medieval Irish populations, rates of 3.9 per cent, 4.2 per cent and 8.7 per cent respectively were recorded (Power 1994, 101). Again, however, the disarticulated nature of the Cloghermore sample does not allow viable comparisons to be made. This is unfortunate, given that the recorded rates of carious lesions in the Cloghermore population appear broadly comparable to data from the post-medieval period in Ireland, although evidence indicates that the use of the cave centres on the period AD 700–1000.

A very small number of teeth had the pits and/or lines indicative of enamel hypoplasia. These defects occur when there is a disturbance to the growth of the organic matrix during childhood, which later becomes mineralised to form enamel. A large variety of diseases and nutritional deficiencies can cause this anomaly (Hillson 1986; Mays 1998, 156). Again, its prevalence in this population cannot be properly assessed; suffice to say that at least some individuals had suffered from physiological stresses in childhood.

A total of 24 of the sub-adult teeth had deposits of calculus, and five teeth had enamel hypoplastic defects. It was impractical to attempt to quantify these in relation to the overall numbers of sub-adult teeth recovered.

## Skeletal pathological conditions

A limited number of skeletal pathological lesions were observed. Degenerative joint disease (DJD) was the most common, followed by traumatic lesions and infectious diseases. Metabolic disease was also recorded.

Although DJD was the most commonly observed pathological lesion, it was confined to adult individuals. DJD is a non-inflammatory disease, involving—in simplest terms—the degeneration of the articular cartilage of various joints. This degeneration can allow a variety of bony manifestations to develop, and it is these bony changes that are frequently observed on skeletal remains. The disease is strongly related to age, although other influences may be involved in its development and/or progress, including trauma and obesity. The vertebral bones were those most frequently affected in the Cloghermore population, and the lesions included osteophytes, porosity, a single case of eburnation, Schmorl's nodes and a single example of intervertebral osteochondrosis. Schmorl's nodes are pressure defects in the superior or inferior surfaces of the vertebral disc. They are caused by a herniation of the gelatinous core of the intervertebral disc and are believed to result from falls or from lifting heavy objects incorrectly (Mann and Murphy 1990, 52; Rodgers and Waldron 1995, 27). Intervertebral osteochondrosis (crescent-shaped depressions on the superior or inferior surfaces of the vertebral disc) are thought to have a similar aetiology to Schmorl's nodes (Coughlan and Holst 2000, 68). Evidence of DJD was observed on the cervical through to the sacral vertebrae and affected both intervertebral discs and apophyseal joints. The vertebrae in the cave were particularly fragmented, which does not allow for accurate assessment of the rates of DJD; however, the numbers of fragments with DJD were recorded. Two cervical fragments were affected, and the disease was confined to the bodies. Thirteen thoracic vertebral fragments had evidence of DJD, and both the arches and the bodies were involved. Schmorl's nodes were also present on a number of thoracic fragments. Twelve lumbar fragments had evidence of DJD, manifested in a similar way to that observed in the thoracic vertebrae. Two sacrums had DJD, one of which was affected by eburnation, which is indicative of osteoarthritis (Rodgers and Waldron 1995, 13). In addition porosity was observed on the distal epiphysis of a proximal foot phalanx and on the lateral end of a clavicle. Owing to a number of factors (disarticulated assemblage, fragmentation, small MNI), it was not possible to quantify the prevalence of this disease in this population.

A number of bone fragments exhibited traumatic lesions. A non-union fracture was observed on the rib shaft of an adult, 30mm medial to the lateral end of the shaft. Extensive deposits of callus bone (fibrous repair bone) were observed, particularly on the lateral fracture site. This indicates that the bone was in the process of healing, but, possibly owing to the lack of or incomplete immobilisation of the ribs of this individual, the repair process was not complete at the time of death. The average duration of healing of the ribs is 6 weeks (Schlosser 1968), which suggests that the injury occurred quite close to the time of death. The intermediate and distal foot phalanges of an adult are fused, which may have been caused by a traumatic episode.

In addition, there are at least two lumbar vertebrae with evidence of a condition known as spondylolysis. This condition involves a separation between the laminae, spinous process and inferior articular facets and the remainder of the vertebrae, typically at the pars interarticularis, and is most common in the lower lumbar vertebrae (Aufderheide and Rodríguez-Martín 1998, 63). The aetiology of this condition is not certain, but it appears to be linked to a genetic predisposition and/or particularly to fractures caused by biomechanical stresses (*ibid.*; Merbs 1996, 357; Arriaza 1997). One of the affected lumbar vertebrae was recovered from the Graveyard (Pl. I), and a single fragment of a superior articular facet and of an inferior articular facet with evidence of spondylolysis were recovered from the Graveyard and from Area V respectively. The latter two fragments represent an actual minimum of one vertebra. However, the fragments with spondylolysis may actually represent one, two or three individuals, of a minimum of fifteen adults from the cave, affected with the condition (representing rates of 6.7 per cent, 13.3 per cent and 20 per cent respectively). The condition is found in 4–8 per cent of

PL. I
*Spondylolysis; fifth lumbar from the Graveyard (superior and posterior view).*

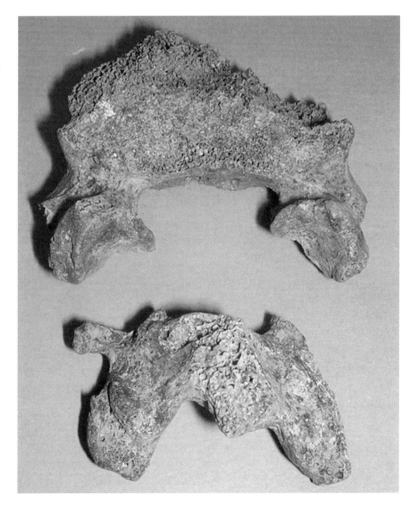

modern populations (Aufderheide and Rodríguez-Martín 1998, 63). The incidence of the condition in the Cloghermore population may either fall within the normal expected modern range or be higher than normal; however, the very incomplete nature of the vertebral remains from the cave significantly hampers this interpretation. At least one of the lumbar vertebrae affected with this condition was a fifth lumbar. It was not possible to identify accurately the other lumbar vertebra(e).

A single traumatic lesion was also observed on the articulated remains of the male from Area W. The distal two-thirds of the left radius were displaced posteriorly, indicating the site of a healed fracture. The left radius was slightly shorter than the right (240mm, compared to 248mm), presumably as a result of this fracture, and there was a compensatory superior extension to the articular facet of the distal ulna. This healed fracture is a classic manifestation of a Colles fracture, which results from a forward fall when the individual extends the arms in an attempt to minimise injury (Ortner and Putschar 1981, 58).

Finally, a single bone fragment from the Two-Star Temple had evidence of sharp-force trauma. A fragment of the neck of an adult right femur exhibited a sharp, narrow, linear cut (a maximum of 0.5mm wide) running for a length of 12mm obliquely across the interior surface of the femoral neck (Pl. 2). The colour and sharp margins of the edges of the lesion (combined with parallel grooves observed by Chamberlain and Witkin 2000, 13), and indeed the fact that it is unique within the assemblage, indicate that it occurred as a result of deliberate sharp-force trauma to the individual rather than taphonomic factors after disposal or deliberate defleshing of the corpse. There is no evidence of healing, and therefore the injury

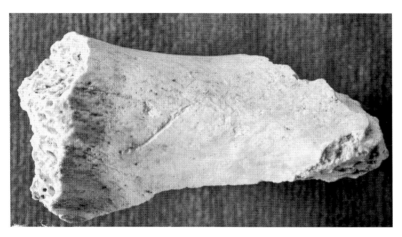

PL. 2
*Sharp-force trauma; right femur from the Two-Star Temple (view of inferior neck).*

occurred at or around the time of death. The position of the injury indicates that a significant amount of major muscle tissue, as well as the femoral artery, was severed. It is probable that the lesion occurred as a result of a violent encounter, presumably with a sword or an axe.

Periosteal lesions were identified on a small number of bone fragments. Periostitis 'usually represents part of, or a reaction to, pathological changes to the underlying bone' (Ortner and Putschar 1981, 129). The condition is most frequently associated with inflammatory processes linked with various infections, both specific and non-specific; however, its manifestation is not restricted to infection (Ortner 2003, 206) The bone may be deposited as a result of an inflammation of the periosteum, which directly overlies the bone surface. The accumulation of pus raises the periosteum, which allows for the deposition of new fibrous bone underneath. Periostitis was observed on the shaft of a left fifth adult metatarsal and two long-bone fragments. This condition was also observed on the anterior mid-shaft of the right tibia of a young child (4.5–5.5 years). Extensive bony growths, sclerotic in nature, were observed in the right frontal sinus of at least one adult and are suggestive of sinusitis (after Armentano et al. 1999; Roberts and Manchester 1995; Aufderheide and Rodríguez-Martín 1998, 257). The extensive nature of the deposits indicates a long-standing condition.

Evidence of metabolic disease was also observed on some of the bone fragments. Healed porotic lesions were recorded on three adult cranial vault fragments, and at least three left (three/four observable left) and one right (one/two observable right) orbits of sub-adult individuals also displayed porotic lesions that were still active at the time of death. The lesions indicate the conditions known as porotic hyperostosis (cranial lesions) and cribra orbitalia (orbital lesions) respectively. The condition is related to an attempt by the marrow-rich bones to increase the output of iron, which results in the expansion of the middle layer of the bone and the thinning of the outer surface of the bone (Stuart-Macadam 1991; Roberts and Manchester 1995); this process can manifest in the type of lesions on the remains from Cloghermore Cave. Although the lesions may be linked to iron-deficiency anaemia, there is substantial evidence that they may also be an indication of a healthy defence system. The body can dramatically increase its output of iron when it is under stress from an invading organism, such as a parasitic infestation of the gut, or from a disease such as cancer (Roberts and Manchester 1995). Again, it is not possible to quantify the condition in this population.

## Articulated skeleton from Area W

The supine and partially articulated remains of an adult male aged 35–39 years (pubic symphysis and auricular surface of the ilium) at the time of death were recovered from inside the entrance to the cave. The thorax, left upper arm, right lower arm and hand, and left lower leg and foot were found *in situ* in relation to the original burial position. These bones indicate that the left upper arm, at least, was extended down the side of the left thorax, the right forearm and hand were extended slightly out to the right lateral of the body (with the forearm presumably extended down parallel to the upper right thorax), and the left leg was slightly flexed to the right. Bones of the right foot were also recovered in a partially articulated state but lying in a prone position to the left side of the left knee. Virtually all of the remainder of the skeleton was recovered and identified in a disarticulated state from the immediate area. No cranial or dental remains were recovered associated with this skeleton. The estimated living stature was 167.6cm. The distal metaphysis of the left radius was misaligned, indicating the location of a healed fracture (as referred to above); no other pathological conditions were present. An anomaly was present, however, on the first cervical vertebra. The left transverse process was present as a separate and unfused entity to the main bone of the vertebra. The unfused process is unusually elongated superiorly/inferiorly and measures 10mm. This fragment usually fuses when an individual is 3–4 years of age (Scheuer and Black 2000). The remains of this individual were in an excellent state of preservation, with minimal post-depositional erosion or fragmentation.

### BONE FRAGMENT ANALYSIS

## Bone preservation

The variations in the bone fragments recovered and the effects on the resulting analysis have been referred to above. The condition of the bone and the completeness of the long bones recovered from the primary areas of the cave (the Two-Star Temple, the Graveyard and the Entrance Gallery) were recorded in order to examine pre- and post-depositional contributions to the current bone assemblage.

### Condition of human bone

In the Two-Star Temple all of the bone was a general yellow colour, with very slight discoloration. The outer cortex of a small number of bones had been eroded by water action. Cave deposits were found adhering to a number of bone fragments.

The bone fragments recovered from the Graveyard were in quite a good state of preservation. The dominant colour again was yellow. Water erosion was visible on a number of fragments and varied from minor to substantial in severity. A small number of fragments also displayed cave encrustations. A very noticeable factor observed in this area was that there were two sets of adult bone, one female and one male, that were radically different in appearance. The bones of the female were gracile and clean yellow in appearance; the bones of the male were morphologically much larger and were discoloured with a very distinctive dark brown, mottled deposit with tinges of green and grey. The latter bones were recovered from Quadrants C and D, in the Graveyard, in particular. In addition, a small number of both adult and sub-adult bones from an area just to the south of Area Z (Quadrant A) displayed similar dark discoloration, some of which overlay surfaces that had already been eroded by water. This suggests that the source of the discoloration originated within the cave. A single adult humeral fragment displayed evidence of rodent gnawing, as did a sub-adult first left metatarsal.

In addition, a number of bones from the Graveyard had breaks that had occurred when the bones were still fresh. These include the distal half of an adult right humerus (possible female) with breaks on the proximal end of the shaft (Pl. 3), the diaphysis of an adult left tibia

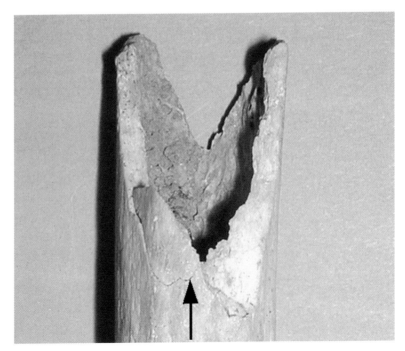

PL. 3
*Bone damage, suggestive of breakage of fresh bone; right humerus from the Graveyard.*

with breaks on the proximal and distal ends of the diaphysis, the distal half of an adult left tibia with breaks on the proximal end of the diaphysis, and two adult rib shaft fragments with extensive crushing and breakage of the cortical bone (Pl. 4). The clear, sharp margins of the breaks indicate that the bones were still fresh at the times of the breaks. However, the appearance of the breaks is not indicative of accidental or violent trauma on a fully fleshed body. Certainly the ribs could not have been damaged in such a manner had substantial amounts of flesh been still adhering to them. The damage to the humerus indicates complete breakage between the proximal and distal diaphyses, the severity of which suggests that the bone was defleshed, or at least partially defleshed, but still fresh. The fact that both diaphyses of the tibiae displayed this break pattern suggests a similar process. The breaks are too definite to have been caused accidentally by activities within the cave, and the indications are that for some reason these defleshed but fresh bones were deliberately damaged. It was apparent on the tibia that consisted of just a diaphysis that, although both the proximal and distal epiphyses of the bone were completely detached, some segments of the very clean breaks had become eroded with time and the sharp edges less distinct and identifiable. It is highly probable that a number of other

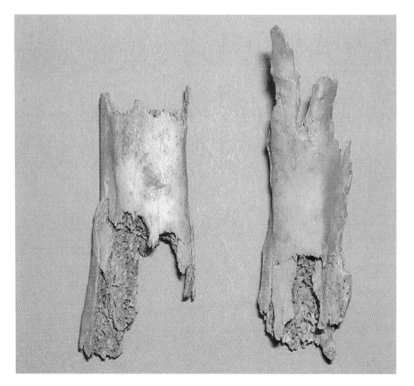

PL. 4
*Extensive bone damage, occurring when bone was fresh; two rib shafts from the Graveyard.*

bones in this area had similar breaks, but the evidence has simply been eroded with time.

In general the bone recovered from the Entrance Gallery was in a very good state of preservation. The concentration of complete long bones in this area was very noticeable. The mostly complete remains, of an articulated male adult and a neonate skeleton, were retrieved from here, as well as the partially articulated remains of a young child. The excellent preservation of these remains is obvious in the examination of the location of complete long bones (Tables 11 and 13). Virtually all of the bone was yellow in colour, although there was some slight discoloration of adult and sub-adult fragments recovered from Area X, sub-adult bones from the entrance shaft and some adult bones from Area U. There was some minor water erosion of the bone fragments recovered from the Entrance Gallery, in addition to minor cave encrustations. These deposits were significant on the sub-adult bone fragments recovered from Area T. A sub-adult first right metatarsal had evidence of rodent gnawing.

No fresh breaks (that is, breaks occurring when the bones were fresh) were observed on any bone fragments recovered from the Entrance Gallery (which does not necessarily mean that such breaks were not originally present—see above); however, another very distinctive post-mortem process was observed on a number of fragments. The diaphysis of an adult left humerus (female) and an intermediate and a distal adult hand phalanx all displayed evidence of charring or burning. The posterior diaphysis of the humerus was slightly blackened, with the cortical bone beginning to crumble in tiny longitudinal fragments (Pl. 5). The phalanges were almost completely blackened (Pl. 6), and the sizes of the bones strongly suggest that they are from a single individual. The nature of the blackening suggests that the bones were burned when defleshed. Both of these bones were recovered disarticulated (but within Area U, as with the humerus), but, given the likelihood that they are from the same individual and combined with the distinctive charring on these two small bones of the extremities, it is probable that the charring occurred when the bones were still articulated but not necessarily when there was still flesh (as opposed to ligaments) attached to them. There were clear indications of *in situ* burning on top of the pit in Area V in the Entrance Gallery. It is possible that the bones became charred here, particularly given the fact that all of the fragments were recovered from the area of the Entrance Gallery.

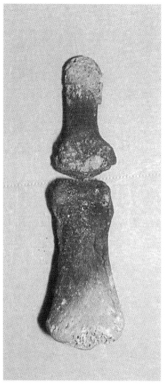

PL. 5
*Charring; left humerus*
*from the Entrance Gallery*
*(posterior view).*

PL. 6
*Charring; intermediate*
*and distal hand phalanges*
*from the Entrance Gallery*
*(palmar view).*

## Complete long bones

A number of complete long bones were recovered from the cave. Five adult long bones were sent for radiocarbon dating without the lengths being recorded (Table 1). The lengths of all of the other complete adult long bones are given in Table 11.

Seven of the thirteen complete bones listed in Table 11 are from the single articulated burial recovered from Area W, again indicating its uniqueness in the context of the human skeletal remains. Two other complete long bones were recovered from the Entrance Gallery (as well as a left and a right femur that were sent for dating); three were recovered from the Graveyard (as well as a left ulna and a right humerus that were sent for dating); and one complete long bone was recorded from the Two-Star Temple (as well as another complete right femur that was sent for dating). It is evident that the frequency of complete long bones increased dramatically from the Two-Star Temple through to the Entrance Gallery. This may reflect differential subsequent trampling in the cave, but it is also certainly reflective of differential patterns of deposition and burial throughout the cave.

The length of each complete sub-adult long bone is given in Table 13. In addition to those bones listed, a left humerus from the Graveyard and a right ulna from the entrance shaft (see Table 1) were sent for dating without the lengths being recorded and are therefore excluded.

| Area | Bone | Side | Age | Length (mm) |
|------|------|------|-----|-------------|
| Two-Star Temple | Femur | L | 4.5–5.5 years | 224.0 |
| Graveyard | Radius | L | Adolescent? | 198.0 |
| Graveyard | Radius | L | Adolescent? | 196.0 |
| Graveyard | Femur | L | 4.5–5.5 years | 230.0 |
| Graveyard | Tibia | L | 1.5–2.5 years | 128.0 |
| Graveyard | Tibia | R | 3.5–4.5 years | 169.0 |
| Graveyard | Tibia | L | 3.5–4.5 years | 174.0 |
| Entrance Gallery | Humerus | L | 1.5–2.5 years | 119.2 |
| Entrance Gallery | Humerus | L | 1.5–2.5 years | 119.7 |
| Entrance Gallery | Ulna | R | 1.5–2.5 years | 98.0 |
| Entrance Gallery | Ulna | L | 1.5–2.5 years | 98.6 |
| Entrance Gallery | Ulna | R | Neonate | 69.6 |
| Entrance Gallery | Ulna | L | Neonate | 69.3 |
| Entrance Gallery | Ulna | R | 1.5–2.5 years | 99.4 |
| Entrance Gallery | Radius | L | 1.5–2.5 years | 89.6 |
| Entrance Gallery | Femur | R | 1.5–2.5 years | 160.0 |
| Entrance Gallery | Femur | L | Neonate | 80.4 |
| Entrance Gallery | Femur | R | Neonate | 80.6 |
| Entrance Gallery | Femur | R | 1.5–2.5 years | 149.5 |
| Entrance Gallery | Tibia | L | 1–2.5 years | 126.0 |
| Entrance Gallery | Tibia | L | 0.5–1.5 years | 120.2 |
| Entrance Gallery | Tibia | R | 4.5–5.5 years | 190.0 |
| Entrance Gallery | Fibula | ? | 1.5–2.5 years | 122.4 |

TABLE 13—*Sub-adult long-bone lengths and estimated ages (after Ubelaker 1989, 70–1).*

A total of 23 complete sub-adult long bones were measured. Again, as with the adult bones, a single complete sub-adult long bone was recovered from the Two-Star Temple. Six were recorded from the Graveyard (as well as a humerus that was sent for dating), and sixteen were recovered from the Entrance Gallery (as well as an ulna that was sent for dating). Again, a prominent feature of the list of bones in Table 13 is that four of the bones from the Entrance Gallery were from a single neonate individual.

*Summary of bone preservation*

The bone fragments retrieved from the Two-Star Temple were

highly fragmented, but the fragments themselves were in a relatively good state of preservation.

The bones from the Graveyard were in a better state of preservation than those recovered from the Two-Star Temple, with a number of complete long bones being recovered. A very noticeable discoloration was observed on a number of the bones, which appears to originate from the cave itself. The fact that a set of female and a set of male remains were observed with very differing colorations suggests that these individuals may have been interred in an articulated, or at least a semi-articulated, state within the Graveyard. The discoloration of the male bones commenced, but in time the remains of both individuals became disarticulated and commingled. Both sets of remains were recovered from the western half of the Graveyard. A number of bones recovered from this area had evidence of breakages that had occurred when they were defleshed but still fresh.

The most complete and well-preserved bones were recovered from the Entrance Gallery. This was particularly apparent in the remains of the articulated male, the well-preserved female neonate and the partially articulated child from Area U, and many of the complete long bones were recovered from these individuals. There was only minor discoloration of the bones from this area. A number of bones were very distinctively charred. Indications are that some of these bones were either wholly or partially defleshed at that time and the charring may have occurred within the cave.

Water erosion and cave encrustations were observed on the bones from all areas of the cave.

## Bone weights

Virtually all of the human skeletal remains recovered from Cloghermore Cave were weighed; the exception was the result of an oversight. A number of bones, as detailed in Table 1, were sent for radiocarbon dating without being weighed and therefore could not be included in the following analysis. However, it is unlikely that their exclusion has altered the results in any significant way. It was decided to analyse the weights of the bone because of the difficulties presented by the significant fragmentation of the skeletal elements. It is acknowledged that the weight of the bones of one individual may differ from those of another owing to a number of reasons: not only normal variations between individuals and between sexes but also differential taphonomic factors. It is probable that some bones recovered from the cave have been subject to a variety of taphonomic dynamics (such as water erosion and cave encrustations), which may have affected the present weights of bones. These differences in bone weight between individuals are magnified with regard to sub-adult remains, given the difference in bone weight between, for example, an infant and a child aged 10 years. In addition, there may have been some mixing of the deposits between the Entrance Gallery and the Graveyard, and therefore the results may not necessarily reflect the original deposition. However, analysis of bone weights is still a useful indicator of distribution rates and rates of representation.

### Adult bone weights

The total weight of adult bone recovered was 15,098g (in addition, 193g was recovered from an unknown location by potholers). Each of the main skeletal elements was weighed individually, and the weights were then combined into the main body parts of skull, torso and limbs.

The weights, by percentage of the total identified, of the main adult body parts recovered from the Two-Star Temple are presented in Fig. 2. These are compared with percentages of the total weight expected from each of the main body parts of the average human adult skeleton: head 18.2 per cent, torso 23.1 per cent, and limbs 58.7 per cent (McKinley 1989, 68).

The total weight of adult bone recovered from the Two-Star Temple was 2060g, or 13.6 per cent of the total adult bone recovered. The most prominent aspect of the chart below is the lack of cranial bones. Clearly, the head is under-represented in this area of the cave.

FIG. 2
*Recovered weight compared with expected weights of adult skeletal body parts, Two-Star Temple; MNI 3.*

FIG. 3
*Recovered weight compared with expected weights of adult skeletal body parts, the Graveyard; MNI 7.*

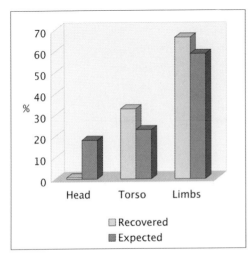

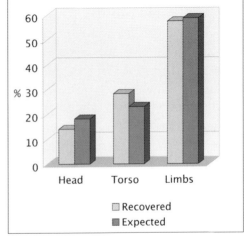

This is supported by bone counts: only one left temporal was recovered from this area, whereas a number of torso and limb bones indicate the presence of three individuals (see demographic profiles). The lack of cranial elements is unlikely to be due to excavation methods as the entire area of this chamber was examined. Neither can it be attributed simply to poorer survival of this skeletal element, given the good preservation of the other body parts. It is probable that the absence is more attributable to human intervention in antiquity, either as part of a death ritual involving intentional exclusion of the head or in later actions such as the deliberate removal of this body part.

The weights of adult bone recovered from the Graveyard are provided in Fig. 3. The total weight was 7006g, or 46.4 per cent of the total. The above chart indicates that all of the body parts are well represented in the Graveyard. There is a slight under-representation of cranial bones and a slight over-representation of torso bones, but the disparity is not significantly great.

The bone weights by body part as recovered from the Entrance Gallery are provided in Fig. 4. The total weight of bone recovered from the area of the Entrance Gallery was 6032g, or 40.0 per cent of the total adult assemblage recovered. It was particularly apparent in this area that the weight of the virtually complete articulated skeleton from Area W was predominant in the sample. At 2106g, it comprised 34.9 per cent of the total adult bone recovered from the Entrance Gallery, though representing only one of five individuals identified in this area. Figure 4 indicates the significant under-representation of cranial remains, most immediately apparent in the absence of the skull from the articulated skeleton. Torso remains are grossly over-represented within the sample; and, again, the limb portions of the skeleton are relatively well represented. This suggests that, as with the Two-Star Temple, there may have been selective deposition of certain body parts in this area. Again, all of this area was excavated, thus militating against factors of selective excavation. Differential preservation is also unlikely to account for the disparity, and other, post-excavation factors are also excluded. It is probable that some of the skeletal elements from the Entrance Gallery and the Graveyard had been mixed, but it is not possible to quantify the degree of mixing given the context of recovery.

A summary of the combined results of the distribution rates of each of the main body parts through each primary division of the cave is provided in Fig. 5. All body parts are poorly represented in the Two-Star Temple, which is probably a reflection of the fact that a

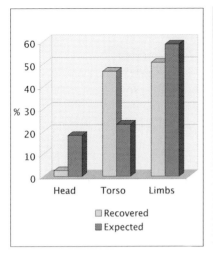

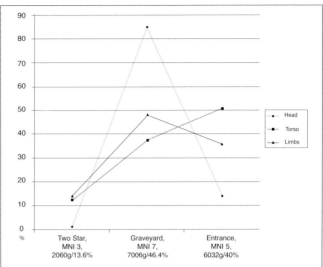

FIG. 4
*Recovered weight
compared with
expected weights of
adult skeletal body
parts, Entrance,
MNI 5.*

FIG. 5
*Distribution of adult
skeletal body parts
by primary cave
division.*

minimum of just three adult individuals were recovered from this area (see above). Negligible cranial remains were recovered from the Two-Star Temple in comparison to the other areas, particularly the Graveyard. The main concentration of bone is from the Graveyard, again probably a reflection of the minimum number of seven adults recovered from this area. The head is most dominant in the Graveyard. The concentration of skull fragments in the Graveyard may be due to the greater MNI in this area but may also be linked with the lack of adult skull fragments in the Entrance Gallery (see above). Torso remains increase in frequency from the Two-Star Temple through to the Entrance Gallery. This is unexpected given that the Graveyard contains the highest concentration of bones, in terms of both MNI and actual bone weights. The distribution of the limbs between the three areas of the cave may be more representative of the expected rates of recovery (as detailed above). Certainly, however, there are strong indications of selective deposition of certain body parts in certain areas of the cave.

*Sub-adult bone weights*
The total weight of sub-adult bone recovered was 4196g (in addition, potholers recovered 170g of sub-adult bones from unknown areas). The weights of sub-adult bone recovered from the primary areas were 1044g (24.9 per cent) from the Two-Star Temple, 2085g (49.7 per cent) from the Graveyard and 1067g (25.4 per cent) from the Entrance Gallery. There is significant variation in sub-adult skeletal weight, and the percentages of weights attributable to the three main body

parts in adults cannot be equated to those of sub-adult remains. The body proportions of a child differ from those of an adult. At birth the head is one-quarter of the total length of the body (Collins 1995, 366). Maintaining a pattern established from the embryonic stage, the head continues to grow at a slower rate than the rest of the body, so that in adults the head is one-eighth of the total length of the body (*ibid.*). Therefore, percentages of recovered sub-adult bone weight cannot be compared with expected rates of recovery as with adults: the results would simply be incorrect. However, in order to gain some insight into the distribution of the three body parts in the three primary areas of the cave, all of the sub-adult bone was weighed (Fig. 6). The chart shows a distribution pattern that differs from that of the adults, particularly regarding the prominence of all body parts in the Two-Star Temple. The Graveyard again shows the highest concentration of sub-adult bones. Cranial remains, particularly in comparison to the Two-Star Temple, are significantly under-represented in the Entrance Gallery.

*Summary of bone weight analysis*

Finally, in order to compare readily the weights and therefore the distribution of both adult and sub-adult bone recovered from the cave, the totals for each group have been summarised in Fig. 7.

Figure 7 clearly indicates that the bone deposits were primarily concentrated in the area of the Graveyard. However, in proportion, more sub-adult bone was recovered from the Two-Star Temple while more adult remains were recovered from the Entrance Gallery. The results regarding the Two-Star Temple are interesting in that the

FIG. 6
*Distribution of sub-adult skeletal body parts by primary cave division.*

FIG. 7
*Distribution of adult and sub-adult bone weights within the cave.*

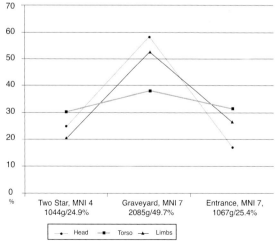

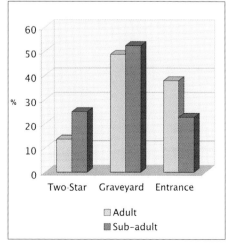

minimum number of adults and sub-adults recovered from that chamber was three and four respectively, with one of the latter four represented by a femur only.

The total minimum number of adults recovered from the cave was fifteen, and the total weight of adult bone was 15291g. The problems inherent in assessing the weights of archaeological skeletons have been examined above and were always a consideration in this analysis. However, the recovered weights point to one paramount factor: the recovered weights are not representative of the complete skeletons of the MNI. Based on the total recovered bone from the cave, each individual is represented by just 1019g of bone. However, the partially incomplete adult male recovered from Area W weighed 2106g. This suggests a gross under-representation of bones within the cave system when compared with the MNI. It was not possible to assess the recovered sub-adult bone weights in a similar manner, owing to the variation in the relative size of the juvenile skeleton as an individual grows.

**Frequencies of representation**
Because of the small MNI of both adults (three) and sub-adults (four) recovered from the Two-Star Temple, it is not feasible to assess the frequencies of representation of individuals by bone type. The combined areas of the Graveyard and the Entrance Gallery, however, were assessed. Table 14 lists the minimum numbers of adult individuals as represented by each bone type, with a corresponding list of the number of bones that are absent from the sample (based on the bone count and not the final MNI). The statistical validity of the results is still questionable in light of the small numbers of adult (and indeed sub-adult) individuals represented in this sample. However, the tables (Table 14 for adult bone; Table 15 for sub-adult bone) illustrate the disparity in the rates of recovery of the various bones, which has also been highlighted above.

It is immediately apparent with regard to the adults that there is a significant absence of bones of the extremities—the hands and feet. This fact is exaggerated when one considers that many of the hand and foot bones recorded were from the articulated adult in Area W. The absence of hand and foot bones cannot be attributed to incomplete excavation, as all areas were excavated. In addition, all of the soil recovered from the cave was sieved, which allowed for the recovery of even the smallest bones. This suggests that many of the remains were brought into the cave originally as disarticulated samples, with the smaller bones of the hands and feet either being mislaid in the process of disarticulation, collection and deposition or deliberately excluded, or that the bones were taken from the cave in later times.

A number of other anomalies are evident in the adult sample from the Graveyard and the Entrance Gallery. The maxilla, femur, cervical vertebrae (C3–7) and fibula are all noticeably under-represented. The virtual absence of the maxilla is unexpected given that the temporal is well represented, although it is acknowledged that the maxilla is a relatively fragile bone and may not survive (but see summary below). The robustness of the femur usually ensures that it survives well. Its scarceness in this sample may be due to the poor survival of the proximal and distal epiphyses, as a number of shaft fragments were identified but could not be sided. The lack of the lower cervical vertebrae is unexpected also, given the high representation of both the first and the second cervical vertebra, and the absence is difficult to explain.

| Bone | Present | | Absent | |
|------|---------|---|--------|---|
| | MNI | % | MNI | % |
| Scapula | 11 | 100 | 0 | 0 |
| C2 | 11 | 100 | 0 | 0 |
| C1 | 10 | 90.9 | 1 | 9.1 |
| Clavicle | 9 | 81.8 | 2 | 18.2 |
| Ulna | 9 | 81.8 | 2 | 18.2 |
| Ilium | 9 | 81.8 | 2 | 18.2 |
| Talus | 9 | 81.8 | 2 | 18.2 |
| Radius | 8 | 72.7 | 3 | 27.3 |
| Temporal | 8 | 72.7 | 3 | 27.3 |
| L1–5 | 7 | 63.6 | 4 | 36.4 |
| Sacrum | 7 | 63.6 | 4 | 36.4 |
| Metatarsal 2 | 7 | 63.6 | 4 | 36.4 |
| Metatarsal 4 | 7 | 63.6 | 4 | 36.4 |
| Humerus | 7 | 63.6 | 4 | 36.4 |
| Calcaneus | 7 | 63.6 | 4 | 36.4 |
| T1–12 | 6 | 54.5 | 5 | 45.5 |
| Mandible | 6 | 54.5 | 5 | 45.5 |
| Ischium | 6 | 54.5 | 5 | 45.5 |
| Navicular | 6 | 54.5 | 5 | 45.5 |
| Tibia | 6 | 54.5 | 5 | 45.5 |
| Metatarsal 1 | 5 | 45.5 | 6 | 54.5 |

TABLE 14—*Frequencies of representation by adult bone type from the Graveyard and the Entrance Gallery combined (adapted from Ubelaker 1974).*

| Bone | Present | | Absent | |
|---|---|---|---|---|
| | MNI | % | MNI | % |
| Pubis | 5 | 45.5 | 6 | 54.5 |
| Patella | 5 | 45.5 | 6 | 54.5 |
| Cuboid | 5 | 45.5 | 6 | 54.5 |
| First cuneiform | 5 | 45.5 | 6 | 54.5 |
| Metatarsal 3 | 5 | 45.5 | 6 | 54.5 |
| Metatarsal 5 | 5 | 45.5 | 6 | 54.5 |
| Fibula | 5 | 45.5 | 6 | 54.5 |
| Manubrium | 5 | 45.5 | 6 | 54.5 |
| Coccyx | 5 | 45.5 | 6 | 54.5 |
| Intermediate hand phalanges | 4 | 36.4 | 7 | 63.6 |
| Metacarpal 3 | 4 | 36.4 | 7 | 63.6 |
| Metacarpal 5 | 4 | 36.4 | 7 | 63.6 |
| C3–7 | 4 | 36.4 | 7 | 63.6 |
| Third cuneiform | 4 | 36.4 | 7 | 63.6 |
| Proximal hand phalanges | 3 | 27.3 | 8 | 72.7 |
| Proximal foot phalanges | 3 | 27.3 | 8 | 72.7 |
| Femur | 3 | 27.3 | 8 | 72.7 |
| Lunate | 3 | 27.3 | 8 | 72.7 |
| Triquetral | 3 | 27.3 | 8 | 72.7 |
| Metacarpal 1 | 3 | 27.3 | 8 | 72.7 |
| Distal hand phalanges | 2 | 18.2 | 9 | 81.8 |
| Maxilla | 2 | 18.2 | 9 | 81.8 |
| Scaphoid | 2 | 18.2 | 9 | 81.8 |
| Metacarpal 2 | 2 | 18.2 | 9 | 81.8 |
| Metacarpal 4 | 2 | 18.2 | 9 | 81.8 |
| Second cuneiform | 2 | 18.2 | 9 | 81.8 |
| Hamate | 2 | 18.2 | 9 | 81.8 |
| Intermediate foot phalanges | 1 | 9.1 | 10 | 90.9 |
| Distal foot phalanges | 1 | 9.1 | 10 | 90.9 |
| Pisiform | 1 | 9.1 | 10 | 90.9 |
| Trapezium | 1 | 9.1 | 10 | 90.9 |
| Trapezoid | 1 | 9.1 | 10 | 90.9 |
| Capitate | 1 | 9.1 | 10 | 90.9 |

TABLE 14 (CONT)—*Frequencies of representation by adult bone type from the Graveyard and the Entrance Gallery combined (adapted from Ubelaker 1974).*

Similar analysis of the sub-adult bones recovered from these areas (Table 15)—again, with the caution of the small sample size—reveals a number of similar features in the frequencies of representation. As with the adults, the bones of the hands and feet are under-represented and the second cervical vertebra is well represented (although the first cervical vertebra occurs less frequently). In contrast to the adult sample, however, the maxilla is well represented in the sub-adult population.

| Bone | Present | | Absent | |
|---|---|---|---|---|
| | MNI | % | MNI | % |
| Maxilla | 9 | 100 | 0 | 100 |
| C2 | 9 | 100 | 0 | 100 |
| Ilium | 8 | 88.9 | 1 | 11.1 |
| Femur | 6 | 66.7 | 3 | 33.3 |
| Mandible | 6 | 66.7 | 3 | 33.3 |
| Clavicle | 6 | 66.7 | 3 | 33.3 |
| Ischium | 6 | 66.7 | 3 | 33.3 |
| C1 | 6 | 66.7 | 3 | 33.3 |
| Calcaneus | 6 | 66.7 | 3 | 33.3 |
| Humerus | 6 | 66.7 | 3 | 33.3 |
| Ulna | 6 | 66.7 | 3 | 33.3 |
| Tibia | 6 | 66.7 | 3 | 33.3 |
| Scapula | 5 | 55.6 | 4 | 44.4 |
| Temporal | 5 | 55.6 | 4 | 44.4 |
| T1–12 | 5 | 55.6 | 4 | 44.4 |
| Radius | 4 | 44.4 | 5 | 55.6 |
| C3–7 | 4 | 44.4 | 5 | 55.6 |
| L1–5 | 4 | 44.4 | 5 | 55.6 |
| Talus | 4 | 44.4 | 5 | 55.6 |
| Pubis | 3 | 33.3 | 6 | 66.7 |
| S1–5 | 3 | 33.3 | 6 | 66.7 |
| Fibula | 3 | 33.3 | 6 | 66.7 |
| Metatarsals | 2 | 22.2 | 7 | 77.8 |
| Hand phalanges | 2 | 22.2 | 7 | 77.8 |
| Manubrium | 1 | 11.1 | 8 | 88.9 |
| Patella | 1 | 11.1 | 8 | 88.9 |
| Metacarpals | 1 | 11.1 | 8 | 88.9 |
| Other tarsals | 1 | 11.1 | 8 | 88.9 |
| Foot phalanges | 1 | 11.1 | 8 | 88.9 |
| Carpals | 0 | 0 | 9 | 100 |
| Coccyx | 0 | 0 | 9 | 100 |

TABLE 15—*Frequencies of representation by sub-adult bone type from the Graveyard and the Entrance Gallery combined (adapted from Ubelaker 1974).*

## Summary of frequencies of representation

As noted above, it is not feasible to analyse the Two-Star Temple in a similar manner to the Graveyard and the Entrance Gallery. This is unfortunate, as these data would have allowed for comparison between the isolated former area, with its earlier burials, and the combined data from the latter areas, which date to the later phase of burial activity. However, the frequencies given above illustrate a number of important points as regards the human remains from the Graveyard and the Entrance Gallery.

The bones of the hands and feet of both the adults and the sub-adults are clearly under-represented. This cannot be linked with factors of partial excavation or partial recovery, owing to the procedures that were followed during the excavation. On the assumption that much of the bone in these areas was deposited in a disarticulated state, the absence of these bones may be linked to accidental loss associated with the processes of disarticulation, to deliberate exclusion of bones during deposition or to later activities in the cave.

In addition, given that the lack of maxillary remains in the adult sample was tentatively linked to the relative fragility of the bone, it is unexpected that this element is so well represented in the sub-adult population. Sub-adult bones are generally not as robust as those of adults, but the sub-adult maxillae recovered from these areas are in excellent condition. It is possible that the disparity is not due to differential preservation alone but also to human intervention.

DISCUSSION

The analysis of the human remains recovered from Cloghermore Cave concentrated on two primary aspects. Firstly, the bones were examined in order to establish osteological information including MNI, demographic profiles and stature and also to consider the various dental and skeletal pathological lesions apparent on the remains. This analysis was quite problematic given the primarily disarticulated nature of the assemblage, its context of origin and post-depositional influences. Secondly, the bones were analysed with a view to assessing the method(s) of disposal and all of the factors inherent in that process. Post-depositional dynamics were also considered, in order to gain an insight into those processes that have contributed to the current sample.

A number of important elements emerged in the process of establishing the MNI. It was evident that, depending on the physical aspect of the cave that one wished to examine, the MNI could vary. The final numbers of adults and sub-adults from the entire cave are fifteen and fifteen (Tables 5 and 8). In contrast, analysis of each individual area within the cave gave combined totals of twenty adults and twenty-five sub-adults (Table 9). It was evident too that these numbers differed if bone counts alone were relied on (see Table 2).

The overall small size of the sample recovered from this site allowed for the detailed correlation of age at death and sex profiles with the initial bone counts, which subsequently allowed for more accurate numbers to be established. Unfortunately, this also led to problems with the statistical assessment of the assemblage; however, although the validity of including such statistics is questionable, a number of interesting aspects were apparent in the results, particularly with regard to the processes associated with the deposition of the dead (see below).

The evidence from the osteological analysis reveals equal numbers of adults and sub-adults (50 per cent; 50 per cent) within the cave. There is a slight bias in the adult population toward female individuals (58.3 per cent of adults whose sex could be determined). Interestingly, both of the infants whose sex could be determined were female (two of four infants). This may suggest a bias toward the deposition of females in the cave, but the sample size is too small and the sexing of infants too tentative for this conclusion to be affirmed. Two young (1–<6 years) male children were also identified.

The age profile of the population also provides some interesting information. Of the ten adults whose age at death could be determined, just one (10 per cent) was an older adult, while four (40 per cent) were young adults and five (50 per cent) were middle adults. There certainly appears to have been a bias toward the deposition of young and middle adults, although this may be due to low life expectancy in the host population. In the sub-adult population 46.7 per cent were aged 1–<6 years at the time of death, with a total of 73.3 per cent of the sub-adults aged less than 6 years. Although two radii recovered from the Graveyard may be from adolescent sub-adults (that is, 12+ years), this evidence alone is not conclusive, and therefore there is no substantial evidence of any individuals aged 12–<17 years. The analysis indicates a clear bias toward the desposition of younger children within the cave.

The estimated stature of the adults suggests that both females and males were shorter than their contemporaries. However, there are a number of factors that may have significantly biased these results. Although short stature is linked to genetic factors, there is strong evidence that nutritional deficiencies in childhood can contribute to stunted growth (Goodman 1991; Larsen 1997). Metabolic diseases were also observed in the skeletal remains, which further suggests that some of these individuals suffered from physiological insults (in particular the sub-adults), and this information can be corroborated to a degree by the occurrence of dental enamel hypoplasia. Unfortunately, it is simply not possible to assess accurately the health status of this population. The limited numbers of other skeletal pathological lesions that were observed on the bone fragments cannot be assessed on a broader scale, nor can the various conditions present on the teeth.

Most of the assemblage of human bone excavated from Cloghermore Cave was recovered in a disarticulated state. A limited number of articulated remains were uncovered, in addition to further evidence of bodies having been interred in an articulated state but with some later becoming commingled with the other bones in the cave (in total, at least five individuals). The Entrance Gallery contained the excellently preserved remains of an adult male and a possibly female neonate. In addition, substantial remains of an adult female and an adult male were evident from the Graveyard (based on preservation, colour and size), and the partially articulated and virtually complete remains of a young child were recovered from Area U of the Entrance Gallery. In contrast were the completely commingled disarticulated bones in the immediate areas of all of these five individuals and in the Two-Star Temple. The articulated/partially articulated remains indicate, as noted above, that these five may have been among the last to have been deposited in the cave.

The commingling of deposits, even between apparently isolated areas of the cave, was one of the main factors to be considered in the analysis. Although it was possible to give demographic profiles for specific areas of the cave, it is highly likely that the remains of each individual were scattered throughout the cave. Thus, although the pit in Area V primarily contained the torso of a child aged 1–3 years, it is possible that the remaining skeleton of this individual was recovered from the disarticulated mass in the Graveyard and the Entrance Gallery. Conversely, however, a single vertebral fragment was the only evidence from the entire cave of the remains of a human foetus. This element of commingling and the possible methods of deposition were examined in detail in the analysis of the bone fragments. The analyses of the preservation of the bones, the bone weights and the frequencies of representation have provided detailed information regarding the burial and/or depositional practices, as well as post-depositional factors.

The evidence indicates selective deposition of a disarticulated assemblage in the cave. For example, there is a significant under-representation of adult skulls from the Two-Star Temple and the Entrance Gallery and of sub-adult skulls from the Entrance Gallery, in addition to noticeable concentrations of body parts in individual and specific areas of the cave. Of particular interest is the pit in Area V, where the remains consisted primarily of the torso of a young child combined with the feet of a number of individuals, both adult and sub-adult: the deliberate deposition of certain body parts in this pit indicates a very specialised ritual. The lack of foot bones, at least, and possibly hand bones, in the main sample may not have been an accidental consequence of the collection and deposition of a disarticulated assemblage or been due to post-depositional factors. The emphasis on the feet in one area suggests that these remains may have been deliberately excluded from other areas as a gesture associated with the deposition ritual. There is the possibility that the remaining skeletons of the four individuals contained in this pit are not scattered around the rest of the cave but may have been kept by the community and/or deposited in another manner, either in the cave or somewhere else.

Excavation evidence has indicated that the human remains in the Two-Star Temple and also some burials in the Graveyard belong to the earliest phase of burial/deposition rituals at this site. The excavation report has described the physical isolation of the Two-Star Temple from the remaining chambers in the cave and the different rates of recovery of finds from this area. The evidence of the burial practice from the Two-Star Temple is somewhat limited owing to both the small amount of bones and the low MNI, but it indicates a different burial/depositional practice in this area of the cave from the disarticulated and articulated assemblages in the Graveyard and the Entrance Gallery.

The uniqueness of the Two-Star Temple is evidenced in a number of elements. There is no trace of human bone in the passage (Area Y) linking the Two-Star Temple and the Graveyard, indicating a clear-cut division between this and the rest of the cave. The Two-Star Temple also contains the least amount of bone and the lowest number of individuals. The bones are considerably more fragmentary than those recovered from the Graveyard and particularly the Entrance Gallery. All sub-adult skeletal elements are well represented in the Two-Star Temple, in proportion to overall sub-adult deposits. Adults in the Two-Star Temple, in proportion to the rest of the adult bone in the cave, are poorly represented. Cranial remains are virtually absent, and, although this factor in particular corresponds with certain observed biases in the Graveyard and the Entrance Gallery, there is the possibility of post-depositional interference with these burials, possibly by the individuals who used the cave for the second phase of burial (particularly including the deposition of the articulated burials). It was apparent also that none of the bone fragments recovered from the Two-Star Temple exhibited the fresh breaks (that is, occurring when the bones were fresh) and/or charring found on the remains from the main area of the cave. However, the rite of this earlier phase was still that of the deposition of selected portions of disarticulated remains. The nature of this initial disarticulation is difficult to ascertain given the low MNI and the fragmentary nature of the bones. In conjunction with other excavated evidence, the indications are that the remains recovered from the Two-Star Temple, and some of those recovered from elsewhere in the cave, belong to a different burial tradition from that of those burials that appear to have been inserted as complete bodies.

Most of the bone recovered from the Graveyard also dates to this earlier phase of use and was deposited as disarticulated remains, with the exception of the five individuals noted earlier. Bones from the Entrance Gallery, on the basis of a single radiocarbon date, also appear to relate to this earlier phase of burial; however, this is not conclusive, and bones in this area may date to both periods, their deposition here being due to later disturbance of the site.

The question arises of the processes involved in the deposition of the bodies in the cave. There is no evidence to indicate that fresh bodies were deliberately defleshed using sharp implement, as no distinctive cut-marks were observed that would typically be associated with this process. An adult femoral fragment exhibited a sharp cut-mark at the femoral neck, but this is the only incidence of sharp-force trauma observed in the entire assemblage, and its origin is therefore attributed to violence rather that to classic defleshing with sharp instruments.

There is a possibility that the bodies were exposed in order to deflesh them, but the evidence is not substantial. A number of smaller bones were under-represented (particularly the hands and feet), which may be a result of accidental loss either during exposure or during transportation of the skeletal remains for final deposition, but, as already mentioned, the lack of these bones in this assemblage may not be as accidental as initially assumed. In addition, there is evidence of rodent gnawing on a small number of bones (three). If fresh bodies had been exposed, it might be expected that more evidence of gnawing would be evident; and if semi-fresh bones had been deposited in the cave, it is highly probable that rodents and other scavengers would have been attracted to the decay that would have permeated from the cave. Exposure of the bodies therefore seems an unlikely origin of the disarticulated state of the remains from Cloghermore Cave.

The bones recovered from the cave were, in general, quite fragmented. A number displayed breaks that had occurred when the bones were still fresh, particularly those from the Graveyard. These breaks are clearly not associated with violent or even accidental trauma. In addition, trampling in antiquity is unlikely to account for all of the breaks. Rather, they would appear to be the result of deliberate acts of breakage. Many other fragments displayed evidence of breaks that had occurred when the bone was no longer fresh, but the coloration clearly indicated that the breaks were ancient. Many of these breaks may be the result of trampling. It is possible that the bodies were initially buried in the ground somewhere in the area surrounding the cave and were dug up after a certain period of time to be deposited in the cave. Certainly, also, there was selective deposition of various body parts, in terms of both which parts were deposited in the cave and where in the cave they were deposited.

The almost complete articulated skeleton recovered from just inside the entrance merits particular mention. The indications are that Area W was primarily reserved for the burial of this male individual. The poorly preserved remains (in terms of both the number of bones recovered and the condition of the fragments) of another adult male were recorded from this area, and there are indications that there was selective deposition of certain body parts of this latter individual. It is possible that this selective deposition of more ancient remains was part of the ritual associated with the burial of the articulated male. Sub-adult remains recovered from Area W are very minimal and suggest accidental inclusion, possibly as a result of later activities.

The positions of a number of the bones of the articulated male reveal some tantalising information. The first and second cervical vertebrae were recovered lying in an articulated state but 60mm superior to the third cervical vertebra. Although the lower portions of this skeleton had been disturbed and disarticulated, there was relatively little disturbance to the thorax area of the body. This suggests that the skull and mandible were deliberately removed from the body after it had been deposited in the cave. The positions of the upper cervical vertebrae suggest that there was still flesh, or at least ligaments, present when this action was undertaken. The lack of any sharp-force trauma to the cervical bones indicates that no weapons or tools were used to remove the head.

In the process of decomposition of the head, the mandible becomes detached from the cranium and subsequently the cranium becomes detached from the vertebrae (Haglund 1997, 383). The period of time involved in this process of decomposition can vary dramatically depending on a wide variety of factors. Considerable research has been undertaken in the United States of America to examine this process. Studies in the north-eastern USA show that the complete skeletonisation of a body buried at 4 feet or deeper (>1.2m) takes *c.* 2 to 3 years, while a body buried at a depth of *c.* 1 foot (0.3m) can become skeletonised in 6 months to 1 year or more (Rodriguez *et al.* 1997, 461).

Given the context of recovery of this individual and the high degree of later interference in the cave, it is impossible to determine when the skull and mandible were removed from this individual. Although the studies noted above may act as general guidelines, it is important also to consider the context of recovery: a cave. The rate of decomposition of a buried corpse is governed by two major factors: the first is carrion insect and animal activity, and the second is the soil environment (Rodriguez *et al.* 1997, 459). Low temperatures significantly reduce the rate of decomposition. It is probable that the decomposition of this individual may have taken a longer than average time for a typical buried body. However, the removal of the mandible with the skull suggests that it may have occurred relatively soon after burial. As the body was covered in soil, and given the likely unsavoury appearance of the corpse at that time, it shows a very deliberate and successful attempt to retrieve these body parts. The reasons for the behaviour remain unknown.

In addition, it was noted earlier that the right foot of this individual was recovered in a prone position to the lateral side of the left knee. It would have been virtually impossible to bury the individual in this position without breaking some bones in the legs, and there was no skeletal evidence of this. A number of the bones of this individual were recovered in a disarticulated state in the immediate vicinity; however, the foot was articulated. Although much of the disturbance to the lower portions of the skeleton in particular may have occurred in much later times, the foot was obviously displaced when there was flesh still adhering. Whether this occurred accidentally during the recovery of the skull or is related to the specialised rituals already noted with regard to foot bones, in particular, in the rest of the cave is unknown. Another factor that should be considered is that this displacement of the foot may be a result of a general desecration of the grave by later people.

## CONCLUSION

The main report includes detailed information on the dating sequence of Cloghermore Cave. The burials in the Two-Star Temple appear early in the sequence (c. eighth century). Indications are that at least some bones from this period were deposited in the Graveyard also. The rite consists of the deposition of selected disarticulated bones, often concentrated in the natural clefts and alcoves of the Two-Star Temple. There appears to have been little post-deposition interference with the burials in this area.

A second phase of burial and deposition occurred in the ninth/tenth century with the burial of fresh bodies, along with large quantities of archaeological artefacts. The lack of stratigraphy militates against the conclusive separation of the two phases of burials in the Graveyard. Both phases of use indicate highly specialised burial and depositional practices, at odds with the apparent pervading Christian burial rites of those centuries. Essentially, the cave acted as both an ossuary for the deposition of dry bones and a place for the deposition of complete bodies in the later phase. The site is examined in its wider context in the main volume.

## REFERENCES

Armentano, N., Malgosa, A. and Campillo, D. 1999 A case of frontal sinusitis from the Bronze Age site of Can Filuà. *International Journal of Osteoarchaeology* **9**, 438–42.

Arriaza, B.T. 1997 Spondylolysis in prehistoric human remains from Guam and its possible etiology. *American Journal of Physical Anthropology* **104**, 393–7.

Aufderheide, A.C. and Rodríguez-Martín, C. 1998 *The Cambridge encyclopedia of human palaeopathology*. Cambridge.

Bass, W.M. 1995 *Human osteology: a laboratory and field manual* (4th edn). Columbia, Missouri.

Brooks, S.T. and Suchey, J.M. 1990 Skeletal age determination based on the *os pubis*: a comparison of the Acsádi-Nemeskéri and Suchey-Brooks methods. *Human Evolution* **5**, 227–38.

Brothwell, D.R. 1981 *Digging up bones* (3rd edn). New York.

Buiskstra, J.E. and Ubelaker, D.H. 1994 *Standards for data collection from human skeletal remains*. Fayetteville, Arkansas.

Chamberlain, A.T. and Witkin, A. 2000 Human skeletal remains from Cloghermore Cave, County Kerry, Ireland. Unpublished report.

Collins, P. (ed.) 1995 Neonatal anatomy. In P.L. Williams (ed.), *Gray's Anatomy. The anatomical basis of medicine and surgery*, 344–73. New York.

Coughlan, J. and Holst, M. 2000 Health status. In V. Fiorato, A. Boylston and C. Knüsel (eds), *Blood red roses: the archaeology of a mass grave from the Battle of Towton AD 1461*, 60–76. Oxford.

Goodman, A. 1991 Health, adaptation and maladaptation in past societies. In H. Bush and M. Zvelebil (eds), *Health in past societies: biocultural interpretations of human skeletal remains in archaeological contexts*, 31–8. British Archaeological Reports, British Series 567. Oxford.

Haglund, W.D. 1997 Scattered skeletal human remains: search strategy considerations for locating missing teeth. In W.D. Haglund and M.H. Sorg (eds), *Forensic taphonomy: the postmortem fate of human remains*, 383–94. Washington.

Haglund, W.D. and Sorg, M.H. (eds) 1997 *Forensic taphonomy: the postmortem fate of human remains*. Washington.

Haglund, W.D. and Sorg, M.H. (eds) 2002 *Advances in forensic taphonomy: method, theory, and archaeological perspectives*. Washington.

Hillson, S. 1986 *Teeth*. Cambridge.

Larsen, C.S. 1997 *Bioarchaeology: interpreting behaviour from the human skeleton*. Cambridge Studies in Biological Anthropology 21. Cambridge.

Lieverse, A.R. 1999 Diet and aetiology of dental calculus. *International Journal of Osteoarchaeology* **9**, 219–32.

Lovejoy, C.O., Meindl, R.S., Pryzbeck, T.R. and Mensforth, R.P. 1985 Chronological metamorphosis of the auricular surface of the ilium: a new method for the determination of age at death. *American Journal of Physical Anthropology* **68**, 15–28.

Mann, R.W. and Murphy, S.P. 1990 *Regional atlas of bone disease: a guide to pathological and normal variations in the human skeleton*. Smithsonian Contributions to Anthropology 28. Washington.

Mays, S. 1998 *The archaeology of human bones*. London.

McKinley, J.I. 1989 Cremations: expectations, methodologies and realities. In C.A. Roberts, F. Lee, and J. Bintliff (eds), *Burial archaeology: current research, methods and developments*, 65–76. British Archaeological Reports, British Series 211. Oxford.

Meadow, R.H. 1980 Animal bones: problems for the archaeologist together with some possible solutions. *Paléorient* **6**, 65–77.

Merbs, C.F. 1996 Spondylosis of the sacrum in Alaskan and Canadian Inuit skeletons. *American Journal of Physical Anthropology* **101**, 357–67.

Moorrees, C.F.A., Fanning, E.A. and Hunt, Jnr, E.E. 1963a Age variation of formation stages for ten permanent teeth. *Journal of Dental Research* **42** (6), 1490–502.

Moorrees, C.F.A., Fanning, E.A. and Hunt, Jnr, E.E. 1963b Formation and resorption of three deciduous teeth in children. *American Journal of Physical Anthropology* **21**, 205–13.

Ortner, D.J. 2003 *Identification of pathological conditions in human skeletal remains* (2nd edn). San Diego.

Ortner, D. and Putschar, W.J. 1981 *Identification of pathological conditions in human skeletal remains* (1st edn). Washington.

Power, C. 1994 A demographic study of human skeletal populations from historic Munster. *Ulster Journal of Archaeology* **57**, 95–118.

Roberts, C. and Manchester, K. 1995 *The archaeology of disease* (2nd edn). New York.

Rodgers, J. and Waldron, T. 1995 *A field guide to joint disease in archaeology*. New York.

Rodriguez, W.C., III 1997 Decomposition of buried and submerged bodies. In W.D. Haglund and M.H. Sorg (eds), *Forensic taphonomy: the postmortem fate of human remains*, 459–68. Washington.

Roksandic, M. 2002 Position of skeletal remains as a key to understanding mortuary behaviour. In W.D. Haglund and M.H. Sorg (eds), *Advances in forensic taphonomy: method, theory, and archaeological perspectives*, 99–118. Washington.

Scheuer, [J.]L. and Black, S. 2000 *Developmental juvenile osteology*. San Diego.

Scheuer, J.L., Musgrave, J.H. and Evans, S.P. 1980 The estimation of late fetal and perinatal age from limb bone length and logarithmic regression. *Annals of Human Biology* **7** (3), 257–65.

Schlosser, V. 1968 *Traumatologie*. Stuttgart.

Schutkowski, H. 1993 Sex determination of infant and juvenile skeletons, 1: morphognostic features. *American Journal of Physical Anthropology* **90**, 199–205.

Schwartz, J.H. 1995 *Skeleton keys: an introduction to human skeletal morphology, development, and analysis*. Oxford.

Stuart-Macadam, P. 1991 Anaemia in Roman Britian: Poundbury Camp. In H. Bush and M. Zvelebil (eds), *Health in past societies: biocultural interpretations of human skeletal remains in archaeological contexts*, 101–13. British Archaeological Reports,

British Series 567. Oxford.

Trotter, M. 1970 Estimation of stature from intact limb bones. In T.D. Stewart (ed.), *Personal identification in mass disasters*, 71–83. Washington.

Ubelaker, D.H. 1974 *Reconstruction of demographic profiles from ossuary skeletal samples*. Smithsonian Contributions to Anthropology 18. Washington.

Ubelaker, D.H. 1989 *Human skeletal remains: excavation, analysis, interpretation* (2nd edn). Washington.

Ubelaker, D.H. 2002 Approaches to the study of commingling in human skeletal biology. In W.D. Haglund and M.H. Sorg (eds), *Advances in forensic taphonomy: method, theory, and archaeological perspectives*, 331–51. New York.

Waldron, T. 1987 The relative survival of the human skeleton: implications for palaeopathology. In A. Boddington, A.N. Garland and R.C. Janaway (eds), *Death, decay and reconstruction: approaches to archaeology and forensic science*, 55–64. Manchester.

Woodward, M. and Walker, A.R.P. 1994 Sugar consumption and dental caries: evidence from 90 countries. *British Dental Journal* **176**, 297–302.

# ANIMAL REMAINS

*Margaret McCarthy*

## INTRODUCTION

The excavations at Cloghermore yielded a collection of almost 17,000 animal bones. Most of these were recovered from a layer of brown soil brought into the cave before the second phase of burial. Smaller quantities of animal bone were recovered from surface deposits within the enclosure constructed around the entrance to the cave. Material finds and radiocarbon dates from human skeletal material place the deposition of the animal bones in the early/mid-tenth century when the cave was used for an apparently short period of time by a Hiberno-Scandinavian group. Most of the artefacts, the surface activity and the construction of the dry-walled entrance shaft also date to this later phase of burial.

The animal bones were well preserved, and careful excavation techniques led to the recovery of the full range of species and elements. Fragmentation rates were high, resulting in large numbers of bones that could only be classified as large and medium mammal remains (Table 1). The high incidence of non-diagnostic bone may reflect butchery and food-processing practices to a certain degree, although the suggested desecration of the site by native Irish populations shortly after the burials were interred may also have led to increased fragmentation rates. Non-cultural taphonomic factors such as roof collapse within the cave probably contributed to the breakage pattern as well. There were scatterings of charred and burnt bones throughout the various areas of the cave, some of which were barely scorched while more had the characteristic blue/grey appearance of bone that had been in contact with fire for a considerable period of time. Some of the burnt bone may relate to joints of meat being roasted over a fire during food preparation, but a collection of cremation animal bone within a stone setting in the Graveyard has been interpreted as a burial ritual deposit. Many of the burnt fragments from the surface may also have originated from the cremation pyre excavated close to the entrance to the cave. It is clear from the human skeletal material that the Hiberno-Scandinavian inhumations were deliberately desecrated, and therefore there is a high probability of mixing of bones from one area of the cave with those from another. The faunal remains reflect this to a certain extent, particularly when fragments of bone from different areas of the cave are cross-matched.

The faunal assemblage was examined and recorded using the modern comparative collections of mammals, birds and fish in the Department of Archaeology, University College Cork. The bones from the surface (Trenches 1, 3 and 4) were recorded by individual context, whereas the material from the cave was examined according to the areas in which it was found. Identifications were taken to species level where possible, but, because of the very fragmentary nature of the sample, almost 70 per cent of the bones could not be positively identified. Fragments for which specific identification could not be made were classed in terms of size and morphological character. The bones listed as 'large mammal' in Table 1, for instance, are likely to belong to cattle but are too small for the possibility of horse or red deer to be eliminated. Similarly, specimens that in all probability were sheep but that may also have originated from goat, pig or large dog were recorded as 'medium mammal'. The separation of ovicaprid material into sheep and goat relied on comparison with reference material and on the discussion in Prummel and Frisch (1986). Only two definite goat bones were identified, and those bones that allowed for the discrimination between the two species were overwhelmingly identified as sheep. Ageing data were obtained using procedures outlined by Silver (1969) for long bones and Grant (1975a; 1975b) for mandibles. The relative proportions of the species present were primarily assessed using the total number of identified fragments. The minimum number of individuals present was assessed for the three main livestock animals by each area, but the totals for the other species were combined before the minimum number was quantified.

## RESULTS

During excavation of the site no selection processes were employed, and all bone was kept for examination. Almost 68 per cent of the assemblage could not be positively identified to species, leaving a total identified sample of 4410 bones. Most of the unidentifiable material consisted of small chips of bone recovered during sieving, which was a routine part of the excavation. The smallest faunal samples were recovered from the innermost areas of the cave system, including the Two-Star Temple, Area Z and Area Y. Outside the cave, bones were collected during excavations in Trenches 1, 3 and 4. The only significant quantities were from Trench 3, for which specific figures are given below. No animal bones were found in Trench 2, and the small samples from Trench 1 and Trench 4 merit little comment.

| Species | Location | | | | | | | | | |
|---|---|---|---|---|---|---|---|---|---|---|
| | Entrance shaft | Area V | Area W | Area U | Area T | Area X | The Graveyard | Area Z | Area Y | Two-Star Temple |
| Cow | 163 | 221 | 20 | 258 | 82 | 27 | 468 | 4 | 8 | 4 |
| Sheep | 244 | 242 | 43 | 346 | 87 | 45 | 886 | — | 16 | 31 |
| Goat | 2 | — | — | — | 1 | — | — | — | — | — |
| Pig | 112 | 65 | 25 | 191 | 16 | 19 | 285 | — | — | 4 |
| Horse | 1 | 1 | — | 2 | 1 | 1 | 4 | — | 1 | — |
| Dog | 20 | 4 | — | 5 | — | — | 17 | — | — | — |
| Cat | 4 | 1 | 1 | 5 | 3 | 7 | 4 | — | — | 2 |
| Red deer | — | — | — | 1 | — | 2 | — | — | — | — |
| Hare | — | — | — | — | — | — | 1 | — | — | — |
| Mouse | 2 | — | 1 | — | — | — | 2 | — | — | — |
| Rabbit | 2 | — | — | — | — | — | — | — | — | — |
| LM | 261 | 318 | 46 | 382 | 86 | 55 | 664 | — | 8 | 45 |
| MM | 437 | 368 | 84 | 696 | 197 | 51 | 1264 | 1 | 48 | 23 |
| Unid. | 642 | 566 | 262 | 547 | 152 | 104 | 1235 | — | — | 48 |
| Total | 1890 | 1786 | 482 | 2433 | 625 | 311 | 4830 | 5 | 81 | 157 |

TABLE 1—*Total numbers of identified mammalian fauna; LM: large mammal; MM: medium-sized mammal. (Cremation and surface trench deposits are not included here.)*

| Species | Location | | | | | | | | | |
|---|---|---|---|---|---|---|---|---|---|---|
| | Entrance shaft | Area V | Area W | Area U | Area T | Area X | The Graveyard | Area Z | Area Y | Two-Star Temple |
| Cow | 4 | 5 | 2 | 5 | 2 | 1 | 14 | 1 | 1 | 1 |
| Sheep | 14 | 5 | 4 | 7 | 4 | 4 | 18 | — | 2 | 3 |
| Pig | 5 | 3 | 2 | 8 | 1 | 2 | 8 | — | — | 1 |

TABLE 2—*Minimum number of individuals: cow, sheep and pig. (Cremation and surface trench deposits are not included here.)*

## The entrance shaft

The various layers in the entrance shaft produced one of the largest assemblages of animal bones from the site. A total of 1890 bones were found, and the largest individual samples came from deposits excavated at the base of the shaft. Most common were the remains of domestic ungulates: sheep, cattle and pig. Sheep and cattle were the dominant species, accounting for 74 per cent of the identified sample. Sheep bones outnumbered those of cattle, and the remains were mostly from juveniles, including fourteen bones from lambs less than 6 months old and a single bone from a neonatal individual. More than 80 per cent of the sheep bones were from individuals that had been slaughtered before 2.5 years of age, indicating that meat provisioning was significant. The entrance shaft produced the only diagnostic goat bones from within the cave: a fragment of a skull and the distal portion of a metacarpus. Cattle were second in importance in terms of number of identified fragments (30 per cent) but ranked a close third to pigs when the minimum number of individuals was estimated (Table 2). A number of mandibles provided ageing evidence, which indicated that young and immature cattle dominated the sample. Ageing data from epiphysial fusion showed a similar pattern of age distribution, with 78 per cent of the bones belonging to individuals that were slaughtered at less than *c.* 2.5 years old. There were 112 pig bones, representing a minimum of five individuals, including a neonatal piglet. Skull fragments, teeth and meat-bearing upper regions of the body predominated, and most of the remains represented individuals slaughtered at around 1 year of age.

All other mammalian species were present in very small numbers, although the largest sample of dog bones from the site came from a layer at the base of the entrance shaft. Twenty bones were identified: all were fully mature and from an individual about the size of a modern sheepdog. The bones came from all parts of the skeleton and included vertebrae, mandibles, teeth, metapodia, limb bones, astragalus and phalanges. Four cat bones were recovered from the base of the shaft and were identified as a vertebra, two astragali and the lateral portion of a skull. They all belonged to a mature individual, and there was no evidence of dismemberment. One astragalus was extremely weathered and eroded and had clearly been exposed on the surface for some time before deposition in the cave. None of the cat or dog bones bore traces of butchery, and all were unburnt. The only other domestic animal present was horse, which was identified from a complete molar of an adult individual.

Wild mammals present in the entrance shaft included rabbit, *Oryctolagus cuniculus*, and mouse, *Apodemus sylvaticus*. There were four rabbit bones, representing an adult and a newborn individual. All of these are assumed to be intrusive as rabbits were not present in Ireland until the thirteenth century, when they were introduced as an additional food source by the Anglo-Normans. Two mouse leg bones were recovered from the base of the shaft, and these represented separate individuals. In the absence of cranial material, the bones could not be used to distinguish between wood mouse, *Apodemus sylvaticus*, and house mouse, *Mus musculus*. They are assumed to belong to *Apodemus* as the house mouse is generally accepted not to have reached Ireland until the medieval period. The only other point of particular interest in the faunal assemblage from the entrance shaft was the occurrence of twenty bones from wild species of bird. These were identified as blackbird, *Turdus merula* (seven bones), fieldfare, *Turdus pilaris* (seven bones), stonechat, *Saxicola torquata* (three bones), greenfinch, *Carduelis chloris* (one bone), starling, *Sturnus vulgaris* (one bone) and golden plover, *Pluvialis apricaria* (one bone). The bones were found scattered throughout the various fills of the entrance shaft, and there is nothing particularly significant about their deposition.

The only point of interest, in terms of ritual deposition, was the recovery of a complete cattle skull at the base of the shaft. The skull was shattered into numerous pieces, and a single horn-core survived attached to one of the cranial fragments. The horn-core represented a short-horned individual and probably belonged to a male. Both lower mandibles were present, and, although the caudal ends were damaged, there was no evidence that these elements had been butchered. No teeth survived in the left mandible, and the incisors and some premolars of the right jaw were also missing. All molars in the right mandible were fully erupted and represented an individual over five years of age. The cow skull was found in the vicinity of nine other cattle skull fragments, which appeared to originate from a single individual. The excavator has suggested that these skulls may have been placed together as a ritual deposit at the base of the entrance shaft, facing out of the cave. Examination of the bones does not refute this theory, although there are no cut-marks on any of the skull fragments to suggest that the two individuals had been decapitated.

## Area V (pit)

This pit was situated immediately inside the base of the entrance shaft and was cut into the sterile sediments that underlay the brown clay that had been brought into the cave. It has been singled out as an area of particular significance in terms of ritual activity as it contained the torso of a child and the foot bones of two other children and an adult. The pit also produced the highest density of artefacts from any area of the cave. A substantial quantity of butchered animal bone was incorporated in the pit, along with the human remains and artefacts. In all, 1786 bones were recovered, but slightly more than 70 per cent of these could not be identified to species level. Of the identified sample, sheep (45 per cent) and cattle (41 per cent) were represented in roughly equal numbers while pigs ranked a poor third (12 per cent). Calculation of the minimum number of individuals indicated that the partial remains of at least five cattle and five sheep were present. The majority of the sheep and cattle bones came from young animals, and there was a particularly high incidence of bones from individuals less than 6 months old. Two neonatal lamb bones were present, and more than 75 per cent of the bones came from individuals under 2.5 years of age. There was no evidence of the slaughter of calves, but, with the exception of a single bone from an animal more than 3.5 years of age, the cattle bones were all from individuals under 2 years of age. At least three pigs were present in the pit, and the identified bones also suggested the slaughter of young individuals. There were several instances of chopping and splitting, with three cases of very efficient mid-line splitting resulting in the division of the carcass into two halves. One cattle horn-core had been severed at its base from the frontal bone by a sharp, heavy implement. The assemblage is interpreted as primarily representing waste from the slaughter and dismemberment of young domestic animals during feasting activities associated with the burial of the partial remains of four humans.

Bones of all other species were found in very small numbers in the pit, and no wild animals were identified. The distal portion of a scapula from an adult horse was recovered, but there were no butchery marks on the bone to suggest that it had been deliberately dismembered as part of the ritual activity. The remains of a juvenile dog, including a portion of a maxilla, a lower molar, a caudal vertebra and a metatarsus, were also present. The single cat bone was identified as the proximal portion of an unfused ulna, belonging to an individual less than 1 year old at slaughter.

## Area W

This small area was situated immediately inside and to the east of the cave entrance and produced the only articulated burial from the cave.

The skeleton was that of an adult male, and its position close to the entrance suggested that it was the last burial inserted in the cave. Excavations here resulted in the recovery of 482 animal bones, of which just 90 (19 per cent) were identifiable. Sheep accounted for 48 per cent of the identifiable sample, and the remains mostly represented young individuals, including six lamb bones and a tibia from a newborn individual. The fused proximal portion of a tibia provided the only evidence of the selection of sheep of more than 3.5 years of age. At least four sheep were present, including a newborn lamb, two individuals less than 6 months old and an adult. The bulk of the bones represented prime meat-bearing areas from the upper regions of the body, although there were sufficient quantities of peripheral elements such as phalanges, skull fragments and metapodia to indicate that the sample represents the remains of complete sheep carcasses and not prepared meat joints. The remains of cattle and pig were recovered in almost equal quantities. Twenty cattle bones represented at least two individuals aged *c.* 1 year old at slaughter. The sample mostly represented meat-bearing elements, including humerus, radius, pelvis and ulna. Pig was second in importance to sheep in terms of number of identified fragments, and ageing data for the two individuals represented indicated that they were less than 1 year old when slaughtered. The only other domestic animal present in this sample was cat, identified through the recovery of the mid-shaft portion of a maxilla. Non-domestic species consisted of a complete tibia from a mouse. This bone belonged to a young individual and is presumed to belong to wood mouse, given the sealed context of the find.

## Area U

This area proved to be one of the most productive parts of the cave in terms of both animal bones and artefacts. Altogether, 2433 bones were recovered, of which just 808 (33 per cent) were identified to species level. Domestic species comprised the major part of the assemblage. Sheep (43 per cent) and cattle (32 per cent) predominated, and there was a high rate of slaughter of young animals, including calves and lambs. Pigs ranked third in importance in terms of number of identified fragments, but an estimate of the minimum number of individuals present indicated that they were the most commonly occurring species. Remains representing at least eight pigs were present, including an interesting collection of 61 neonatal bones representing four individuals. These may be of significance in terms of ritual deposition of animals in the cave. In common with the other domestic ungulates, the long-bone fusion evidence indicated that young pigs, including perhaps neonatal individuals, were deliberately selected for slaughter.

Most of the livestock remains show evidence of some form of butchery, and the assemblage consists of a mixed accumulation of waste from all stages of the slaughter and subsequent consumption of the animals during suggested feasting activities. There was evidence of the splitting of cattle and sheep down the mid-line of the vertebral column, and two pig skulls were chopped axially to give access to the brains. Several metapodia were also split down the mid-line for the extraction of marrow. Two cattle mandibles had been chopped through, suggesting that the lower jaw had been removed, perhaps to give access to the tongue. There was plentiful evidence of the slaughter of lambs and calves, and the presence of almost entire carcasses for these animals suggests that slaughtering, food preparation and consumption were carried out locally, perhaps at the entrance to the cave where surface activity was identified in Trench 3.

The remains of other animals accounted for a small proportion of the sample. Two horse bones were identified as a mandible and a tarsal. The cranial portion of the mandible survived and included most of the incisors and two canines, suggesting a male horse aged *c.* 8 years. The collection of cat bones included three vertebrae and two tibiae, representing an individual less than 8 months of age. There were five dog bones, similar in size to those of a modern sheepdog, which belonged to an adult individual: a complete humerus, an axis, a phalanx, a metapodial and a tooth. Area U is most notable for producing one of the few red deer, *Cervus elaphus*, bones from the excavation. This was identified as the tip of an antler tine that had been sawn halfway through and then snapped off.

## Area T

A relatively small sample of 625 bones was recovered from the north-east corner of the Entrance Gallery. The various categories of unidentified material again formed a large proportion of the sample, with just 190 bones (30 per cent) being positively identified. Domestic sheep and cattle formed the major part of the assemblage, and, unlike in other areas of the cave, cattle were only marginally less significant than sheep in terms of both number of fragments and minimum number of individuals. The majority of the cattle and sheep bones were from juvenile individuals, but seven cattle limb bones pointed to the occasional slaughter of animals of more than 3.5 years of age. The sheep remains included a complete femur, an astragalus and an ulna from a newborn lamb. There were just sixteen pig bones, representing an individual less than 1 year of age. A pig skull fragment was chopped axially, presumably to give access to the brain. Horse was identified through the recovery of an incisor belonging to an old individual. The only other species identified was cat—two humeri and the cranial portion of a right maxilla represented a single individual less than 8 months old.

## Area X

This area was situated at the northern end of the Entrance Gallery in a long, narrow passageway that sloped steeply toward the Graveyard. The faunal sample consisted of 311 bones, of which 210 (68 per cent) could not be identified to species level. Livestock remains dominated the identified sample, and almost all elements of the skeleton were recognised, suggesting localised butchery of the carcasses. In terms of identified fragments, sheep (45 per cent) were the most commonly represented species, followed by lesser amounts of cattle (27 per cent) and pig (19 per cent). Calculation of the minimum number of individuals confirmed the dominance of sheep, with the remains representing at least four individuals, including a neonatal lamb, two juveniles and an adult. Ageing data showed that the bones predominantly represented animals that were slaughtered at 1–2 years of age. There were 27 cattle bones, representing two individuals of less than 2 years of age at slaughter. Pig remains ranked third in order of frequency, and the bones represented two individuals: one was a young pig of less than 1 year old, and the distal end of a scapula indicated a neonatal piglet. Other domestic animals present included horse and cat. The horse was identified by a molar from an adult individual. Area X is most noteworthy for producing the largest amounts of cat and deer bones from the cave. The cat remains represented a single adult individual and were identified as a mandible, a radius, three vertebrae, a metatarsus and a rib. None of the bones bore any traces of burning or dismemberment. Red deer was attested through the recovery of two antler tines.

## The Graveyard

Excavation in the area of the cave designated the Graveyard resulted in the recovery of the largest sample of animal bones from the site. These consisted mostly of the remains of the major domestic livestock species scattered in a random manner across the surface of the cave. The total number of fragments examined was 4829, of which 1666 were positively identified. This does not include the large collection of animal bones from the cremation deposit within the stone setting, which are reported on separately in the next section. The sample of bones from the Graveyard was similar to those from all other areas of the cave in that it represented a selection of both meat-bearing and peripheral parts of the skeleton. This indicates that the animals present were slaughtered and butchered in the immediate vicinity of the cave and subsequently eaten during feasting activities. It is presumed that the food remains and the primary butchery waste were brought into the Graveyard to be incorporated with the human burials.

Sheep was the dominant species, contributing 886 fragments and representing 53 per cent of the identified sample. At least eighteen individuals were present, and ageing data provided plentiful evidence of the slaughter of young animals, including neonatal lambs, individuals less than 6 months of age and sub-adults. The mandibular tooth-wear pattern and epiphysial fusion data indicated that almost 80 per cent of the bones were from animals of less than 2 years of age at slaughter. The only other animals present in any quantity were cattle, the remains of which accounted for 28 per cent of the identified assemblage, representing at least fourteen individuals. All parts of the body were identified, but there were more vertebrae and skull fragments than any other elements. Meat provisioning was again significant, and ten of the fourteen individuals present were less than 2.5 years of age. At least two calves were selected for slaughter, and there was evidence of one adult individual of more than 4 years of age. Pigs were the least frequently occurring of the three main meat animals, and all of the bones were from animals less than 2 years of age. At least eight individuals were present, including a neonatal piglet. The sample included the remains of 33 pig teeth, including three tusks from a boar. Two of these were sufficiently large to have originated from a wild boar. The excavation records indicate that two boar tusks were recovered from beneath an articulated row of ten animal vertebrae, and these were recognised as a 'special', perhaps ritual, deposit. The remains inadvertently became included with other bone samples from the Graveyard, and therefore it proved impossible to separate the vertebrae and tusks from the remainder of the assemblage. Butchery evidence was widespread on the fragments of the three main livestock animals and mainly took the form of heavy chop-marks on the skull and limb bones. There was very little evidence of fine knife-marks that would suggest careful filleting of meat from the bones.

Other mammalian species were present in very small numbers. The Graveyard produced the most horse bones from the site. Two of these were found close to the cremation deposit, and a horse tooth was contained within the stone setting itself. The bones found in association with the cremation deposit were identified as the distal portion of a tibia and a complete molar. A crude chop to the lateral portion of the shaft of the tibia was the only evidence of the deliberate dismemberment and consumption of horse carcasses at the site. The other horse bones from the Graveyard consisted of a portion of a mandible and three teeth. There were seventeen fragments of dog, which represented all parts of the skeleton, although limb bones predominated. A complete femur indicated a medium-sized individual with a shoulder height of 56cm. Another complete femur represented a juvenile dog less than 1 year old. The cat bones were identified as a fragment of a skull, a mandible, a maxilla and a radius; these belonged to a mature individual. The only species of wild mammal present was wood mouse, *Apodemus sylvaticus*, identified through the recovery of a mandible and a tibia.

*The cremation deposits*
The cremated remains were recovered from a subcircular stone setting filled with animal bone, ash and charcoal. The excavator has suggested, on the basis of the recovered artefacts, that a female burial, probably also cremated, was associated with this deposit. Although the analysis of the cremated animal bone did not reveal any human remains, it is possible that the cremated burial had been contained in a pot that may have been removed on the abandonment of the cave as a place of burial (see main volume).

A total of 3748 bones were recovered from within the stone setting, of which just 182 were identified to species. Some of the cremated bone varied from slightly blackened to brown/grey and blue/grey in appearance. These bones had been in contact with heat for a period but not sufficiently long for the fragments to become totally burnt. Other bone fragments were white and cracked from extreme exposure to fire, and these must represent bones that remained in the pyre for a sufficient time to become totally calcined. Fragmentation rates, not surprisingly, were very high, and 95 per cent of the sample could only be classified as tiny pieces of unidentifiable long bone. A few of the animal bones, including a horse tooth, were unburnt, but the circumstances of the find indicate that these bones are contemporary with the primary deposition of cremated bone. The pyre where the animals were cremated was uncovered on the surface close to the entrance to the cave.

| Body part | Cow | Sheep | Pig | Horse | Hare | Large mammal | Medium-sized mammal | Unidentified |
|---|---|---|---|---|---|---|---|---|
| Horn-core | — | 1 | — | — | — | — | — | — |
| Skull | 21 | 4 | 1 | — | — | — | — | — |
| Mandible | 2 | 1 | — | — | — | — | — | — |
| Tooth | 2 | 1 | — | 1 | — | — | — | — |
| Vertebra | 32 | 6 | — | — | — | — | — | — |
| Scapula | — | 3 | — | — | — | — | — | — |
| Humerus | 2 | — | — | — | — | — | — | — |
| Radius | 1 | — | — | — | — | — | — | — |
| Ulna | — | 1 | — | — | — | — | — | — |
| Pelvis | 3 | 4 | — | — | — | — | — | — |
| Femur | — | 1 | — | — | — | — | — | — |
| Tibia | 3 | 2 | — | — | 1 | — | — | — |
| Metapodial | 1 | — | — | — | — | — | — | — |
| Astragalus | 1 | — | — | — | — | — | — | — |
| Carpal/tarsal | 4 | 7 | — | — | — | — | — | — |
| Phalanx | 1 | — | — | — | — | — | — | — |
| Patella | 1 | — | — | — | — | — | — | — |
| Rib | 19 | 55 | — | — | — | — | — | — |
| Long-bone fragment | — | — | — | — | — | 230 | 186 | 3150 |
| Total | 93 | 86 | 1 | 1 | 1 | 230 | 186 | 3150 |

TABLE 3—*Animal bones from the cremation deposit.*

Identification of the bones revealed that domestic animals formed the greater part of the assemblage. Cattle and sheep bones were the most numerous, and diagnostic fragments of vertebrae and skulls predominated (Table 3). Most elements of the body were identified, including fragmented sesamoid bones and a complete second phalanx that belonged to an individual a little more than 1.5 years of age. Young individuals dominated the collection of cattle bones, and there was evidence of the ritual slaughter of calves in the form of a distal tibia from an individual less than 3 months old. Sheep bones were also well represented, accounting for 47 per cent of the identified assemblage. Most parts of the skeleton were recognised, including the main meat-bearing, upper elements of the body and the lower extremities such as carpals, tarsals and metapodial bones; however, rib fragments dominated. The only evidence of pig was a section of the zygomatic arch of the skull. Other species identified in the cremation deposit were horse and hare, *Lepus timidus*. The horse molar was unburnt and came from an adult individual. Two unburnt horse bones that were found around the stone setting and are referred to in the previous section may be associated with this cremation deposit. The only evidence of the hunting of hare was a distal portion of a femur from an adult individual.

## Area Z
Excavation was undertaken at the north-eastern end of the Graveyard, where a large boulder partially blocked the entrance to a short adit. The faunal sample was minimal, consisting of just five bones. Cattle were the only species identified, and the remains included two complete horn-cores from a probable bull. The horns displayed chop-marks along the base where the sheath had been removed, possibly for artefact manufacture. Other cattle bones consisted of the proximal portion of a metatarsus and an incomplete sternbra. The remaining fragment was identified as a rib from a medium-sized animal, probably sheep. The sample was too small to merit further comment.

## Area Y
A small sample of animal bones was collected in a narrow passageway leading from the Graveyard to the Two-Star Temple. Altogether, 81 bones were examined, which represented a selection of both meat-bearing and peripheral elements. Almost 70 per cent of the sample could not be identified to species level. Some of the limb bones were noticeably weathered and eroded as if they had been redeposited from elsewhere. The results are only summarised here, as the sample is too small for a detailed analysis to be undertaken. Sheep, cattle and horse were all positively identified in that order of frequency. There were sixteen sheep bones, including teeth, vertebrae, foot bones, pelvises and two long bones. The remains came from at least two individuals less than 1.5 years old at slaughter. At least one cow was present, and the bovid sample included various

limb bones, vertebrae and individual fragments of a skull and a scapula. Horse was identified through the recovery of a complete patella belonging to an adult individual. The remainder of the sample was classified into two size categories: 48 fragments from medium-sized animals and eight from large mammals. These fragments probably belong to sheep and cattle, given that they are the only two species represented in the sample with any frequency.

## The Two-Star Temple

Excavation in this chamber revealed a very thin soil cover sealing a solid stalagmite floor. The quantity of animal bone in the Two-Star Chamber is negligible, and it is probably intrusive, as the human burials from here are associated with an earlier, native Irish period of burial. A total of 157 bones were recovered, and a little more than 74 per cent of these could not be identified to species. The sample of identifiable bone was very small, and consequently only a few comments are in order. Sheep were by far the most common species, accounting for 76 per cent of the identified bone. Three of the sheep bones were charred, and all belonged to individuals less than 2 years old at slaughter. Apart from a number of chop-marks associated with butchery, little else can be said about the sheep remains. Cattle and pigs were also identified but in negligible quantities of just four bones each. These belonged to young individuals, and none bore any traces of butchery. The only other animal identified in the Two-Star Temple was an adult cat, represented by the mid-shaft portion of a maxilla and an upper molar.

## Trench 1

Excavation outside the entrance to the cave revealed a D-shaped enclosure and an associated linear cut. The samples from these features were too small to study in depth, and the bones were generally badly preserved. The fill (C105) of the enclosure ditch yielded a total of twenty bones. Cattle, sheep and cat were identified from seven fragments, and the remainder of the sample was too fragmentary to be identified to species. Cat was represented by a right mandible from an adult individual. Bone material from a linear cut (C112) outside the enclosure bank was equally small in quantity and was in an eroded and weathered condition. Cattle was the only species identified, and the remainder of the material consisted of eleven fragments of bone from large mammals and five from smaller animals.

## Trench 4

Excavation in this trench yielded a total sample of 210 bones, of which just 51 were identified to species. Seven of these were totally calcined, and they may have originated from the cremation pyre close to the entrance to the cave. Sheep again dominated the sample, with 21 bones being identified to this species. Most parts of the skeleton were represented, but teeth, vertebrae and peripheral elements were more frequent. An astragalus had been chopped horizontally during the removal of the lower legs, and all of the vertebrae came from individuals less than 2 years of age. Cattle (thirteen fragments) and pig (eleven fragments) were also identified in the sample, and the bones included meat-bearing elements and teeth. There were three dog bones, all from an adult individual. The final point of interest regarding this sample is the recovery of the only red deer bone from the surface deposits. This was identified as the tip of an antler tine, which appeared to have been removed by hand.

## Trench 3

The animal bones were recovered in small numbers from various pits, post-holes and deposits on the surface close to the entrance to the cave (Table 4). Some of the post-holes have been interpreted as representing a wooden mortuary house that had been dismantled, with the pyre on which the animals were cremated constructed in its place (see main volume). The majority of the bones came from a charcoal-rich black layer, the sealing layer of cobbles and the fill of the cremation pyre pit. The remainder of the contexts produced fewer than twenty fragments each. The bones from the cremation pyre were mostly unburnt and must have been deposited in the pit after the fire had been extinguished. Just one fragment was sufficiently calcined to indicate that it had been subjected to intense heat, and thirteen bones were blackened from being in contact with fire but not for any great length of time. There was evidence of more burning among the remains from C2, the topsoil layer, with 35 of the total sample from the trench having the white, cracked appearance of totally calcined bone. These presumably originated from the pyre and became scattered in a random manner across the surface of the ground during the cremation process. Some of the specimens from C11, the layer of cobbling, were also slightly scorched.

| Location | Cow | Sheep | Goat | Pig | Horse | Large mammal | Medium-sized mammal | Unidentified |
|---|---|---|---|---|---|---|---|---|
| Topsoil | — | — | — | — | — | 1 | 2 | — |
| Black layer | 63 | 53 | — | 22 | 1 | 169 | 124 | 314 |
| Cobble sealing layer | 29 | 18 | — | 18 | — | 46 | 39 | 85 |
| Stone socket 1B | 1 | — | — | — | — | 4 | 4 | 3 |
| Cremation pyre site | 22 | 29 | 1 | 18 | — | 30 | 68 | 95 |
| Stone socket 2B | — | — | — | — | — | — | — | 4 |
| Post-hole 1 | 1 | — | — | — | — | — | 1 | — |
| Post-hole 4 | 1 | 3 | — | | — | — | 1 | — |
| Post-hole 6 | — | 1 | — | — | — | — | — | 6 |
| Post-hole 19 | 1 | 2 | — | — | — | 1 | 1 | — |
| Long slot-trench | — | — | — | — | — | — | 7 | — |
| Post-hole 5 | — | — | — | — | — | — | — | 3 |
| Post-hole 23 | — | — | — | — | — | — | 2 | — |
| Post-hole 20 | 6 | — | — | — | — | 6 | 8 | — |
| Ditch feature | 2 | 1 | — | — | — | 4 | 8 | — |

TABLE 4—*Number and location of identified fauna in Trench 3 (see Fig. 12 in main text for feature numbers).*

The faunal samples were, not surprisingly, dominated by the remains of cattle and sheep, which together accounted for almost 80 per cent of the identified assemblage. The remains were very fragmented, and loose teeth formed a large proportion of the identified assemblage. The bones originated from all parts of the skeleton, and a high mortality rate was again evident in the ageing data. The patella of a calf and the pelvis and metatarsus of a newborn lamb were present in C2, the topsoil layer. The only butchery evidence was from a sheep radius, which had been chopped along the mid-line. Pig remains accounted for 20 per cent of the identified assemblage and were dominated by loose teeth from juveniles and adults. Skull fragments and lower limb bones were also well represented, and the tusks of at least two boars were also identified. The only other species were horse and goat, each represented by a single fragment. An adult horse molar was found in the topsoil layer (C2), and a fragment of a goat horn-core was recovered from the cremation pyre pit.

## The horse remains

In all, fourteen horse bones were identified in the cave; most were recovered from the Graveyard, including an unburnt tooth from the cremation deposit within the stone setting (Table 5). Loose teeth and skull fragments were the most prevalent. Two of the three post-cranial bones came from the lower hind leg: a patella from Area Y and a tibia from the Graveyard; the distal portion of a scapula was recovered from Area U. Only one of the bones had been broken in antiquity, and the absence of butchery marks on the other remains made it difficult to determine whether breakage had occurred before or after deposition in the cave. With the exception of the horse tooth from the stone setting in the Graveyard, it proved impossible during excavation to associate the horse remains with any particular burial. The excavator has suggested that the bones may be associated with the prime adult male from the Graveyard, although the recovery of a mandible and a tooth close to the stone setting may be of significance regarding association with the cremation burial.

| Location | Body part | | | | | |
|----------|-------|----------|---------|-------|---------|--------|
| | Tooth | Mandible | Scapula | Tibia | Patella | Carpal |
| Entrance shaft | I | — | — | — | — | — |
| Area V | — | — | I | — | — | — |
| Area U | — | I | — | — | — | I |
| Area T | I | — | — | — | — | — |
| Area X | I | — | — | — | — | — |
| Graveyard | 5 | I | — | I | — | — |
| Area Y | — | — | — | — | I | — |
| Total | 8 | 2 | I | I | I | I |

TABLE 5—*Location and identification of horse remains.*

The human skeletal report (Appendix 2) indicates that the inhumations had been subjected to considerable disturbance and dispersal. It is suggested that the burial site was deliberately desecrated by native Irish groups, and this would also have led to the animal bones becoming scattered across the cave (see main text). If the entire sample of horse bones is taken as a single depositional event, it indicates the presence of one mature individual. Fusion data and tooth-wear evidence show that the remains represent an animal that had reached 5 years of age at slaughter. An estimation of stature by comparison with modern skeletal material indicated a modern-day pony of 13–14 hands. The combination of parts of the skull and the bones of the lower extremities of a horse has parallels in Viking cremation burials in eastern Sweden. The circumstances of the finds from Sweden suggest horse sacrifice.

## DISCUSSION

The faunal assemblage from Cloghermore is unusual for archaeozoological studies. On-site sieving of the entire contents of the cave ensured the recovery of the complete deposited sample, and the bones can therefore be confidently used to answer certain questions that are raised concerning the interpretation of the site. Overall, a picture emerges of a highly fragmented collection of bones becoming incorporated with Hiberno-Scandinavian inhumations in various areas of the cave. Analysis of the human skeletal material demonstrated that the bodies had been broken up and dispersed shortly after burial, possibly as a deliberate desecration of the site (Lynch, Appendix 2). This activity undoubtedly led to fragmentation and dispersal of the animal bones as well. In interpreting the various faunal samples from within the cave, therefore, it is probably best to see them as a single assemblage associated with a relatively short period of burial, perhaps less than two years.

The vast majority of the identified bone fragments from Cloghermore originated from domestic animals. Although the results could be seen to shed light on aspects of contemporaneous economic practice, the unusual nature of the site precludes any definitive assessment of local diet and farming methods. If the remains are regarded as representative of the economy, the animal husbandry system seems to have been one that made maximum use of the immediate environment through a concentration on sheep rearing. The occurrence of the bones in association with at least seven human burials merits an alternative interpretation, however, and indicates that the animal remains from the cave accumulated as a result of ritual activity. The age profiles of the domestic animals make little economic sense, with a very high incidence of animals that were killed at less than 2 years of age. Calves, lambs and piglets were regularly selected for slaughter, and the percentage of young livestock animals is considerably higher than for most contemporaneous settlements. Meat provisioning was clearly the only purpose, and it is suggested that much of this relates to ritual feasting before the insertion of human inhumations in the cave. The bones derived from all stages of the processing of the animals, indicating that the slaughter and dismemberment of animals were undertaken in the vicinity of the cave, probably close to the entrance, where excavations provided evidence of a wooden mortuary structure and a cremation pyre pit. Butchery evidence was plentiful and mainly took the form of chop-marks uncharacteristic of careful butchery. Heavy chopping tools seem to have been more frequently used than knives, although superficial marks associated with filleting were observed on a few ribs and upper limb bones. The bulk of the bones, however, were crudely chopped and smashed, and little care seems to have been taken in preparing suitable joints for consumption. Metal artefacts recovered from the cave include an axe, knives and blades, and these may well have been used for the slaughter and subsequent division of the carcasses into suitable portions for consumption. Several long bones had been split longitudinally for the extraction of marrow, and quite a number of skulls had been chopped axially, presumably to allow access to the brains.

A number of other observations concerning the mammalian remains from Cloghermore Cave merit discussion. The majority of the bone assemblage is interpreted as the remains of festive meals relished by funeral guests, but the ritual deposition of the partial skeletons of certain animals should also be considered. The disturbance of the burials shortly after the site had been abandoned made it difficult for the excavators to recognise 'special' bone deposits within the cave. The only sample that could confidently be assumed to have had a ritual meaning was the collection of cremated animal bones from the stone setting in the Graveyard. Two partial cattle skulls at the base of the entrance shaft seemed to have been deliberately placed at the passageway leading to the Graveyard. The burial of parts of horses is known from some Swedish Viking sites, and a selection of bones, mostly comprising skulls and extremities, was often included with the human burials (Gräslund 1980). The consumption of horses as part of the ritual feast before human burial has also been observed on Scandinavian sites. There is some evidence from Cloghermore of the dismemberment of horses before the placing of part of the skeleton in the cave. The recovery of teeth and mandible fragments, as well as lower leg bones, provides an interesting parallel with the Scandinavian sites. The presence of unburnt horse teeth in cremation deposits is common in central Sweden, and the recovery of an unburnt horse tooth from within the stone setting in the Graveyard at Cloghermore is therefore not insignificant. Dog bones often occur with horses in Viking burials, and the dismemberment of dogs is known from many sites in Scandinavia. At least three dogs were present in the identified sample from Cloghermore. Two of these were adult individuals of medium size, and the other was less than 1 year old when it died.

Cat bones were scattered in a random manner across all areas of the cave. A total of 27 bones were recognised, representing at least three cats: two juveniles less than 1 year old and an adult. All of the remains were unburnt, and there was no evidence of deliberate dismemberment, as is found on contemporaneous Scandinavian sites, where cats seem to have held special significance in relation to buried humans. Cats are generally regarded as important in Viking burial practices, and the bones are often interpreted as offerings to the god Freyja (see main text). The presence of cats in Scandinavian burials is recorded as a substitute for a human body. At Cloghermore the cat bones were dispersed across all areas of the cave, and nothing to indicate a 'special' deposit was found during excavation.

Of the wild fauna at the site, there was evidence of red deer, hare, wood mouse and a few species of bird. The only evidence of the exploitation of deer came from the recovery of four antler tines, three in the cave and one on the surface close to the entrance. The absence of post-cranial deer bones indicates that venison did not make any contribution to the feasting activities at the site. There was just one hare bone, recovered from the cremation deposit within the stone setting in the Graveyard. It is a matter of speculation whether this bone has a ritual meaning. A small sample of bird bone was recovered from the entrance shaft, which were identified as small passerine species all of which are resident locally. More exotic bird species such as peacock have been recorded in Scandinavian graves such as the Oseberg ship burial, but domestic fowl also occur as sacrifice as well as food remains (see main text). Although the ritual context of bird bone in Scandinavia is strong, the collection from Cloghermore Cave does not appear to be significant. The very capture of these birds alone would have proved difficult, and the few recovered bones are interpreted as incidental occurrences. The few wood mouse bones are likewise regarded as incidental finds.

The evidence of other Scandinavian burial in Ireland is limited to the two cemeteries at Islandbridge and Kilmainham and records of a burial mound at Donnybrook, which was excavated in the 1700s (Hall 1978). With the exception of the Donnybrook site, few parallels for the method of burial at Cloghermore can be found in Ireland. The occurrence of animal bone intermixed with human burials has many parallels in Scandinavian and Manx Viking graves, although there is little evidence of the incorporation of human burials in caves. The composition of the faunal assemblage from Cloghermore is similar to that recorded in funerary contexts in Sweden, the Isle of Man and the Donnybrook site in Dublin. At all of these sites cremated and unburnt animal bone are variously interpreted as refuse from the meals of funeral guests and the deposition of parts of the carcasses with human burials. The collection of bones from Cloghermore Cave should also be seen as deriving from a purely ritual source, and the choice and age of animals were clearly dictated by activities relating to the burial of the Scandinavian or Hiberno-Scandinavian individuals.

## REFERENCES

Grant, A. 1975a The animal bones. In B. Cunliffe (ed.), *Excavations at Porchester Castle. Vol. 1: Roman*, 378–408. London.

Grant, A. 1975b Appendix B: the use of tooth wear as a guide to the age of domestic animals. In B. Cunliffe (ed.), *Excavations at Porchester Castle. Vol. 1: Roman*, 437–50. London.

Gräslund, A.-S. 1980 *Birka IV: the burial customs. A study of the graves on Bjorko*. Stockholm.

Hall, R. 1978 A Viking-Age grave at Donnybrook, Co. Dublin. *Medieval Archaeology* **22**, 64–83.

Prummel, W. and Frisch, H.J. 1986 A guide for the distinction of species, sex and body size in bones of sheep and goat. *Journal of Archaeological Science* **13**, 567–77.

Silver, I.A. 1969 The ageing of domestic animals. In D.R. Brothwell and E.S. Higgs (eds), *Science and Archaeology*, 283–302. London.